⌐·⌐

NAVAJO TRADING

⅃∙L

NAVAJO TRADING
The End of an Era

Willow Roberts Powers

UNIVERSITY OF NEW MEXICO PRESS

Albuquerque

© 2001 by the University of New Mexico Press
All rights reserved.
First paperbound edition © 2002

Library of Congress Cataloging-in-Publication Data:

Powers, Willow Roberts, 1943–
     Navajo trading : the end of an era / Willow Roberts Powers.—1st ed.
     p.   cm.
Includes bibliographical references and index.
   ISBN 0-8263-2322-7 (pbk. : alk. paper)
     1. Navajo Indians—Commerce.   2. Trading posts—Southwest, New—History.
   I. Title.
   E99.N3 P68 2001   381'.089'972—dc21
                                                             2001001998

Cover photo: Rug woven by Lorraine Wilson, owned by Elijah Blair,
photograph ©Frank Talbott

Robert Johnson Coyle
in memoriam

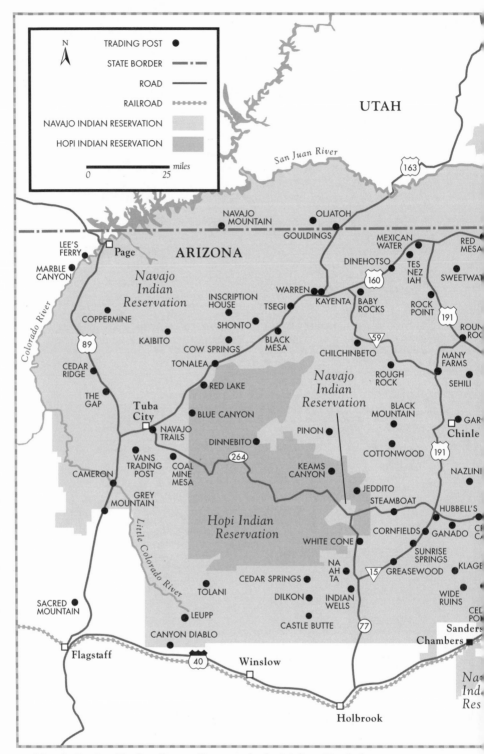

Navajo Region Trading Posts. Cartography by Melissa Tandysh.

J•L

CONTENTS

◢∎◣

LIST OF ILLUSTRATIONS

Except where noted, all illustrations are from Northern Arizona University's Cline Library, Special Collections. Illustration section begins on page 81.

J·L

ACKNOWLEDGMENTS

This book is part of a collective project to document the history of trading with Navajos, funded by a grant from Northern Arizona University Foundation through a donation from the United Indian Traders Association. Elijah Blair, long-time trader at Dinnebito Trading Post, dreamed up the idea of a history of trading that would draw on memories and details still vivid, and other traders joined him. The results include videotaped interviews and transcriptions, archival papers, and photograph collections, as well as this written account.

The work was therefore a joint effort, and I have many people to thank. But before I start that most enjoyable task, I have a confession to make: I did not want to write this book. I thought I had said all I wanted to say on the topic of traders in an earlier book, *Stokes Carson*. In addition, I felt hesitant to take on such a history at the request of those about whom I was writing. Ed Foutz, a trader whom I knew and respected, asked me to consider applying, and I went to be interviewed for the project, although I had no real interest in doing the work. Several people helped change my mind. I felt I could work with Elijah Blair, Bruce Burnham, and Hank Blair— partly because their view of their own history was interesting and I shared it, and partly because of their integrity and the challenge they offered. They perceived that there was a difference in economies—theirs, that of the Navajos—and thought that the events of the 1970s were a critical juncture in trader history. Rather than focus on a faded past and what Frank McNitt calls "the glory days of trading" they wanted a book that examined more recent events in the light of the whole of trading history. This was the challenge: could I write a book on the complex history of the 1970s, from the traders' perspective, without being just a mouthpiece of traders? But anthropologists have learned to work ethically in partnership with the people they write about, and I felt those ethics would stand me in good stead. By the second interview, I had decided to take on the book. Lije, Bruce, and Hank wanted me to get the facts, to give primary focus to Navajos and Navajo history, and, in Bruce's words, "to give it heart." They kept sight of that goal. Together with Claudia Blair, Victoria Blair, and Virginia Burnham, they contributed factual corrections, stories, and many questions and discussions, while never for one minute forgetting the right I had claimed (in writing) as author to say what I wanted.

The other person who indirectly helped to change my mind was Karen J. Underhill, head of the Cline Library's Special Collections and Archives Division. Karen was responsible for the collection of oral history interviews on which the book would draw. Karen and I had already been colleagues in an effort to recognize Native American archival issues, and I trusted her advocacy of Navajo perspectives and came to know and trust everyone else working on the oral histories. In addition to Karen, the interviewing was carried out by Bradford Cole, Special Collections Manuscripts Curator, and videotaped by Lew Steiger and Gail Steiger, the audio-visual team of Steiger Brothers. At the same time, Laine Sutherland, Photo Archivist in Special Collections, obtained photograph collections documenting trading history. Karen, Brad, Lew, Gail, Laine: thank you—I hope I have done your work justice.

The interviews, so freely given by many different traders and others involved in trading, are an integral part of this book: I have tried to let people speak for themselves by quoting them extensively. There is a list of everyone who is quoted in the book on page 264: to all of you, thank you. The reader may view the interviews, as well as trader photograph collections, on the Cline Library's Special Collections Web page.

There are many other traders who've contributed to my knowledge, some of whom I interviewed years ago, others more recently. Though they are no longer here, Jo and Sam Drolet started my feet on this path. Thank you, Andrea Ashcroft, Bob and Theta Cooke, Raymond and Melissa Drolet, Ed Foutz, Mildred Heflin, Nina Heflin, Sharon Heflin, and Alice and Walter Scribner.

The history of trading isn't completed just by interviewing traders, and I have asked DNA lawyers and Navajos for their views on trading and the events of the 1970s. In both cases, I've interviewed only a small number of the people involved. Many thanks to Martha Blue, Paul Biderman, Mike Gross, Bruce Herr, Robert Hilgendorf, and Eric Treisman for helping me to understand DNA and its activities in those years; and to Grace Brown, Gloria Emerson, Richard Mike, Arlene Tracy, Cecilia Yazzie, and Peterson Zah for helping me to understand Navajo perspectives, in all their broad variety. I have presented my view of the situation and in some cases it may not reflect your own, but I hope I have done it fairly. Archival sources have been important also. Thanks to John Paul Deley, archivist at the Federal Trade Commission, I was able to see old FTC records.

Several people have contributed their expertise. Thank you, Beth Hadas, for constant support and high standards of writing, as well as editing. Thank you, Jane Kepp, for instrumental editing and comments on the manuscript's anxious first chapters. Thanks to Jocelyn de Haas, who transcribed my tapes for me. Thank you, Laine Sutherland, for ever-ready help with the illustrations. And thanks to Peter Iverson, for comments and suggestions for improvements to the manuscript's first draft.

The Northern Arizona Foundation and the United Indian Traders Association funded the project, and we are all grateful. Thank you, Susan Casebeer, Foundation official, for such cheerful, prompt assistance. Though the initial idea for this book was to focus on the history of the United Indian Traders Association, I looked at a much broader picture and paid most attention to the stormy years of the 1960s and 1970s rather than the narrower history of the UITA; I was given the freedom to do this. Thank you, Lije, Claudia, Bruce, Virginia, Hank, and Vicky, for this freedom and for your time, trust, and patience.

Last but not least, thanks to those good friends who have supported me and listened to my endless conversations about the book: Barbara King, Peter McKenna, Janet Patterson, and Robert Powers.

There are many different perspectives and different political views of the more recent history of the Navajos, and the role of trading in that history. These are my own views, and any errors here are mine also.

PART ONE

⌐▪⌐

THE WAY TRADING WAS

1

J·L

TRADERS

The next morning we started off and arrived at Fort Defiance before noon. At the store we sold our wool—I don't know what we got for it—and then they told us to go to the next store. When we got there the door was open, and that was the store. Lots of things were in that house. On the shelves lay bundles of red flannel and white cloth, and dishes, and from the ceiling hung buckets of different sizes and scarfs of all colors. Everything was new to me. I stood and looked, thinking, "What wonderful things they are." While we were in the store a tall white man came in. He had on a pair of pants with a big patch of red buckskin on the seat. He was walking around in the store and whistling, and I was looking at him. I was afraid of the white people.

> *Left Handed, 1938: Son of Old Man Hat. Ed Walter Dyk, 56.*

One hundred and thirty years ago, a handful of intrepid peddlers, men with wagons of miscellaneous goods, went onto the Navajo Reservation and bartered these items for the wool from Navajo herders, a few sheep, a rug, or a piece of silver jewelry. Trading between the two cultures continued to evolve, and by the twentieth century had become a steady and vital exchange of goods and services. It was a Navajo institution, although it was run by Anglo-American traders who learned how to deal across the cultures. Nevertheless, Navajos shaped the institution, dealing in their own manner and in their own community with outsiders, their unfamiliar goods and foreign manners, customs, and means of exchange. This is an account of Navajo trade and traders, how it grew and settled down; most of all, it is the story of how it changed and finally how it ended.

The first traders went onto Navajo territory a few years after the signing of the Navajo-U.S. Treaty of 1868, the last Indian treaty signed by the federal government. Recognizing that Navajos not only had a valuable resource but liked the utility of the products of industrial America, traders bartered tinware, tools, flour, coffee, and fabric for wool and sheep. A hundred years later, trading was an important part of reservation economy, a source of goods, services, and information, a currency exchange, a labor exchange, a center for the purchase of crafts, a pawnshop, and a point of contact with the larger society. Trade took place in stores that were often part—even the core—of a settled, if far-flung, community, in buildings that reflected the needs of both traders and Navajos. Navajos shaped trade—and traders—to the way they lived and worked. Traders who did not accept Navajo ways were not very successful, and often did not last long. Even though traders were part of the dominant culture, and though problems (of misunderstanding, of bad behavior) constantly arose, Navajos stamped the style of their own culture and social mores on trading posts, traders, and trade.

Traders occupied a special niche, exchanging culture as well as material goods, bringing new ways to the Navajos and, eventually, preserving the old ways. In 1962, Frank McNitt published a book on trading entitled *The Indian Trader*, the first serious account of trading and its many characters. In his opening sentence, McNitt commented on the lack of recognition given to traders.

> In the history of the Western frontier the Indian traders have received little attention. When mentioned at all they usually have been presented as almost shadowy figures moving in a scene changing but unchanged and scarcely touched by their own actions.[1]

But if Frank McNitt's book was the first real history of Navajo trading posts and traders to note some of the interesting details, traders were recognized in different ways. They are mentioned quite frequently in the nineteenth century correspondence of Indian agents, in the few books by agents, and in a variety of reports to or by federal agencies. As individuals, they are quoted as experts in these reports and histories. As a group, they were acknowledged (sometimes reluctantly) by other non-Navajos as active participants in the Navajo world. Traders were agents for change, but change on the reservation in turn affected them, too.

A few traders published the stories of their lives—rare and atypical traders, whose tales usually covered experiences beyond trading. One of the first traders to write an autobiography was Joseph Schmedding, a colorful character who was in turn ranch hand, trader, diplomat, and writer. He had worked as a wrangler for Richard Wetherill, a rancher and amateur archaeologist best known for attracting the attention of academic archaeologists to the ruins at Chaco Canyon, New Mexico, where he had a ranch and a trading post. Later, Schmedding himself turned to trading, and ran Sanders and then Keams Canyon Trading Posts, and went on to have many adventures in foreign lands.

There were also women who wrote about trading. One was Louisa Wade Wetherill, wife of the trader at Kayenta Trading Post, John Wetherill. John, who was the brother of Richard (and had a similar interest in ruins), traded at Kayenta from 1906 until the late 1920s, described by Louisa (with help from Frances Gillmor) in *Traders to the Navajos*. Elizabeth Compton Hegemann published a book called *Navaho Trading Days* the year after McNitt's book appeared. It was an autobiography, and it described several years of trading with her second husband at Shonto Trading Post in the late 1920s. Her photographs and prose captured some of the day-to-day details of trading, as well as for those unacquainted with the Southwest, the unknown, even exotic, life of an outsider trading on the Navajo Reservation. Franc Johnson Newcomb, wife of the trader at Newcomb's Trading Post, also wrote about her life and her acquaintance with Navajos and Navajo medicine men in *Navaho Neighbors*. Newcomb's trading post, where the Newcombs traded from 1914 to 1930, lay at the foot of the Chuska Mountains, in the valley that ran south of Shiprock, New Mexico, very different country from Kayenta and Shonto.[2]

Then came criticism. In 1963, a book on Shonto Trading Post was published by William Y. Adams. Originally a doctoral dissertation, it described in detail the economics of a "modern Navajo community" and the role of the trader in this community. Adams saw the trading post and the Navajo economy as interdependent and complimentary, but he viewed the trader as anachronistic, paternalistic, and, like older, traditional Navajos, unable to adapt to change—quite literally stuck in the trading post situation without the means or the desire to alter his circumstances. Where Hegemann celebrated a romantic solitude mixed with an unusual crossing of cultures, Adams viewed traders as holding back Navajo modernization, controlling their spending, their work, and their ways of making a living.[3]

By 1963, change was speeding up on the Navajo Reservation. At the end of the 1960s, traders, their Navajo customers, and departments of the Navajo tribe and the federal government became embroiled in a dramatic fight: a fight over regulations, legal formalities, and the proper way of doing business, especially when that business crossed the boundaries of different cultures. During these years, the old federal trading regulations and leases for trading posts were examined by the Bureau of Indian Affairs (BIA) and the tribe and new ones drawn up. The traders, who saw themselves as fitting the description of rugged individualism, turned to the United Indian Traders Association, an organization created in 1931 to fight for authenticity in Navajo arts and crafts, for help in facing legal attacks on the way they carried out their business. Though the weapons were lawyers and paper, bureaucracy and class action suits, the battle was hotly political and, as in all politics, was concerned with economics and the ways in which the Navajo economy was to be organized. The roots of the problem lay in change, and resistance to change, and in some of the disjunctions between Navajo culture and the culture of the dominant society.

This fight over the way in which Navajo trade was conducted came to a head in 1972 with a series of hearings carried out by the Federal Trade Commission (FTC), followed by a scathing report. New regulations were eventually put in place. Pawn, a constant of the exchange between Navajos and traders, ceased altogether. Trading continued for the next twenty years, but its real basis—the exchange of sheep and crafts for food and goods—was mostly gone. With little to differentiate itself from regular stores, the trading post itself began to disappear, its place taken by convenience stores and eventually supermarkets.

By 1990, the clamor of criticism raised by the crisis had died down, but in effect the trading post era was over. At the beginning of the twenty-first century, although a few trading posts, mainly those in distant communities, continue to do a good business, there is almost no trade. Few sheep and less wool are exchanged or sold for goods. Gas stations with convenience stores line the highways, selling soda pop, fast food, and a few basic necessities; supermarkets have appeared in larger towns such as Tuba City, Kayenta, Window Rock, and Chinle. In the border towns of the reservation, such as Flagstaff, Gallup, and Farmington, stores that often call themselves trading posts, and are frequently owned by people whose families once were traders, deal in Navajo arts and crafts and in pawn. Sometimes they carry items that are favored by their Navajo customers, who come in to buy good jewelry and other items, but more often they stock goods that appeal to the tourist.

This book is an account of the closing decades of Navajo trade, trading posts, and traders. It is the story of a set of entrepreneurs and their closing years; it is specific to the Navajo Reservation, but it has something to say about small business in general. Much of this tale of economic change involves details of bureaucracies, a tale of our times, but it is anything but dull. Since the 1970s, Navajo life has changed, and trading posts are no longer part of it. The decline of trading posts—a decline that traders themselves acknowledge as inevitable—was accompanied by dramatic action and events, as this book will describe, which left their mark on the reservation and on everyone involved in its life. In the chapters that follow, I describe trading post life, its beginnings and evolution, and its changes, crises, and conclusion.[4]

This is not the first book I have written about traders; I have known some of the best, and it has given me an interest in, even a bias toward, them. I have also had the honor of knowing and working with Navajos in different communities, which has led to friendships and to some familiarity with—and much respect for—Navajo life as it used to be and as it is now. Most of all, I am interested in the connections and relations between different cultures and the ways in which they interact. I want this story to show all sides: that of the traders, that of the Navajos, and that of the legal aid attorneys, and others who were engaged in the changes of the 1970s and the conflict over trading. It seems to me that the different sides were not only in conflict, they were often not even talking about the same subjects. That is, in fact, the way the events in history occur, and I want to put in the details of this small history as part of a larger picture of economic shifts.

First, I want to give the traders' stories of the early days of trading in their own words: the days of their grandparents and sometimes great-grandparents, and parents, and their own trading post childhoods and trader beginnings. In subsequent chapters of Part I, I'll explain the details mentioned in these accounts, and fill in the background and the history, both Navajo history and trader history, and the intricacies of the trading business. In Part II, I'll describe the events of the last thirty years—the last real years of trading, the end of the era.[5]

In 1870, trade began out of wagons, but as Navajos began to raise larger and larger herds of sheep, a more settled exchange started. Settler families, moving into the area, built trading posts. Trading was combined with ranching, and sometimes with missions: settlers represented Mormon, Catholic, and Protestant sects. Mormons in particular settled all across the Southwest, around Navajo territory, and there were several many-branched, well known trading families: Ashcroft, Bloomfield, Burnham, Dustin, Foutz, McGee, Tanner.

Seth Tanner was born in Bolton, New York, in 1829, and went to Salt Lake City with Brigham Young. He came down to the Southwest—to the territory of Arizona—in the early 1870s to explore and homestead. He was a big man, said to be something of a loner, unafraid of anybody. He became known as *Hasteen Shash*—Mr. Bear. He explored, settled, mined—in the Grand Canyon and elsewhere, trying to find coal, silver, turquoise, whatever there was—and traded. He worked with his brother and later with his son, Joe—Joseph Baldwin Tanner—who was known as *Shash Yáázh*, Bear Cub, or *Shash Yázhí*, Little Bear. Both father and son spoke good Navajo. Seth, who undoubtedly had a Navajo as well as a Mormon wife, possibly more—polygamy was permitted and encouraged by the Mormon fathers—also spoke Tewa.

Seth's son Joe was born around 1868, and carried on his father's way of life: mining, trading, working with Navajo and Pueblo jewelry. He too spoke English, Navajo, and possibly another Southwestern language, and he too traded in the typically marginal fashion of the 1880s, when trading was mixed in with other endeavors. He ultimately owned a trading post at Mancos Creek and, briefly, at Hogback. He took an intense interest in Navajo silversmithing. Joe's grandson, Joseph Elwood Tanner (Joe, also a trader), said that his grandfather brought in turquoise for the smiths and was instrumental in the marriage of silver and turquoise.

> He was at the height of his career at that great opportunistic time, when all of these early traders were trying to figure out ways to trade—what were the goods of trade? The obvious one, the Navajos had the hottest commodity in America, in the West. Before the white man ever showed up, the Comanches wanted their blankets, the Utes wanted their blankets, the Mexicans wanted their blankets. That weaving art was the obvious most sought-after thing, whether you were an army soldier, or whatever you were. . . . All of these guys, whether it was my Grandpa Joe or whether it was Cotton in Gallup, or Moore at Crystal, or Hubbell—they were all

just trying to figure out ways that these people could best make a living. And turquoise and silver became one of those important things. And my granddad was toe-to-toe with those names—my Grandpa Joe was toe-to-toe with Hubbell and Moore. . . .

Grandpa Joe started mining turquoise down between Bisbee and Morenci, and he had a really important turquoise mine down there. And what he would do is mine the turquoise, then he would bring the turquoise up to the bead makers. And they were Navajo bead makers, Hopi bead makers, Santo Domingo bead makers, and Zuni bead makers. The technique of trade was that half of what was created out of the turquoise belonged to the bead maker, and the other half belonged to Grandpa. And so he'd leave them an important stash of turquoise, and when he came back at a designated point in time he would sit there and get first pick. Grandpa got first pick, the bead maker would get the next pick, and they would just satisfy it that way. And then of course Grandpa would try to then buy the bead maker's piece, and sometimes he had success and sometimes he didn't. The Zuni, the bead makers, were always traders themselves. And this was a great commodity, a great *jackla*—the earring that goes on the bottom of a necklace—a really good one of those was fair trade for the best steer in the herd or thirty head of ewes. [Joe Tanner Sr., Cline Library interview, March 1999]

By the turn of the century, trading posts were already scattered across the landscape, all across the reservation, and around its edges, wherever there seemed to be a congregation of Navajos.

Grace Herring was born at Shiprock in 1910. Her parents, George and Lucy Bloomfield, took over the lease of Toadlena Trading Post from the Smith brothers in 1911 and ran it until about 1943.

In 1910 my father [George Bloomfield] was working for the government service, and they sent him to Toadlena to build a school there. . . . Merritt Smith and Bob Smith had the trading post . . . and they went and applied to put a post at Toadlena, and Mr. Shelton [BIA superintendent at Shiprock] said he would come out and help them pick the spot where they could put it . . . and that's where it is right today. . . . [Grace Herring, Cline Library interview, February 1998]

Bloomfield and his neighbor Noel Davies became interested in weavers, and began to build a trade in rugs. The weaving tradition of the area, now known as Two Grey Hills, and the interest in it by outsiders, dates to this time.

Mother tended the store, took care of eight kids—I don't know how she did it, no water in the house, no electricity, no conveniences like we have today, but we loved it. It was beautiful. . . . The canyon was close by, there were always things to do that were fun. I remember especially that Mother just let us kind of do what we wanted to do. The only thing that she would say when we left the house was, "Don't go on the right side of the canyon, because it's dangerous. And watch out for rattlesnakes." As we were growing up, Dad would not let the girls work in the store. The boys worked there. . . . I didn't work in it until after we [she and her husband] bought the store, and I had to learn because Charles was gone and I had to run the store. I'm not fluent [in Navajo] by a long ways yet, but I can talk a little.

I remember Dad had a [Navajo] man who took his team with a four-horse team on it, and Dad would give him his money and the grocery list to go to Gallup to Kirk's [wholesaler] and other places. The man would take the money and go and get everything and bring it back by team wagon. You never had to worry about it, everything was taken care of the way it should be. . . .

When Dad first moved to the trading post, he was immediately interested in the rugs. He never bought a rug in the store, he would take it to the front room . . . he put the rug down on the front room floor. I've seen him on his hands and knees many times, showing [the weavers] how they could make them better, how they could make them finer, and to use the patterns from the potsherds into the patterns of their rugs. He and Mr. Davies did that together. They worked very close together. He had the trading post at Crozier, which is actually Two Grey Hills now, but it was called Crozier then. They were very good friends, and they worked close together.

Now, when they first went there, the rugs were very rough . . . they were heavy. But they started to try to tell [the weavers] to make them finer. They did use to use some blue and red [wool] in there, but Mr. Davies and Dad told them to keep it the natural colors, and Dad and Mr. Davies are the ones who started to show them not to put any color into their rugs. . . . [Grace Herring, Cline Library interview, February 1998]

Trading posts began with bachelor traders, in part because of the distance, the solitude, and the possibility of attack. By the turn of the century, it had become a family undertaking. Not only were trading posts built and worked in by fathers and brothers, uncles and cousins, but husbands and wives worked together. It was still a lonely occupation. Stella McGee, daughter of a Mormon family living in Kirtland, married Rule Lehi–Chunky–Tanner in 1924, and after a short time working in Phoenix for a dairy, Chunky Tanner gave it up, bought a Model T Ford and drove Stella and their baby, J. B., up to New Mexico to see family.

His brother-in-law, Willard Stolworthy, had a store down at Montezuma Creek, and he needed somebody to run that store. So we traded our Model T Ford as a down payment on that. . . .

There was no road . . . got down there, and then had to turn the Model T back to Willard, and he drove it back. . . . You'd never see a white person for eight months. You'd just sit right there. The store was in pretty bad shape, but my husband was a real good Navajo talker, and he really built it up. We got 1,400 head of lambs that first fall, in 1926. . . .

I remember how frightened I was at first. But you know, those Indians became my best friends, and they're the ones that really taught me a little bit. I'd follow Chunky around, and I'd say, "What did he say, What did he say?" And he said, "Get this girl to tell you what they said." That's how you picked up the language. . . .

So we were there for two lamb seasons. That's how they did it way back then. They'd have two seasons: wool season and lamb season. And the traders would carry them [the Navajos] on the books. And then when they would make a rug . . . they would bring them in and the trader would tell them how much it was worth, and write it down on a paper bag. They would buy one thing at a time. And after they'd buy one thing, why, they'd have to know how much they had left. And then it would just take them all day to trade out that rug. . . .

That was the end of nowhere, as far as I was concerned. The only way you could get any freight in or anything, was in big wagons. I remember I'd watch over that hill, when I thought there was going to be a load of freight coming in, which would only be about once every two months. You'd see that team of wagons coming. It just seemed so good to be able to see somebody. . . .

I baked bread for every day, about twelve. We had an old wood stove, and I'd bake the bread and the Indians would stand around waiting for that bread to come out of the oven, and we sold loaves of bread. And I made the cookies for the store, because as I said, we only got supplies in about every two months. I made their skirts, sewed them up. We had a machine, and I'd charge them so much for sewing up a skirt. [Stella Tanner, Cline Library interview, July 1998]

A year or two later, Stella and Chunky Tanner bought a half interest in the lease at a trading post called Tsaya, where they stayed for about eighteen years.

They [Navajos] would come in and start to pawn a little bit. That's the first recollection I have of pawn, is they'd bring a bracelet or beads or something in, and Chunky would tell them how much they could have on it. Then he'd roll it up and put it in a paper bag and put it in a drawer. We didn't have too much pawn. We carried it mostly on the book from one season to the other. That was in 1932 when the Depression started, you know, when all that happened. [Stella Tanner, Cline Library interview, July 1998]

There were trading posts that were at confluences of different tribes, different activities. Piñon Trading Post, for example, was on Black Mesa, south of the Hopi pueblos, and Tuba City was near Moencopi, another Hopi village. Tuba City was originally part of a Mormon settlement, named after a Hopi—Tuba, or as other spellings have it, Tuve or Tivi—who apparently gave Mormon families permission to settle there some time after 1872. By the 1890s, Tuba City had become an Indian Agency town and was a busy settlement, with a school, a hospital, and several trading posts. Jot Stiles was a trader who at one time worked the posts at Piñon, Tuba City, and Castle Butte. Like all traders he could turn his hand to many things and had been in turn a cattle rancher, in the military, a border patrolman on the Mexican border, and an Indian trader. In 1924, he took his family to Piñon trading post. His daughter, Mary May Bailey, was three when he took them to Piñon.[6]

We had a car, which was an old Dodge, and that's my first memory, being asleep in the front seat between Mother and Daddy, and hearing that car gear down and gear down, like they used to, and then come to a stop, and seeing my Dad take off his shoes and socks and his pants. And then we could see him go down the wash and wade and see if he could find a rock bottom or something we could cross on. And if not, then he came back and he said, "All go to sleep, we're here for the night." And we'd have to wait till the wash went down, to cross. . . .

And of course we didn't get any mail, much, and no fresh groceries. But occasionally they would send them out from Flagstaff or Winslow or Holbrook on the mail route. So we did get some connection. Lorenzo Hubbell brought Daddy a wet battery radio—one of the first ones—but they could never get it to work. . . . [Mary May Bailey, Cline Library interview, July 1999]

About a year or two later, Stiles took a partnership in the Tuba City Trading Post, so that his elder daughter Betty, then six, could go to school.

The store was a big hexagon, and all the way around was shelves—they had a big opening where the big double doors opened and came in, and that was always called the bullpen, and there was a big stove in the middle, to get warm in the wintertime. And they all managed to—there was always a coffee pot going. And on the counters there was always a cigar box with a spoon tied with a string, and made permanent with that box. The box was filled with tobacco, and there was always papers.

There was always an odor about a Navajo trading post that if I was to go in one today, I would recognize it immediately. There was a mixture of wool, ground coffee, and all of these other wonderful smells—oh my!— and hides. Some smells not so good, some smells good. It made it just wonderful. And cheese—they always had a big block of cheese that they could cut off. And then all mainly canned goods. Lots of pawn. Lots of big heavy safes. [Mary May Bailey, Cline Library interview, July 1999]

The Stiles children, Betty, Mary May, and Roger, moved between trading and ranching. Roger served in World War II and was killed in Aachen, in Germany; "that nearly killed my folks, when they lost him, but we went on." The Stiles daughters had not been allowed to work in the trading post either, but after Roger was killed both of them went on to run trading posts after the Second World War, despite lacking any knowledge of Navajo language.

So it really made it doubly hard. I remember one day I was left at the store with my little girl. She was just a baby, and I was there alone, and this Navajo man came and all he wanted was *toh 'azis*. Now, *toh* means 'water.' *'Azis* is a sack. So it was over an hour that we went through everything in that trading post, and I'd say, "This?" "*Dooda*" [No]. Anyway, what he finally wanted—he found a potato, I took him back to the back of the counter, and he found a potato, and there was an empty pop bottle, and he put them together—and then I knew he needed kerosene in a bottle with a potato stopper. Now how you get from *toh 'azis* to that, without knowing the kerosene part, was a real battle! . . .

We bought saddle blankets by the great gross, and they either brought in a saddle blanket to sell, or a blanket—they wove lots of better blankets. And hides, we bought hides. We'd buy mutton sometimes. A lamb or a goat was the best thing in the world they could bring in, and we would have fresh meat. And then we finally got an Electrolux refrigerator so we could keep it without having to hang it up every night. Oh, those were the most delicious things to eat! Mother would do them outside with the ribs. But that's what they would trade, or they would pawn something. . . .

I was down at the store in town [Winslow] one day when Daddy had a New York banker sitting by his desk, and he was watching all of this, and he thought it was the most amazing thing he had ever seen, because one of Daddy's best customers, or some of them, had come in and they wanted to borrow their pawn. So Daddy went back to the pawn room, and he had shown the guy the pawn room before. And he picked out their pieces that they wanted, and he sent them on their way. Now this is stuff taken in as collateral. That banker nearly died! "How in God's world can you ever make a profit?" So Daddy told him, "You have to know your customers." And he said, "They're as honest as the day is long, and they'll be back, and they'll bring it back in." And so they did. But, oh, there was a huge amount of pawn, and that was one of your big items.

There were some people that lived out around Leupp, and I can't recall their name . . . but they fought. Over the drop of a hat they'd fight. Well, there were two of their family in the trading post, and I don't know what precipitated it, but one girl walked up to the other and she knocked her clear over the stacked-up flour in the middle of the store. You stacked them, you know, so that they were real high. And she knocked her clear across there, and then all the rest of the Navajos just sat back there and laughed. And it was all over within a twinkling of an eye. . . .

When they first started the draft—that was before we were in the [Second World] War—they sent all kinds of flyers out to all the trading posts to open up a place where these men could come and register to sign up for the draft. So Daddy thought that was a real good idea. We had a big ceremonial hogan that he had bought after one of the ceremonies close to Castle Butte. He bought the whole thing and had the men come up and set it up by Castle Butte. . . . So he put up a flag pole and flew a flag, and put a big Navajo rug out there on the side of the hogan, and that's where the men signed up. Well, that morning that they were to sign, this young Navajo man came. One of the first ones, and he had a bedroll on the back, and a rifle mounted in a scabbard on the side of his saddle, and he hung around all day long after he signed up. He was still there when we were eating supper. And Mom said, "You know, I think you ought to go out and ask that man what he's waiting for, Jot." So Jot asked him what he was waiting for. He said, "I'm waiting to go to war. I'm all ready. Just as soon as they tell me where I can go I'll go."

I think this was in the forties: Mother and Daddy had decided they would take a vacation and go out to Los Angeles to visit with my sister. She was living there at the time. So Daddy says, "Well, as long as we're going, let's take a whole lot of pawn and see if we could peddle some of it." So he got all the dead pawn. Now pawn goes dead after a certain time. But these bankers that would come by . . . were astounded, "You mean you keep that stuff for a year without any payment at all?" "And longer if they're good." You know, if they're good customers. . . .

Anyway so they filled a big boot box and took it to Los Angeles. Daddy loved the horse races, so they went to Santa Anita . . . and they had the best time. They took their boot box and put it under their seat, and they spent the whole afternoon there watching the races. They left, and they got out quite a ways from the racetrack, and Mother said, "Jot, did you put that box in the car?" And he said, "No, did you?" "No." "Well let's go back and get it." So they went back, looked and there it was. In Los Angeles, in the forties. So they still had their jewelry to peddle. [Mary May Bailey, Cline Library interview, July 1999]

Traders love stories, and the stories go round and round. Many of them are concerned with travel, tales of the naive and ignorant travelers who would drive the dirt tracks and stay at trading posts, or with the mistakes—their own, their customers'—in language or business. Sometimes, when traders spoke good Navajo, they would try to translate the jokes and stories they were told by customers, but these were so often word puns that translation was impossible, or they were richly bawdy and required a well known audience.

Traders purchased their goods from wholesalers in Albuquerque, Gallup, Flagstaff, or other border towns. Some time after the turn of the century a group of Mormon traders got together to form a buying cooperative, the Progressive Mercantile Company. Alma Luff Foutz, born in the mid-1880s,

was one of the Mormon settlers in Tuba, before it became an Agency settlement. He moved to Kirtland, following his brother in a partnership in
Progressive Merc, as it was known, in the early 1900s. His son, Russell Foutz,
began his trading career working as a teenager for his father.

That was a little wholesale supply store at Kirtland, New Mexico. They
furnished financial backing and merchandise to quite a few of the stores
on that part of the Reservation. I think at one time there were probably
about twenty-two stores. There were four partners involved, all of them
were ex-Indian traders.

There was Burt Dustin, his brother Shel Dustin, and my dad [Al
Foutz], who the Indians called 'Ashkii biwoo bitsilí. His brother [Jim Foutz]
was one of the founders of this business, and he was known as "the man
with the big teeth"—'Ashkii biwoo—so naturally my dad went as "the
brother of the man with the big teeth." The Indians would have a name
for practically every trader that came on the Reservation, they would
attach a name to him. Like one of the old traders was Shash yázhí, and that
was Joe [Joseph Baldwin] Tanner. . . . Burt Dustin did a lot of freighting
and hauling merchandise to these stores, and they named him. He had a
real nice team of horses they freighted with, so they named him łíí bidziilii,
"the man with the big strong horses." The other partner was Willard
Stolworthy who was married to one of Joe Tanner's daughters, so he was
known as Shash yázhí bidoni [Little Bear's Son-in-law].

The four partners had an unusual working agreement. Two would
work for six months, and then the other two would work for six months.
Dad and Shel Dustin would work for six months, and then Willard
Stolworthy and Burt Dustin would work for six months. There wasn't
enough work for them. They had other interests—ranches or interest in
other stores to look after. . . . The arrangement . . . lasted for the entire
time from the early 1900s till they sold out in the forties.

So it was a fairly small Mormon community in those days, and I started
out working there [at Progressive Mercantile], helping to buy the rugs and
keeping the dry goods straightened up. In those days, when we started out,
we were buying these Navajo rugs by the pound. I would set them out and
put them in the different stacks. I think, as I remember, they went from
about 75 cents to $4.50 a pound. And then they would weight them out,
and there would be a few special rugs that would be bought by the piece. I
would get either Dad or somebody to help put a price on one of those. . . .

Chee Dodge [first Navajo Tribal Chairman, 1923–28] had died and there was one of the daughters that had some of his things, and one of those rugs would come through every once in a while. So the rugs in those days ran from a dollar a pound saddle blanket up to a real high priced rug, if it went to a hundred dollars it was right special. [Russell Foutz, Cline Library interview, 1999]

Trading posts were not owned by traders—they belonged to the Navajo tribe—but their leases were. Leases were often bought in partnership, so that each trader might own a half or quarter share of a lease, and such shares were frequently held by relatives. Al Foutz, in addition to working for Progressive Merc, went to trade at Teec Nos Pos with his wife, Harriet Dustin Foutz, when he was about twenty (around 1905). He spent half his time there and half in Kirtland. Luff's eldest son, Edwin Luff Foutz, bought a half share of the Teec Nos Pos store, which he ran with Kenneth Washburn. Russell, a younger son, worked at Teec Nos Pos and Red Mesa Trading Posts in the summer breaks during high school so that the resident trader could take a few days off. Much later on, when his brother Ed died from meningitis in 1939, Russell inherited his share of the Teec Nos Pos lease, and went out to work at the store.

It was a good life. We needed the Indians, and in those days, the Indians needed us. All of us old-timers at one time have helped bury their dead, been their banker, been their advisor. Most of us was sincere, we had their interest at heart. I do recall one winter day that they came into Teec Nos Pos. . . . Old Growler was from up there at Sweetwater. His son had died, and he wanted us to come up and help bury him. That was quite an education for me, because I had always heard that they were reluctant to dress and to have to do much with one of the ones that was buried, that had died. But when we went up there, his face was painted with war paint, and they had made him white pants out of white calico, and he was all dressed for burial.[7] They buried him, they said their prayers over the grave, they asked us to say a prayer over the grave for him. [Russell Foutz, Cline Library interview, 1999]

Russell eventually bought the whole lease of Teec Nos Pos and his daughter Kathy now owns it. The store burned down in the 1960s.

It burned down, and it burned down all the pawn . . . it caused some problems. I replaced: I bought beads, jewelry, and stuff from all over the country to replace that pawn with. I still have a drawer full of wrinkled up [burned] pawn. After that store burned down, they were starting to build the road on there where the Teec Nos Pos store is now. Every time I'd stake out a place to build the store they'd move the road. But before I could build it, I had to get permission from the community to rebuild that store there. So Indians, they always liked big, long meetings, so they had to have a big meeting to decide whether they were going to let me rebuild the store out there, or whether I was going to replace their pawn and all that. So they had this meeting and everybody got up and talked. And finally old Fred Todachini got up and he said, "We know all the white men cheat us. But this man we know. He just cheats us a little bit. I think we better keep him." This was all in Navajo. Then he sat down and laughed. So they all voted they would keep me, "because he just cheated them a little bit." [Russell Foutz, Cline Library interview, 1999]

Trading posts dealt in anything and everything Navajos had to trade, but traders had two major interests, and tended to follow one or the other: sheep and wool, or arts and crafts. The skills and knowledge and work required in each were entirely different. Often a store would have two people, each of whom would take one strand of the trading business: two partners, or a partner and a hired manager, or (more often) a husband and wife. In the Tanner family, Seth Tanner and his son Joe were primarily interested in arts and crafts; Joe's son, Chunky, was a sheep man.

Dad's idea was to buy the Navajo sheep. . . . In a batch of Navajo sheep you'll have the little starving dogie lamb that weighed 30 pounds, and the pet lamb that weighed 120 pounds, and everything in between. . . . My dad was a sheep man to the bone. He loved the sheep business. That was his passion. What he'd do is, buy the bulk of them, or as many as they could, take them up to this big ranch [Tanner property in Durango, Colorado], and start organizing them and cleaning them up. [Joe Elwood Tanner, Cline Library interview, March 1999]

Sheep and wool divided trading into two seasons, buying wool in spring and lambs in fall. In the early days, the traders herded the sheep they had purchased across the reservation to the nearest railhead. They had to be fed and watered, kept together, and sorted out from other sheep encountered on the way. In later years, trucks would come and pick them up from the trading post, but it was still a difficult job. Grace Herring describes the sheep season.

Sheep season was in the fall, and that was a busy time because they'd bring all their sheep and then you had to herd them out every day to get them to pasture. When you got all the sheep out, then they had to be taken to town or someplace to ship. . . . In those days they herded them across [the reservation]. . . .

When we first went out there, the roads were all mud, the wind blew, the rains came, and you didn't go. If it rained, you just didn't go, because the washes get so full you didn't dare to. The roads were so terrible you couldn't ride on them. [Grace Herring, Cline Library interview, February 1998]

Jewel McGee was another trader interested in sheep. He started out at Tsaile, then went to Red Rock Trading Post in Arizona, which remained his main store. He went into partnership with his brother Roscoe McGee on Dinnehotso, Mexican Water, Sweetwater, and Red Mesa trading posts, all in Arizona.

It was about 1933, along in there, when I first went there [Red Rock Trading Post]. . . . We raised our family out there, and that was the most enjoyable parts of our lives, being out there at that time. . . .

Sure I learned Indian [Navajo language], and I learned the store talk, but when you get out to any other places, why, I get lost pretty fast. But very few Navajos spoke English. So you communicated by pointing. Pretty soon, he [the customer] would say the name of the can of tomatoes, and you had to learn to remember that. And you just gradually pick it up. . . .

It was good stock country out there, you know, between those creeks and mountains and the woods. There was lots of stock in there. I used to buy about 4,000 lambs and 400 bags of wool every year, talking about big bags, not little ones. . . .

[During the depression] one time we took a bunch of lambs to Denver, couldn't sell them here so we shipped them to Denver, and I think we got three dollars a dozen for them, above the freight. I think we'd paid a nickel a pound for them [approximately $5.00 an animal or $50–60 dollars for a dozen lambs]. . . .

We tried to get [Navajos] to improve their stock. I used to buy good bucks and rams, take them out and put them out with [ewes] every year. When they first started, why, they were all old long hairy creatures—their wool was more like a goat's. They [weavers] liked it for that, because it was good for weaving. Of course, we didn't like it much to market [or] sell, it wasn't good because it was too hairy. . . . I helped them in their stock business. I built some of the best sheep herds on the reservation. [Jewel McGee, Cline Library interview, February 1998]

Trading posts, even in the late 1930s, were without frills or conveniences. Newly wed young couples went off to work at a trading post together. Jewel and Leona McGee began married life in 1937 at Red Rock, which was built of adobes. Leona remembered the early years.

We'd be just fine until it rained, and then here would come little mud puddles down the walls. Oh, it wasn't a real elaborate, fancy place, but it was very comfortable, and we had a big living room and a post in the middle of the room to hold the roof up, and a fireplace. When we first went out there, we didn't have a bathroom, any convenience like that . . .

But anyway, afterwards we added on a little bit and had a new kitchen. . . . Of course when I first went out there, it looked kind of rough—the men had been batching [bachelor living] there, you know, and things weren't too nice! When I went in the bedroom, the bed had all four legs sitting in a tin can, with kerosene inside, in the bottom of the can. And I said, "Jewel, what in the world is that?" Well, he said he did that to keep the bugs from crawling into bed with him. . . .

Then every time I prepared a meal and we'd sit down to eat, Jewel, before he ate, he'd always do this [a sweeping gesture] on the top of the table. I said, "Why are you doing that?" "Oh," he said, "that's habit. I had to rake off the sand." I nearly had a fit, but I finally got him to quit doing that.

But we enjoyed it, and our children enjoyed it out there. Lavoy, when he was a baby and I had him in the bedroom in a crib, I went in to check on him. He was asleep, and what should I find in there but along the baseboard was the biggest bull snake you ever laid eyes on, four or five feet long. . . . I ran in the store, I told Jewel, "Come quick!" But they would come in the house hunting birds. . . .

But the evenings were wonderful. You could, oh, before it got dark, you could hear an Indian singing away, riding on a horse, going somewhere and just singing at the top of his voice. You could hear the coyotes, and it was really quite nice. [Jewel, Leona, and Lavoy McGee, Cline Library interview, March 1998]

In the early decades of the twentieth century, traders' children sometimes went to schools for Navajos, and sometimes formed a small school themselves. Ruth McGee, George Bloomfield's daughter—Grace Herring's sister—went to such a school when she was a child. But eventually children's education usually required a separation for trader families, and Ruth had to leave the reservation.

> Went to school there until the eighth grade. Then we had to be farmed out to go to high school and college. I lived with some friends that had Newcomb Trading Post, which is about fifteen miles from us [at Toadlena]. . . . I lived with them for two years, and then I lived in Springville, Utah, one year with an aunt, and went to Albuquerque one year, and went to Provo, Utah to BYU [Brigham Young University] to college, one year. [Ruth McGee, Cline Library interview, February 1998]

By the 1930s, when the children were old enough to need to go to school, it was the custom for the men to stay at the store, while the women and children went to live with relatives, or bought a house, in the nearest border town. Separation was a constant in trader marriages. Ruth McGee said when her third child was born, "I was in the hospital with him, and Roscoe was bringing the sheep from Mancos Creek, which is the other side of Shiprock. He didn't come to see me the whole ten days, and I was sure mad at him at that time!"

Traders knew the power of medicine men, and their importance. Older traders remembered the ability of certain Navajos to divine where things—or people—had gone. Sometimes medicine men gave trader wives advice on cures for sick children, and sometimes traders gave Navajos what they knew from their own knowledge of herbs or medicines. Families holding a Sing—the Navajo ceremonial that lasted three, five, or nine days and nights, depending on the kind of ceremony—had special needs, for gifts, for extra food, which were catered to by the trading post. Traders believed in the efficacy of ceremonies and medicine men and women, even if not for themselves.

> Dad told me this story. He said there was a little boy, he was probably eight. He had impetigo [a skin disease] all over his face, all over his hands. And impetigo can just be a running sore. It used to be very prevalent on the Reservation. They had him into the PHS hospital, and Dad said this little kid was just pitiful to see. And so the family went out to the

Mountain behind Red Rock. They had a three-day Sing. He said when the kid came back, his skin was like mine. He said there wasn't a blemish on it. And he said from then on, it wasn't particularly for him, but anytime anyone came in and said, "We need money for a Sing," he said, "If at all possible, we made sure they had it." [Jack Manning, Cline Library interview, March 12, 1998]

2

◢▪◣

NAVAJOS

I'm taking care of my father's horses . . . give them salt and water. He comes here once in a while and asks about his horses. He goes around to different hogans and sings, and he makes his own living that way. I stay right here at my home and take care of my folks. . . . I work pretty hard to get food for my children to eat.

Vogt, 1951: Navaho Veterans, 79

Trade was always a vital part of Indian America. Prehistoric trade routes of great antiquity existed all over the continent, as archaeology shows. Extensive networks connected groups in the Southwest to those in the east, south, west, and north to the Great Plains. There were major centers of trade at Zuni and at Pecos Pueblo at the time Spaniards entered what is now New Mexico. Europeans—from Spain, France, Holland, England, Germany—walked into old trade networks from the first time they set foot on the continent bringing new goods and eagerly accepting Indian products.

Trade between different societies is always an exchange of culture as well as goods, and the exchange between Indian groups and Europeans was no exception. Every object has a practical (or occasionally a ceremonial) aspect, but objects also have meanings attached to them: there's a difference between cowboy boots and hiking boots, for example, partly function, partly culture and style, partly history. Fur and skins formed the major basis of trade between Native Americans and Europeans, but they were obtained as much for prestige as for practical clothing. Beaver, for example, was used widely for a variety of hats worn only by European elites. Indian people bartered furs for tools and food, but they, too, traded for prestige items, for materials that were unusual, different, rare glass beads made in Africa, metal disks from Europe, and used them for decoration or status symbols. And, of course, underneath these major items of furs and metals, other sorts of goods were exchanged: corn, wheat, liquor, meat, cloth, clothes, horses. Other things are exchanged as well, like customs, language, beliefs, sex, and spouses. These are not thought of as trade, but trade usually involves a larger slice of life than is obvious, especially across cultural boundaries. Trade with Navajos brought—and was important for—an exchange of information in both directions.

I want to sketch briefly some Navajo history before going on to describe Navajo-Anglo trade. First, the name that Navajos call themselves is Diné, the People, though they recognize and use the word Navajo, given them by outsiders. Because it is used by traders, and fits with trader history, and is not pejorative or disliked by Navajo people, that is the term I shall use. Navajos are Athabascan speakers, related to the Apaches, and together they are believed to have migrated south from western Canada, perhaps as early as the twelfth or thirteenth century.[1] In 1626, the Spanish noted that there were people known as "Apaches of Nabahó" who grew corn in the Chama and San Juan valleys of northern New Mexico. This area was known to Navajos as the Dinétah, the old Navajo heartland of long ago. In addition to farming, Navajos also gathered wild plants and hunted, possibly in large communal hunts away from their homes; they may have had some sheep but no mention is made of them, and agriculture was basic to their livelihood. They were not purely nomadic, nor particularly unified, rather they lived in sedentary groups, belonging to clans whose names were often place names, traveling widely within their regions. As Navajos adopted the horse and the sheep from the Spanish they began slowly to rely upon sheep herding for subsistence, and to travel between different areas for new grazing.[2]

Relations between the Navajos, relative newcomers to the Southwest, and the long-resident Pueblos were sometimes close, sometimes hostile. During the Spanish return to and reconquest of New Mexico in 1692, twelve years after the Pueblo Revolt, Pueblos and Navajos banded together to escape the Spanish. They moved onto the inaccessible mesas in the Dinétah, living high up on the crags and cliffs. In the early 1700s, Navajos continually raided Spanish settlements, and Spaniards responded, a state of hostilities that lasted until a relative peace set in around the mid-eighteenth century. These calmer years ended around 1770 when Utes and Comanches began to raid the Dinétah, and the Spanish began to move west into the Rio Puerco valley, to the south of where the Navajo then lived. This meant Navajos were surrounded in a kind of pincer movement by different groups, and conflicts mounted again. Gradually the Navajos moved west to the Chuska and Cebolleta Mountains, the core of their current lands.

Trade already existed between all those who lived in the area. Navajos are known to have traded with the Pueblos, Utes, Comanches, the Mescalero, Chiricahua, San Carlos, Jicarilla and White Mountain Apaches, the Hualapais, Yavapais, and Havasupais, Spanish Americans, and later on, the Anglo-Americans. Trading partnerships may have existed at this time, as they did later with Ute groups, as well as with particular Pueblos. They traded livestock, deer hides, baskets, and weavings for corn, meat, pottery, jewelry, and metal. Navajos were known to be fine weavers, and their textiles were much sought after. During the late eighteenth and early nineteenth centuries, Navajos were known as herders of sheep, cattle, and horses. Raiding—but not warfare—was an ongoing activity: raids occurred sporadically, against Zuni, Rio Grande Pueblos, Utes, and Spanish Americans. By the early 1800s, Navajos were primarily herders who also farmed, especially in areas where runoff and water were plentiful, such as Canyon de Chelly, Kayenta, and around creeks and arroyos that drained off the higher areas.[3]

Navajos had no central political structure in the early centuries, nor was it necessary: the focus of life and decisions remained mainly at the level of the small groups making up the larger Navajo population. These groups might have a head man, whose skill was proven in hunting and raiding, and who was accorded respect. His leadership depended on trust and agreement, on the needs of the situation and upon personal ability.

Political changes of the United States throughout the 1800s, although they did not immediately affect Navajo life, were leading slowly toward the incorporation of the Southwest into the new nation. American society began to expand, in territory, in trade and economics, and in technology and entrepreneurship. Mexican independence from Spain in 1821 brought little change to Navajo life in the region. However, when the Americans took possession of the area in 1846 they began a more concerted effort to restrict and control Navajos. In 1848, a peace treaty, the Treaty of Ojo del Oso, was signed with the Navajos. But little was done to support the treaty obligations, and, on the Navajo side, little respect was accorded to the American presence. Raids continued.

Navajos were skilled adversaries, bold fighters, and familiar with the territory. In 1851, Colonel Edwin Sumner built Fort Defiance (a high point of land north of present-day Window Rock) to try to bring an end to the fighting through a military presence in the heart of Navajo country. This met with some success. However, by the 1860s, life in New Mexico was in turmoil. Many years of guerrilla warfare had disrupted Navajo life. Despite the armistice with the Navajos, several groups, including Utes, Zunis, Apaches, Spanish-Americans, and Anglo-Americans, took vengeance against them.

In 1861, when the Civil War began, troops stationed in the West were sent immediately to the field of battle in the South, and Fort Defiance was abandoned. Navajos took advantage of the absence of the military to intensify their raids, and in 1863, despite the Civil War, Colonel Kit Carson was dispatched to lead an all-out military campaign against them. He invaded Navajo territory, and in a short, destructive war, over by the winter of 1863–64, defeated the Navajos. The campaign is well known for demolishing the peach orchards and fields of Canyon de Chelly, and at the close of the winter, Carson rounded up all the Navajos he could find and marched them down to Fort Sumner, known as Bosque Redondo, or in Navajo, Hwéeldi, a Navajo word that carried the meaning of imprisonment and dread.

Many Navajos were taken on the Long Walk to Fort Sumner in 1864. Other Navajos, discovered by the military as they scoured the territory, were sent there later on. A total of over 7,000 Navajo men, women, and children—there were additional Apaches and Utes as well—were kept captive, although some Navajos, living in the inaccessible parts of their country, never surrendered. Fort Sumner lay in the east central portion of New Mexico, east of Albuquerque and north of Roswell, three hundred miles from the very eastern edge of Navajo country. Here Navajos, Apaches, and Utes were kept for four years, from 1864 until 1868.

Army officers tried to encourage agriculture to sustain the captives. Although Navajos farmed in suitable areas of their homeland, the Bosque Redondo area was then poor farming country. The troops dug irrigation ditches, but the effort was a failure.

Sometimes it was insects, again, drought; or again, a flood in the Pecos, or lashing winds or unseasonable cold. . . . Starvation and want were never beyond sight, with rations habitually short and unpalatable; for the Navaho found it hard to accustom themselves to wheat flour, the staple of diet. . . . In the spring of 1868, utterly discouraged and demoralized, the Navaho planted almost nothing, determined at last to meet fate unresisting.[4]

Rations were supplied to keep people alive, and the cost mounted: over $1,000,000 was being spent annually to maintain troops and captives. The military recognized all too quickly that the attempt to "colonize" and turn the Navajos into farmers on unfamiliar soil was an expensive failure. Failure of the crops made reliance on new food necessary and during this unhappy, ill-fated incarceration, Navajos eventually became familiar with foreign foods and goods. They were also quick to pick up the use of new tools and the exchange of new goods—one or two Navajo smiths first learned their skills at Fort Sumner.[5]

By 1868, the cost of keeping the captive population was prohibitive, and after years of a costly civil war the federal government could not continue this support. A treaty was drawn up between the Navajos and the United States that set conditions of peace. It also set conditions of a new life for the Navajos. The treaty was signed on June 1, 1868, by General William Tecumseh Sherman (better known for his Civil War exploits) for the United States. The military personnel divided the Navajos into twelve bands, and recognized "chiefs" or headmen of each band: Armijo, Delgado, Herrero, Ganado Mucho, Muerto de Hambre, Hombre, Narbono, Narbono Segundo, Chiquito, Largo, Manuelito (who had never been made a captive), and Barboncito. Each "chief" signed for the Navajos. The treaty negotiators attempted to give the Navajos land in Oklahoma, but the Navajo headmen firmly resisted, and the military was too eager for resolution to insist. By the terms of the treaty, Navajos were to return to their original lands, though reduced in territory (and later expanded considerably by a series of executive orders).

The federal government agreed to give Navajos rations to get them through the winter of 1868, seeds and tools for planting the following spring, and fifteen thousand sheep and goats. They also agreed to give annuity goods up to five dollars per person for the next ten years. The Navajo people trekked back to their lands, some heading for old homes, some settling in new areas on the way. Fort Defiance was re-established as the Navajo Agency center for administration and distribution of annuity goods, but it lay on the very southern edge of the newly drawn up reservation. Rations were handed out once a week, but Fort Defiance was not an ideal location for Navajos, and many people camped around the fort that first winter in order not to have to constantly travel back and forth to obtain essential commodities.[6]

The Navajos returned as much as possible to their own way of life, to herding and raising livestock. The years at Fort Sumner, coupled with the need for rations when they returned home, had broken up the old ways and led to new habits. Now, Navajos were familiar with and reliant on flour, lard, and other foods, and factory goods. These were at first essential, and then, increasingly, seen as convenient; and from this familiarity and need, trade was born. As people settled down and built homes, and returned to the patterns of herding and farming, a few traders came out onto the reservation to barter goods for wool and sheep. So begins the trader story.

Navajo life and the location of their homes influenced the manner in which trade developed and the placing of trading posts. Navajo homes are called hogans, octagonal or round log or stone houses, in which people sleep, eat, and spend the few hours when they are not working. Navajos built in very loose association with one another, never too close, and never concentrated in villages as the Pueblo people lived. Families might live closer together: the ideal was parents living with their younger children, one or two married daughters with their husbands and later their children, in a cluster of two or more hogans, a shade for the summer, a sweat house or even two—one for men, one for women. Clan relationships held people together, and created kinship ties with strangers. These traditions held strong.[7]

> The Navajo society, we are made up of a matrilineal clanship system, meaning that we will carry on our mother's clan. . . . In the Navajo way, we're told that in order to know who you are, you must know four clans . . . my maternal grandfather's clan, my mother's father's clan. My mother . . . carries on her mother's clan. I must also know my paternal grandfather's clan. His clan will be different. Dad's clan is the same as his mother's clan, he carries on his mother's clan. . . . Name doesn't really mean anything to the Navajo society. In order to identify yourself to another person, who you are, these four clans—that's the way you get to know each other. [Paul Begay, Cline Library interview, February 1998]

The association of a small family or several family members in a loose cluster of hogans, which traders referred to as camps, made settlements on

Navajo lands far-flung, almost solitary. Navajos did not like to live too close together; they also moved between winter camps and summer camps, often quite distant from one another, to give the herd new pasture. Families gained use-rights to their areas, but if they did not use it, others could come in. Traders' choice of location for a post was determined by the routes most traveled by Navajos. As all wagon roads eventually led to water, so most trading posts were also built near water, and many trading post names contain the word *toh*—water.

Navajos in these early times worked extremely hard, and life was often difficult and always required discipline.

> We just ate cornmeal and some kind of weeds, and wild plums, and little wild potatoes. And I didn't have any shoes to wear like these I have on today. And not any kind of material to wear . . . or any kind of velvet. What we used to wear for dresses was just plain white material, and just cut along the sides to make a straight dress. . . . When I was a little girl we didn't have any kinds of dolls or any toys like we have today, so we used to go out and herd sheep. [Nanabah, a woman growing up around 1910, interview from Rapoport, 1954, 115–16]

Critical to Navajo life and survival was mutual assistance and sharing of food and other resources. People were asked to help in building hogans, in hoeing corn, and in herding sheep. Clan relatives were the first to be called on to work, but no one was exempt, and shared work meant shared resources. Navajos helped each other with labor, food, meat, and wealth, and there were strong social sanctions to encourage this cooperation. Children were expected to work—their help was essential—and were taught their responsibilities early.

> Sometimes I herded the sheep. They [his parents and older relatives] chased me around all the time. "Go do something! Get some wood! Get some water! Herd the sheep!" Sometimes I cried when it was cold. It was hard for me to get the wood. We had a hard time to get along. [Pedro Miguel, interview in Rapoport, 1951]

Sheep belonged to individuals, both women and men. Everybody herded, from the youngest child to the oldest woman, taking the sheep out to graze at sunrise, bringing them back to a corral at sunset, or sometimes staying with them at night. Children were sometimes given sheep to care for, to help them learn how to raise them, but in any case they were sent out with the sheep when they were very young.

Men and women had separate responsibilities, though there was little that either did that could not also be done by the other. Life was lived largely outside. In the summer, a ramada for shade was built, a square frame of posts roofed with piñon and juniper branches, for working outside in the summer or for cooking under during a ceremonial gathering. Women had critical roles as central figures in family decisions, as well as taking care of homes and children, and carding, spinning, and weaving wool. Women gathered corn and ground it, prepared all the meals, cooked, and wove on looms set up outside.

Men hunted, farmed, and took care of the herds. They were concerned with their children, too, teaching them the things they needed to know.

> My daddy . . . used to talk to us in the hogan every night. He used to talk
> and talk about all the things we shouldn't do. And while he was still talk-
> ing it used to make us very sleepy and I used to fall asleep while he was
> still talking. He used to teach us how to take care of our home, and how
> to take care of ourselves, and how we should take care of all our horses,
> and sheep. . . . He used to encourage us to live this way so that when we
> grew up and had a home of our own, we would have some sheep and
> horses, and have food to eat and meat to eat, and wouldn't be hungry.
> [Nanabah, interviewed in Rapoport, 1951, 116]

Men could follow a religious path, become apprentice to a Singer (the name for medicine men), and learn the long, intricate prayer chants for one or more of the ceremonies called Sings, chants whose words must be said precisely right for the prayer ritual to be effective.

These ceremonies were important. They brought everyone together from distant homes for healing rituals and feasts. Summer, in particular, was a time for traveling to Sings and their accompanying dances, horse races, and social gatherings. Sings have names—Beauty Way, Night Way, Enemy Way—and each one is responsible for curing certain kinds of illness or trouble. Sickness can result from exposure to danger—ritually powerful animals, perhaps snakes or bears, or hazardous events or materials—lightning or blood—sometimes unknowingly encountered or even placed in a person's vicinity by those wishing to do harm. The patient's family, having had a diagnosis of the symptoms, searches for a well known

Singer who knows the chants for the prescribed Sing. Each ceremony lasts for a specified number of nights: three, five, or nine. These were days of seriousness and pleasure, of religious duties and gift-giving, matchmaking and storytelling, gambling and talking. The primary purpose of a Sing is to heal, to bring harmony, and restore balance, and everyone is invited. In Navajo beliefs, most, if not all, of nature had certain powers, and these could be tapped by specialists who spent years in training to learn the philosophical teachings and prayers. However, there were also people who tapped these forces for evil, and such people, witches, were suspected from their actions and feared by everyone.

There was a winter dance, the Fire Dance, but during the summer there were many sings, both the short three-night sings and the long ones, attended by great gatherings of families.

> Many ceremonies on the reservation began to use materials, fabrics, that the trading post began to use. . . . Ceremonies were done all the time on the reservation. And so what they began to do was buy these fabrics, and they began to use it in the ceremonies. They would have this patient. Towards the conclusion of the ceremony on the last night, they would fold these blankets, fabrics, within about one yard square, and the patient will sit on top of that, and the singing and the prayers go on all night. And in the morning, the patient gets up and the medicine man rolls this fabric and the blankets together and he puts it on his horse, ties it on the back of his saddle, and he rides off. It's used as part of the payment for the job or the service rendered. [Paul Begay, Cline Library interview, February 1998]

In the decades following the signing of the Treaty, Navajos became increasingly self-sufficient, a self-sufficiency encouraged and fostered by the agents and the policy of the Bureau. Farming was taken up again, and herding once more became the central element of Navajo economy. Trading continued with other Indian groups, Spanish traders, and new Anglo-American (especially Mormon) traders, operating out of small trading posts. Navajos, after building up their herds of sheep and goats, turned to cattle and horses, and increased the numbers of all their live-stock. Women continued to weave, and men to make silver, in between herding and hoeing. By 1890, Navajos were enjoying an economic revival, despite areas of poor soil and the problem of droughts or flood. Herds grew as never before and trade prospered.[8]

Slowly, traders learned the needs and occupations of Navajos, and began to supply them. Navajos had incorporated into their everyday life the variety of manufactured items they had encountered, useful tools and equipment such as knives and hatchets, rope and wire, buckets and kettles, tinware bowls, basins, cups and coffee pots, as well as cloth, needles, and thread. The agent at Fort Defiance supplied the first tools and material for weaving and silversmithing, and for raising, shearing, and caring for sheep and horses. Navajos devised ingenious tools from other materials: shearing scissors, for example, were cut from pieces of tin from food cans. As time went on, these items—along with tinned food, coffee beans, sacks of flour, lard, and other foodstuffs—became basic necessities for Navajo life, changing little over the following decades. They became stock items, obtained first at the agency and subsequently carried by traders.

By 1890, Navajos were enjoying an economic boom in sheep and cattle that fostered trade, and more trading posts had been built (as chapter 3 will describe). The number of sheep and goats owned at this time has been estimated at well over 1,000,000, horses at 250,000, cattle at over 9,000. This economic high point, based on a traditional livelihood of farming, trading, and herding, was not seen again. By 1900, there was a sharp decline in wealth, not only because the livestock grew too numerous for the land base but because of economic depressions prevalent in American (and other) capitalist economies.[9]

The reservation was enlarged throughout the 1880s, but not in the 1890s when the number of sheep was greatest. Navajo social mores for sharing did not prevent the development of wealth. Although all families had sheep, some families owned thousands, others hundreds, and some had only a few. It takes about forty-five sheep to support one person, or between 400 and 500 sheep for a family. As the Navajo population increased, the ratio of sheep and goats to people dropped. That is, the number of people increased more than the number of sheep, so that the number of sheep per person decreased. And the land remained the same, so more sheep (and more people) shared the same area. Traders suffered, too, and many trading posts were abandoned where trade was minimal.[10]

Navajo life was influenced by trading in the late nineteenth century. Both Indian agents and traders sought to bring new stock and different practices to Navajo herders. Navajos began to raise herds more with an eye to trading—to selling the wool and eventually the lambs—than to meet strictly local, Navajo-oriented needs. Their economic system had its own organization of wealth and needs, status symbols and cooperation, but it was nonetheless linked to the outside world. The fluctuation of wool prices between 1890 and 1925 affected all ranchers, Navajo and non-Navajo alike, but Navajos were restricted in range to the reservation, while other herders could move more widely. Sheep herding was more and more dependent on and constrained by outside factors. As wool prices fell in 1900, and poor grazing began to affect the herds, Navajos were again destitute.[11]

The year 1900 marks a low point in Indian life and affairs across the continent: population figures were at an all-time low, deprivation and poverty widespread. In 1905, agents with the BIA made an effort to obtain more employment for Indians, usually with railroads, building irrigation structures, or picking crops. Traders, even more than agents, sought work for Navajos: their economic well-being was by now tightly woven together. Traders and agents, somewhat at odds by this time, saw themselves in special relationships with the Navajos, but agents came and went—traders were there for the long term. Inevitably, when a new agent came to the Southwest, the traders knew more: they knew names, families, patterns of buying and selling, they knew some of the camps and sheep herds, and agents often relied on their knowledge.[12]

Traders filled a niche in Navajo life. They provided the foods, tools, and clothes, as well as the means to acquire them—through credit. Traders also brought information on opportunities, rules, paperwork, and regulations sent from Washington and carried out by Indian Office agents. Trade was one way in which Navajos learned about the United States, and the way of life of the outside world. Sometimes they chose to copy it—acculturating themselves to a different society—sometimes they chose to ignore it.

Traders saw many details of Navajo life, the small but integral features of a culture that are only the visible parts of much deeper sets of beliefs and values. They described the avoidance, in the early days, of mothers-in-law and sons-in-law, who should not see or speak to each other, a practice that ended long ago. Other taboos were stronger. Such danger surrounded death and dying that, if a person died in a hogan, it had to be burned, or at least abandoned, and those who took care of the dead had to remain in ritual isolation for four days. If death occurred, a building—of any sort, hogan, barn, trading post—was *ch'įįdii*, that is, the place in which the spirit of the dead could linger and cause harm to others. Traders had occasion to be concerned about this.

We had a [Navajo] man by the name of Tom Johnson that worked at Barnard's as long as I can remember. He burned down three homes—when a person would die in the home, they'd burn it down and take nothing out of it. . . .

I can remember a lady one time having a seizure in the store. . . . Bruce [Barnard] couldn't get her out of the building. He was trying to be kind, but also in the back of his mind was "If this person passes away in this store, I'm out of business." And they got the lady out . . . but had she passed away in the store, he could have burned it down and started over. That's how rigid the Navajos were. [Jack Manning, Cline Library interview, March 1998]

Navajos often asked traders to take care of burials for them, having found out that traders, too, had practices surrounding death: traders, following their own religious beliefs, would build simple coffins and bury the body. Navajos were buried with personal belongings—jewelry, a saddle. John W. Kennedy remembers his father burying a Navajo during the 1918 flu epidemic in which "we had to lead his saddle horse, which was a mare, over by the grave and shoot it so he'd have his horse on his next trip, his next journey."

Education was another and more critical factor in change. By 1892, great effort was taken by the Bureau to make sure children went to schools. Children were usually sent off to faraway (often out-of-state) boarding schools. At the end of the nineteenth century, boarding schools were built closer to the reservation, in Phoenix and Albuquerque; and between 1900 and 1913 such schools went up near trading posts, in places where trading posts had been operating for some time, such as Tohatchi, Tuba City, Shiprock, Chinle, Crownpoint, and Toadlena. Even so, going off to school was a terrifying formative experience for young children. Though Navajo discipline was strict, boarding school discipline was even more severe.

I was taken from my Navajo people. Then, the Government just went out and just took kids to put them in school and so on—I don't know why they picked me, I was just a baby. But I was placed at Tuba City. . . . I was there till I was about four—going on four [about 1920]. They were very mean to us. I never did like it there. They just treated us like prisoners. . . .

I was going on that summer, then, a lot of the Navajo kids . . . they just didn't send them home like they should, like to go to school and you'd go home in the summers. They didn't do that with us, they just kept us right there at Tuba. . . . So Mother [Louisa Wade Wetherill, Betty Rodgers's foster mother] put an end to all that, because she just knew that they were really being very abusive to all the children. [Betty Rodgers, Cline Library interview, July 1999]

This was a period in which Navajo children were taught that they should not speak their language, nor respect their traditions, their ceremonies, or their Navajo culture, but to change their ways—to disobey their parents, even. Many children were virtually kidnapped from their parents, and many tried to escape and come home. Children returned to their homes after a few years, their language and knowledge of Navajo ways lost. One man remembered the words of a medicine man who had talked to him during a sing held upon his return from school, in 1906, when he was twelve.

You're not a white man. What are you going to do when you have learned white men's ways? That won't make you white; you'll still be Navaho. Now, white man's way is one way, and Navaho way is another, and you better learn the Navaho way.[13]

Navajo children were taught very different things as they grew up at home. They learned discipline by rolling in the snow early in the morning, by running, by obeying their parents, and carrying out many tasks from their earliest years. Traditional life was hard, and parents strict: children were taught early on to work hard, to take care of livestock, to endure many dangers and discomforts. Navajo education took place in two ways: first, stories full of history and humor, philosophy and values were told for instruction, example, and entertainment.

The old grandfathers would sit around and tell the children all of the old stories of the old days . . . [they] would sit around in the hogan with the kids gathered around him and the family and they would tell stories. And they did that at night for entertainment. So their stories and legends have been handed down to the younger generation. [Edith Kennedy, Cline Library interview, March 1998]

Second, children learned specific skills through experience. They were sent to herd, or set up to weave, and they were not told how—the experience itself was the method of teaching. The young person might watch and observe, but never asked questions. And though boys and girls had separate responsibilities, and were indeed kept separate from very early on, for propriety and modesty, they were equally relied upon to manage resources, to become leaders, or to raise large herds and responsible children.

> When the baby is older we catch some birds, maybe a bluebird, and we hold it on a buckskin. Then we put corn pollen all over its feathers and we shake it onto the buckskin. Then we let the bird go and we give some of that pollen to the baby to eat. That makes the baby a leader, both boy or girl, and makes them healthy.[14]

By the time of the First World War, Navajos could no longer live well and remain independent of the economic framework of the rest of the country, despite additions of land to the reservation granted after 1900. The demand for wool during the First World War for army coats and blankets, as well as better prices, meant that Navajo sheep were once again a salable commodity for both traders and Navajos. Traders were essential middlemen between Navajos and the market, managing the conversion of Navajo herds into goods, and selecting the kinds of commodities available to the Navajos. Barter of wool and sheep, rugs and silver, gave traders and Navajos a shared interest from the beginning, each from their own side of the counter.

Trading posts were small showcases of industrial culture, even though the range of goods might sometimes be limited. Traders brought the Navajos new tools, foods, and wares, and showed them how to use them. Canned food was a staple, and cans with pictures of their contents were easily understood, but how, for example, to translate a label on a can of condensed milk that carried a picture of a carnation? The preferred brand—Pet—had a picture of a cow on the label. Trade was carried out by gesture, and by trial and error, until traders learned to speak some Navajo and Navajos learned what the goods were, and what they wanted.

At first, it was flour, sugar, lard, knives, and cotton or velveteen fabrics. Then candy, cough mixture, canned peaches and condensed milk, Pendleton blankets, sheep bells, kettles, basins, buckets, bridles, lanterns, dyes for weaving, carding combs, wagons (though these were ordered specially), and saddles. As time went on, new items crept in: jeans, hats, boots, shoes, writing implements, new canned goods. All of the purchases were bartered for Navajo products, much of it barter on credit since sheep and wool came at definite seasons.

The seasons of trading, which determined the Navajo year, did not, in fact, come naturally to Navajos. Navajo sheep husbandry began to change around the beginning of the twentieth century, in response to attempts by agents to improve herds and inculcate Anglo husbandry practices in Navajo herding. Traders, too, especially those who were also interested in sheep raising, began to bring in new breeds and practices such as keeping rams penned apart from ewes, and annual sheep dipping. Originally, Navajos let the rams run with the ewes year round, welcoming the birth of lambs at any time and taking care of winter lambs in the hogan. This was not the way traders worked, a lamb here and a lamb there. Bulk and the economies of scale affected the traders, and they set out to change Navajo practices so that lambs were bought in large numbers. Wool, of course, is seasonal, as sheep grow thicker wool in winter, then shed it in summer. But before 1868, wool, too, was a product solely for Navajo use, not a commodity until traders sought it out, sacked it up, and shipped it out. Traders made the seasons more marked.

With the increase of trade, the desire for goods, and the encouragement of BIA agents and traders, Navajos began to follow new livestock rearing practices, such as timing the birth of lambs for spring so small animals did not have to struggle through cold, snowy winters. Rams were either separated from the rest of the herd, or had a sort of apron tied around their bellies to prevent mating, until the late fall. Then lambs were born in spring, and kept in small corrals, for safety from coyotes and easier care of orphaned lambs or lambs rejected by their mothers.[15]

Shearing now took place in spring, when the wool was still at the peak of winter growth and full of lanolin, the oil that made it waterproof and thick. Although some shearing for wool to be spun and woven might have occurred at different times in earlier decades, by the twentieth century the season for shearing was March, April, and May. Timing was important for shearing: the breed, the condition of the fleece, and especially the weather were all factors. As the weather warms up, the fleece becomes permeated with lanolin, the oil that gives wool its characteristic condition and increases its weight. When the weather becomes too warm the sheep start to shed their coats. New spring grass affects the digestive tract, and, as a result, much of the fleece on the hindquarters gets covered in manure and has to be clipped off. Shearing took place at the point when the fleeces were in their peak condition, but the weather was warm enough to prevent the shorn sheep from catching cold.[16]

Sheep have various diseases, one of which is scabies, an infectious, parasitic disease. Dipping of Navajo herds began in 1895 at Fort Defiance, when scabies was first noticed. The agency set up sheep dips in certain places across the reservation, often at or near trading posts. The dipping solution was a combination of lime and sulfur, which required boiling for two hours, and outdoor vats were set up for this. The solution was then diluted and poured into large dipping troughs. Mature sheep and goats were herded into corrals and guided into the troughs. Navajos were not enthusiastic at first, but agents persisted (white stockmen were using the outbreak of scabies to argue for Navajo herds to be removed from public lands and returned to the reservation). And so dipping became a social event. Families gathered at the dipping stations with their herds, and pooled labor for the intense job of getting sheep into the dip. Men and women used long cottonwood branches with forks at the end to help immerse the sheep in the trough so that the solution would soak their coats and eradicate the scabies parasite, as well as ticks and lice.[17]

> Because of government regulations, when shipping sheep from the Navajo Reservation, for years they had to have two dippings to qualify. . . . So these dippings had to occur about ten days apart, and there was a dip at Kayenta, and one at Bidihochoo, and one at Chinle and one north of Tohatchi, and then we build one there at Rock Springs. . . . I can remember we'd have as high as 17,000 head of sheep there at one time. We dipped every day. We'd have to go down, haul loads of wood, and heat the water for the dip, and had a crew running these sheep through the dip, and so forth. I was usually right at the head of the dip where, if they threw them in or they jumped in, you got splashed real well, so I was covered with Black Leaf 40 dip and bath water all day long. [John W. Kennedy, Cline Library interview, December 1998]

After the burst of World War I prosperity came the depression, and Navajos, like people in other communities beyond the reservation, felt the pinch. They were now beginning to be reliant on wage work, and there was little to be had. In 1928, a blue ribbon committee published a report on Indian Affairs—the Meriam Report—that described miserable conditions on reservations and laid the responsibility for these conditions at the door of the BIA. In 1933, John Collier was appointed Commissioner of Indian Affairs with a mandate to implement the recommendations of the Meriam Report.

John Collier brought to the position of Commissioner a respect for

Indian life and a desire to support Indian self-government and economic development. He put in motion the Indian Reorganization Act to begin a new political structure for the tribes, instituted work programs on reservations, and planned to build new schools on reservations and also bring medical and agricultural programs.

Two of Collier's programs, stock reduction and the plan to develop tribal governments, were especially influential on the Navajo Reservation. The Stock Reduction Program planned to reduce Navajo sheep herds by two thirds in order to solve the problem of soil erosion. The growth of livestock and people meant a reduced carrying capacity—the ability of the land to regenerate herbage quickly enough to support the number of livestock being run on it. The Navajo Reservation had been considerably enlarged, but more land was needed, a solution that was politically unacceptable at the time. The soil, without plants to hold it down, was washing into Lake Mead and threatening Hoover Dam. Collier planned to give the Navajos more land in return for reducing herds, but this plan was not approved by Congress.

To the Navajos, the Stock Reduction Program was the most tangible, most detrimental, and most hated aspect of the New Deal, and the only one most Navajos saw. All other change was interpreted in light of this program, and Navajos rejected many of the New Deal programs because of their resistance to the government's plan to destroy that most important economic element of Navajo life: livestock. Navajos and traders, especially those in the communities far from Window Rock, knew that the traditional basis of Navajo life would be taken away. Fewer sheep meant economic disaster, a radical change in livelihood. Despite the very real problem of overgrazing, the lack of grass, and low weight and poor fleeces of sheep, stock reduction was more obvious in its negative effects. Range riders not only took away livestock, in a few isolated cases they slaughtered a herd because it was not worth trekking it across the reservation for sell. The assault to a Navajo cultural icon was never forgotten. Navajos did not share the philosophy or conservationist approaches of Anglo-Europeans. Now smaller, less well-to-do traditional families had no livelihood, nothing to do, and less to trade with. "John Collier" became an epithet, a curse word, among Navajos.[18]

> It's something the Navajos still resent. It's high on their priorities of things they dislike from Washington . . . because Navajos measured their wealth in the amount of livestock they had. . . . When they were told to reduce

to 200 head, if they had 800 or 900, it was a devastating blow to them. I know I worked for the Atarque Sheep Company south of Zuni Reservation in the spring of 1931. They had had to kill hundreds of sheep. Over behind one ridge, there was a mountain of old sheep carcasses and bones. . . .

Oh, it was serious because they were so dependent on their sheep that when you took away sixty or so percent of their income, it was a real blow to them, and they never did recover. [John W. Kennedy, Cline Library interview, December 1998]

Collier's respect for Indian life and traditions was new in the federal government, and timely. The other element of John Collier's dynamic, radically different approach to Indian affairs was passage of the Indian Reorganization Act, which gave all tribes the ability to develop their own government, write a constitution, and to develop their own political and administrative system. Each tribe had to vote on whether to accept or reject this plan for itself. As a result of anti-Collier sentiment, the Navajo Council rejected the Indian Reorganization Bill.[19]

However, Navajo political development had already been pushed by the need for a formal body to bargain with the oil companies who discovered oil on the reservation in 1921. Navajo tribal government began during those years, and its development was swift during the following twenty years. The members of the Navajo Tribal Council set up a bureaucracy and a sophisticated political machine. On the local level, each community of a certain size, called a Chapter, built a Chapter house and local Chapter organization to deal with community needs and develop community leadership.

The effect of these years was a radical change in livelihood. By the 1950s, herding was not so much a family occupation as that of large stock owners. In the meantime, young Navajos educated in the new Bureau schools became interested in a wide range of occupations, from education to politics, both on and off the reservation. During the early 1930s, federal programs filled in the economic gaps. But the stability of the Navajo economy was gone and, like the rest of the nation, people were hit by the depression in a distant business world. In 1936, after a second wave of stock cuts and a bad winter, malnutrition was reported on the reservation, and by 1937 the situation was dire.[20]

Relations between Navajos and traders were an important aspect of Navajo life. Traders had to know their main customers, and get along well with people if they were going to stay and prosper in the community. They needed to know the size of an individual's herd of sheep, and something about their herding skills and practices. They also needed to know the members of a family, to know who was who, and names were no help. Traders needed to know something about Navajo names and the etiquette that went along with them. It was rude to ask a person's name directly; in fact, Navajos were given traditional names at birth, which were never supposed to be given out to any except close family, used only ceremonially. They called each other by relationship terms—mother, brother, daughter. In addition, people were given descriptive names, which might change over time with the individual's changing appearance or status.

Traders had to learn this. Other Anglos, in the BIA, and especially in the school system, did not understand either the language or the naming practices, and they gave Navajos names that fit their own cultural practices, a first and last name. Sometimes these names were humorous, or came from a historical figure—George Washington was a favorite. Navajos in their own society would be called a different name at different ages, by different people, and might have several names. The first exchange between people who did not know each other was (as Paul Begay explained above) to give the four clans that set an individual in place, and identified each person and their relation to every other person. Clan names, used as last names, undoubtedly reflect the proper response of a child in school to the question of identity: who are you?[21]

The Bureau of Indian Affairs instituted census numbers for Indian people in 1927. Traders never used them; each customer had a name, reflecting something that might be recognizable—a limp, a style of dress or talk, a Navajo nickname heard by a bilingual trader. Most of the names on the accounts of the 1920s and early 1930s were in English: Bent Knee, Braided Hair, for example, at Kin Teel Trading Post. Others were Navajo: Yanabah, Agiltha Dinnison; Peshlakai (a Navajo word, somewhat anglicized, meaning silversmith); Tsinnajinnie (a clan name, appearing in ledgers at many different posts, in many different spellings; clan names appear often for Navajo names). By the end of the 1930s and especially by the 1940s, names were becoming a mixture of Anglo practices (first and last names) and Navajo words (like Begay, "son of," or "Yazzie," little, often meaning a younger relative). Names were used that seemed to fit Navajo language, like Jim or Dan, as well as Navajo words that were pronounceable in English, like Ason. Often the trader's name or that of his wife was taken as a name.

This was not the only cultural etiquette that traders had to learn. Navajos were very quiet: "they are very low-speaking people. They don't speak loudly . . . you just speak very softly and just wait for them to make the move most of the time." Much of the trader interaction depended on each side understanding the other's manners.[22]

> In the Navajo culture, you don't have this eye-to-eye contact, so it was very hard for us. You had to learn to do that. You had to learn to look at a person in the eye and feel good, feel comfortable with it. It takes a long time. Even when I was in high school, I still had difficulty looking at a person in the eye. [Paul Begay, Cline Library interview, February 1998]

Trading was not a hands-off enterprise. The exchange was as much part of Navajo life as it was part of a Southwestern occupation.

3

J·L

THE WAY TRADING WAS

The Navajos are self-supporting. They do not receive pensions, subsidies, treaty payments, or other financial help from the government. To be sure, such assistance was promised them at various times. . . . Whatever material wealth they may possess comes mostly from stock raising. Sheep are by far the greatest source of revenue, although a number of Indians have sizable herds of cattle and horses. . . . the sale of lambs, sheep, wool, and pelts brings him a fairly steady income.

Joseph Schmedding, 1958: Cowboy and Indian Trader, *159*

The first peddlers who drove out onto the Navajo Reservation with a wagonload of goods established the beginning of a unique, and in some ways a specialized, exchange. Anglo-American and Spanish-American traders had traveled among the Navajo before 1864, and there were traders with recorded government licenses (George H. Richardson, Joseph Alexander LaRue, Oscar M. Brown, and William White Martin) who operated at Fort Sumner during the Hwéeldi period. There were traders at Fort Defiance, the center for annuity goods, as well as the headquarters of the first (and for a while the only) Indian agency on the Navajo Reservation, after the return from Bosque Redondo in 1868.[1]

Customers at the forts would have included Navajos, but Navajo trade really opened up on Navajo lands, in Navajo communities, when the first

Navajo trading posts were built around the late 1870s. Half a dozen traders moved into Navajo country and operated out of small, one-room stores of wood or stone, still trying out the response, the danger factor, the possibility of barter, and, above all, whether Navajos would come to them to trade. Ten years after the wagon-and-tent excursions, the exchange was still tentative, and these posts were easily abandoned: an agent reported eight or ten traders on the reservation in 1878, though it seems likely that there were many others on the borders, especially Mormon traders on the northern boundary.[2]

Tentative they may have been, but traders still had to obtain and pay for a license and abide by regulations drawn up by the Bureau. Trade between Native Americans and European Americans was regulated from the very first by the American colonies' Articles of Confederation. Trade with Indian tribes was, of course, a long entrenched exchange, beginning with the fur trade and expanding into every aspect of Indian and immigrant life. After 1779, Congress passed acts and amendments and dealt with trade as an integral part of Indian-American relations. Early on, the federal government attempted to prevent trappers, traders, and trading companies from selling alcohol and firearms, and from engaging in dishonest transactions and rapacious dealings with Indians. From 1790, an Indian agent, who was, of course, a federal official, lived in or near each tribe, supervising the different areas in which Indian people lived. As the organization of the Office (later, Bureau) of Indian Affairs was developed—part of the War Department in 1824, and part of the Department of the Interior in 1849—one of the agent's duties was to manage and regulate all trade, which he did with varying degrees of success.

The Indian agent had to approve the license, and was responsible for overseeing trade in general. Some regulations applied only to on-reservation traders; others, such as the sale of alcohol and firearms to Indian people, applied to all traders, whether on or off a reservation. Traders initially supplied goods to an agency, as well as the Indians served by the agency, and thus were assured of good business. During the first half of the nineteenth century the tie between traders and Indian agents was close. Between 1796 and 1822, the government supplied and managed trading houses (known as factories) for Indian business in the west, and agents were often managers. After government factories were closed, agents frequently became traders themselves, during, as well as after, their service as agents. This practice ended in 1878 when it was ruled that neither agents nor any other employee of the Bureau could have either a direct or an indirect interest in trade at the agency.

Trade of all kinds came to the Southwest by wagons that went out west from St. Louis. By the nineteenth century, the railroads had an enormous effect on isolated regions like the Southwest, connecting them to the economic centers of St. Louis and points further east. Towns and businesses sprang up. Buying through mail-order catalogues boomed. In the early 1880s, the railroad was extended across New Mexico and Arizona, running along the southern border of the Navajo Reservation, with stops between Albuquerque, New Mexico, and Flagstaff, Arizona, and small spur lines running a few miles to various points to draw off the resources—coal at Gallup, carrots at Grants, timber at Flagstaff. More settlers, more businesses, and more goods poured into these railroad towns, and most trading posts operated on the borders of the reservation. Wholesalers opened at these major points, supplying the Navajo trade and taking in steadily increasing amounts of wool: 800,000 pounds in 1881, over 1,000,000 pounds in 1882, 1,050,000 in 1886, 750,000 pounds in 1887, and 1,370,000 pounds in 1890.[3]

There were few criteria for choosing a spot for a trading post, but most important was that it was, or could become, a gathering place for Navajos. A second criteria, not always achieved, was that the post be near water, a spring or stream. Last of all, traders had to be able to bring in horse-drawn wagons. Later traders, inheriting or acquiring trading posts, did not always know exactly why the spot had been chosen. Trader, or Navajo, oral history sometimes passed down the original reasons—good water, the words and permission of a Navajo headman, protection for sheep, and cliffs against which to build sheep corrals—but these reasons were forgotten as generations of people become accustomed to that location for the trading post.

The first trading posts in and around the Navajo Reservation appeared in the 1870s and 1880s. A store, now well known, was built in 1870 at a place then called Pueblo Colorado—now Ganado—in Arizona, in an area that, when the store was built, bordered the reservation and later became part of it. This post was bought a few years later by Lorenzo Hubbell, and it was known as Hubbell's Trading Post from then on. In the 1870s, posts in New Mexico included Becenti Springs, Bibo's, Manuelito's Spring, Tiz Na Tzin, Trubey Canyon. The same time period in Arizona saw The Gap, Lee's Ferry, Tuba City, Chambers (some of these were, like Hubbell's, not then on reservation land). In New Mexico, other off-reservation posts, such as

Cabezon and Chaco Canyon Trading Posts, were also in operation at this time. Around 1875 an Englishman named Thomas Varker Keam built a post at the foot of the Hopi Mesas in Arizona, in a spot known as Keam's Canyon, where he traded also with Hopis. But these on-reservation posts were not all open during the same years, and opened and closed rapidly; much more trade was done from border posts. Fort Defiance remained popular for trading posts—in 1885, there were three trading posts there— as did Gallup. Traders set up stores on their own homestead land, avoiding regulatory oversight of agents and able to attract non-Navajo customers, as well.[4]

In 1881, Red Lake Trading Post, in Arizona, was built. Naschitti, in New Mexico below the Chuska Mountains, was built in 1880. In Aneth, Utah, several trading posts were built, all operating around 1880. Sam and Charles Day operated a trading post at Chinle, Arizona, in 1886. And in the next decade, more trading posts were built that became well known: Tohatchi in 1890; Lukachukai Trading Post, under the Lukachukai Mountains, around 1892; a post on Washington Pass in the Chuska Mountains, later called Crystal, in 1894; and Two Grey Hills, in the Chuska foothills, in 1897. All of these posts operated, though perhaps not continuously or in the same building, at the same spot or nearby, for the next hundred years.[5]

Many of the names of these first posts were, of course, Navajo names, and remained so, either in Navajo or translated. Teec Nos Pos (written in Navajo, *t'iis názbas*) meant "cottonwoods growing in a circle"; Lukachukai, (*Lók'aa'ch'egai*), "reeds spread out white"; Oljato ('*Ooljéé'tó*), moonlit water; and its sister, Shonto (*Sháá'tóhí*), sunlit water. Posts were also named after traders, of course, such as Hubbell's and Keam's Trading Posts, and, much later, Newcomb, Drolet, Carson, and Barnard.[6]

The earliest trading posts were tiny, ephemeral buildings consisting of one room for living, trading, and storage, with a fireplace, a door, and a small high window. Those of the late nineteenth century were still small, perhaps two rooms—a room for trading and a room for living in—and a storage shed or just a root cellar for storage. They were all made of logs or stone, sometimes adobe, had dirt floors, sometimes a metal stove, sometimes an outdoor oven. During this period, Spanish traders continued their earlier presence in the area; there was also the rare Navajo trader— Little Mustache on Black Mesa, Chee Dodge at Crystal.[7]

As time went on, trading posts became somewhat more substantial. Living and storage rooms were added, as well as outbuildings, corrals, and barns. The store, as distinct from the living area, had wooden shelves and counters, and a cast-iron stove. Each new post started as a small building and grew larger over time through the accretion of rooms and outbuildings. The entrance door to a trading post typically opened directly into the store, into what was known as the bull pen, an area in which the customers gathered, surrounded by high, broad counters on two or three sides of the room. A wood stove in the bull pen area heated the store. Shelves lined the walls behind the counter, and the floor was often raised, so the trader was a little higher than the Navajos. The design of this main part of the store was a combination of advertising and defense. The goods could be seen, but not taken. The trader was aware of his outsider status and not at ease until he had been in the area for some years. Robbery and violence were possibilities, and traders were cautious.[8]

Violence was, in fact, unpredictable, as incidents from the twentieth century illustrate. In 1918, a young man, Pat Smith, who was working for the trader at Tucker's Store—a small trading post in New Mexico, south of Chaco Canyon—was killed and the post burned. There did not appear to be any animosity toward the trader, and certainly not toward young Smith who had been working only a few months. The same thing happened to Frank Dugan at Cross Canyon Trading Post, not far from Fort Defiance, Arizona, in 1922. The then Deputy Marshal Sam E. Day, Jr., who had grown up on the reservation (he was also a trader—we shall hear more about him in a few pages), wrote to Howard Bursum in 1924 claiming that "in the last twenty-five years there have been in the neighborhood of twenty such murder cases where the trader has been murdered and his store burned." This statement is likely to be an exaggeration: Day was writing to complain about Peter Paquette, the Indian agent, who he claimed "to be opposed to punishment of Indians, no matter what the crime." But between Paquette and Day there was deep personal animosity, and Day's statements on this, as on other matters, may have stretched the truth. Violence existed, however, in the Southwest, and occurred against Navajos by settlers also.[9]

The 1880s and 1890s were good years for the Navajo, as their sheep, cattle, and horses increased in number, and their economy prospered. More trading posts were built in response to this, and trade blossomed. Traders bartered for sheep pelts, goat skins, piñon nuts, corn, and weavings. Navajos continued to trade rugs with other Indians through the 1870s, but by the late 1880s, at least C. N. Cotton and Lorenzo Hubbell had begun to trade blankets and to engage heavily in Navajo weaving, and by the turn of the century, weaving was a staple trade item. Agency reports give weaving sales in 1890 as $25,000, in 1899 as $50,000; by 1913 the figure for weaving sales was $500,000.[10]

Many of these earliest buildings formed the core of a trading community that brought people in from their scattered homes. Traders began to set up guest hogans for their traveling customers to stay in. Over time, trading posts became focal points where people met and traded, and where missions and Bureau agencies, schools, and clinics were set up. When the agents, responding in the 1920s to the Anglo ranchers' complaints that Navajo sheep carried scabies, an infectious mite, set up sheep dips around the reservation they often put them up near trading posts, drawing on the natural convergence there of Navajos. In the 1920s, the Navajos in trading post communities built meeting places for political organization. These centers were called Chapter houses, part of the growing political structure of the Navajo tribe. But I am jumping ahead in time.

Navajo traders of the turn of the century were usually independent, though some were part of, or staked by, larger trading concerns. Traders associated with, or encouraged, missions of their various denominations, Mormon (most often), Catholic, or Protestant. Gradually, trading became one of the occupations that Southwesterners did for a livelihood, work that required some knowledge about livestock, wholesale dealers, and the lay of the land. Young men learned about trading from fathers, uncles, or in-laws, and families often went about the business of making a living in a more cooperative fashion, pooling resources, know-how, and information. There were always figures (like Joseph Schmedding and Elizabeth Compton Hegemann) for whom trading was one of many interesting, often unrelated, adventures in life. Solitary figures also cropped up in trading, men who came from somewhere else and rolled into an out-of-the-way post and sometimes stayed. Isolation was part of the picture of trading—a geographical isolation, as well as an isolation from one's own culture and people: in the ebb and flow of seasons, days or even weeks would pass without another person entering the store.

The trading post wares were basic and standard: flour, coffee, lard, sugar, salt, baking powder, bolts of cloth, tinware basins, plates, bowls, cups or mugs, tools (hatchets, rope, buckets, knives, shears), weaving materials (carding combs, dyes), shoes and hats for men, and later on (in the 1920s) jeans, shirts, and even later still (in the 1930s) clothes for schoolchildren. Also sold were salt bacon and salt beef, crackers, candy, cough mixture, and various chest rubs for coughs, soda, and its predecessor, a sweet syrup, sewing needles and lanterns, canned milk, canned tomatoes, and canned peaches. There was a wide variety of goods sold for sheep and wool production: bells, shears, wool carders (to which the Navajo took readily, though they preferred to make their own hand spindles, rather than use spinning wheels).[11]

Many commodities came in containers—cans, boxes, sacks—which were not always obvious indicators of their contents, and the trader had to explain what they contained. Over time these very containers became familiar—traders tended to stick with brands Navajos knew—and very useful. They were reused for household purposes (by Navajos and traders): Arbuckle's coffee came in boxes that made useful tables and dressers, lard cans turned into chimneys or buckets, flour sacks made curtains, dresses, or covers. The trader, depending on his or his wife's intuition about the habits of their customers, would also bring in new brands or items to be explained or even demonstrated.

In the absence of a shared language, Navajos pointed out the goods they wanted—with the lips, since pointing with a finger was bad manners. Most traders learned a little Navajo, and a few were, then and now, fluent. Every item was fetched by the trader and his wife or occasionally an assistant or partner, and examined by the customer. If after careful thought the item was felt to be necessary, it was added to the growing pile of goods, to be reckoned against the value of wool brought in by the family, or listed on their account to be paid off with later trade. Money was rarely used; Navajos more frequently made silver coins into jewelry, prized by Navajos and traders alike.

Navajo wool was the main attraction for trade. Navajo sheep were originally those descended from the Spanish sheep brought by Oñate in 1598 and raised by Spanish settlers and by Pueblos. They evolved into hardy, small, tough animals, known as churros, well adapted to the dry Southwest. There is some debate about the breed of sheep portioned out by federal government officials to the Navajo in 1868 after the Treaty: they may have been American-bred English sheep, or they may have included some old churro sheep from New Mexico. As the herds increased so did trade. Agents began attempting to improve the sheep, to cross breed the small Navajo sheep with breeds that would improve the size of the animal and the quality of its wool. At the turn of the century, Navajo sheep were certainly small and hardy, with rather coarse fleeces, less oily than that of other breeds, and, therefore, easier to weave and much liked by Navajos because of this.[12]

Traders played a role in fostering Navajo crafts, and this is the aspect of trading that attracted early attention and continues now that the trading era is over. In the next chapter, I will give an outline of trade in arts and crafts, how traders fitted into this and how the birth of the United Indian Traders Association (UITA) came from the link between traders and crafts. Here, let's note that development of the craft trade was also due to the Fred Harvey Company, the railroad and automobile, and museums, especially those whose directors—such as Edgar L. Hewett and Charles Lummis—were vigorous promoters of the Southwest. Traders were in the business of turning any and every Navajo product into a commodity, because if Navajos did well, so did the trader, and some had an aptitude for this market. Traders who were successful enough, even fleetingly, to create headed stationery for themselves always included "Dealer in Navajo blankets and silver" on it. The traders' more mundane, but no less fruitful, services or equipment, such as automobile repair (this, for the border town trader, was aimed at non-Navajo business) or livestock supplies, were usually added as well, in smaller, lighter type. A few even listed "furs, wool, skins, hides," a last vestige of the trade in fur and skins that had been carried on for two hundred years on the northern reaches of the American continent.

Between 1905 and 1911, more than thirty new posts appeared: in New Mexico, Beclabito, Bisti, Black Rock, Blanco, China Springs, Crownpoint, Dalton Pass, Huerfano, Newcomb's (it was also known as Nava, and later as Drolet's), Pueblo Pintada, Tocito, Sheep Springs, Shiprock, Toadlena; in Arizona, Cameron, Castle Butte, Chilchinbeto, Cornfields, Dilkon, Dinnebito, Dinehotso, Greasewood, Indian Wells, Kayenta, Leupp, Mexican Water, Piñon, Rock Point, Sawmill, Steamboat, St. Michael's, Sweetwater, Teec Nos Pos, Tolchico, Oljato, and Warren's. Some of these were on land that was not yet part of the reservation. Most of these posts stayed in business, and although in many cases an old building was abandoned and a new one built in a slightly different spot, the old name was transferred to the new post.

Trading posts tried to keep at a distance from each other, drawing on customers within a radius of a few miles, but some locations, especially where there was a Bureau headquarters, supported several trading posts. There was some competition between stores. Older posts had become known to Navajos and could be guaranteed customers. New posts—especially with new traders—would be built tentatively and, if unsuccessful, would be abandoned; many small stores opened only to close a year later.

Everything was exchanged on a barter system, worked out across the two languages. There were a few rituals of trading. A generous trader of the turn of the century and later might keep a pot of coffee on the stove, and almost all traders kept a can of tobacco nailed down on the counter, along with cigarette papers, for customers to use. McNitt notes that traders "studded the bottom of the free-tobacco box with nails pointing up to encourage a pinch with the fingers rather than a scoop." Trading was slow, as each item was taken down for the customer to consider. It was seasonal. However little Navajo a trader spoke, he or she would at least greet customers, shake hands, try to call them by a name—perhaps any name— laugh at jokes, tell stories. Whatever was understood in these exchanges, goodwill and good manners were certainly required.[13]

Money, which Navajos had encountered before with the Spanish, was not a new concept, but at trading posts, even in Fort Defiance, there was no hard cash. Traders often created their own tin counters for currency— called *seco*—good only at the trading post. Credit was an element of trade from the start. It was not just the Navajo who lived on credit; the trader relied on it also. Credit was a reason for the underlying tension between Indian agent and trader. Leupp, referring to an earlier period, described "the severely critical attitude assumed by the Indian Office toward the traders who allowed their Indian customers to run up unconscionable debts." Little changed, in this regard, over the decades. Traders saw credit as necessary for the Navajos, because of the seasonality of their goods and the fragmentary nature of wage work. However, once they had extended credit, traders were not eager to let customers slip off to another trading post. Agents saw this as troubling, forever linking a Navajo to one post, leading people into bad spending habits and deeper debt.[14]

As silversmithing developed and, by the turn of the century, became a recognized craft of high value, silver and jewelry became another element of trade. Navajos wore jewelry for adornment and status, and traded it widely with different tribes, as well as with Anglo traders. Silver was also used as wealth: given to a trader as a pledge against a credit account, or pawned for groceries or cash, to be later redeemed.

It is hard to know exactly how the idea of pawn arrived on the Navajo Reservation. In western society, pawn goes back to the late 1400s, when the Catholic order of Franciscans, originating in Italy, opened pawnshops, known as *monti di pieta*—banks that take pity—to combat usury (loans for interest) that was forbidden by the Catholic church. The Franciscans gave small loans to the poor, taking personal items as pledges and making no profit. Pawnbroking as a charitable institution continued throughout Catholic Europe to the present; at the same time it also developed into a profit-making enterprise, especially in England, associated with dealers in second-hand goods who were also moneylenders.[15]

In America, pawnbrokers existed in seventeenth-century New York, and later on Philadelphia, and were present in most of the cities of the northeastern United States by the early nineteenth century. It was an institution almost always associated with urban centers, since profit came from volume and people who pawned could not afford to travel far, and with people who had few reserves and little portable property. Pawn was an alternative to the growing system of banks.

In the Southwest, pawnbroking was in existence by 1880, and it was observed among the Navajo by 1881. In Santa Fe in 1891, the merchant Jesus Sito Candelario—and no doubt others—was acting as a pawnbroker. Candelario's pawnbroking was typical: he handled between three and twelve pawn transactions a day, of pledges ranging from gold watches ($3) to pistols, stoves, rings, and shawls ($1.50). The loans varied from twenty-five cents to $3.50, and the pledges were usually redeemed anywhere from two days to three months later, often to be pawned again and again. Navajo pawning followed a similar pattern. The practice, however introduced, was swiftly adopted and soon became an economic pattern especially well adapted to Navajo needs and a seasonal economy. It became a standard practice at trading posts: a temporary exchange of silver bracelets, necklaces, *getohs* (bow-guards worn by men), and *concho* belts to obtain credit or cash. The piece could be reclaimed, and if there was a loan against it, this was paid off over time. Indian agents criticized pawn heavily from early on.[16]

Traders and agents were uneasy allies, connected by culture, divided by practices. Traders played a considerable role, after the Treaty of 1868, first as providing Navajos with an incentive for keeping the peace, then bringing essential goods for survival and barter, and finally serving as an agent of change and a broker of culture, as well as of goods. Traders provided Navajos with wage work, and wage work linked Navajos to the dominant economy. Indian agents in particular recognized the influence of the trader—on any reservation. Their recognition was tempered with concern: the influence could be for good or for bad, that is, traders could support or defy the policies of the agent. Traders had a long tradition of defying the government. In the eighteenth century many, if not most, traders throughout the continent had dealt in whiskey and guns, despite regulations. While this practice tailed off in the nineteenth century, regulating the trader was like regulating the wind. In 1910, a former Commissioner of Indian Affairs, Francis Ellington Leupp, noted rather dryly that "there are few parts in the drama of reservation life which a trader of the older generation has not been called upon to play, and the stock character in his repertory is that of Everybody's Friend."[17]

The agent's acknowledgment of the trader's role was often tinged with resentment for his competing influence. The agent and the missionary were eager to change Navajo ways, their values and beliefs, their habits and ways of life. Traders were a force of a different kind, interested in supplying (and in the process altering) their material wants, and bartering for Navajo resources to gain their own. The long tenure of many traders brought them into the Navajo universe, especially if they learned to speak Navajo. Some traders married Navajo women. Leupp summarized similarities and differences between agents and traders: "Most of what the traders did for the Indian could have been done by the agents, but he [the Indian] knew that an agent would be more inclined to hold him to a strict account than a trader. . . . Besides, agents were changed from time to time, whereas a trader might stay on for a whole generation." Thus the trader, outlasting missionaries and agents, became a fixture, and between 1890 and 1920 the trading post gradually became an institution: a Navajo institution, in Navajo surroundings, responding in varying degrees to Navajo needs.[18]

The trader was both an agent of change, a link between the world outside and the world inside the reservation, and the means to continue traditional life. Through the trading post—even more than at the agency—Navajos learned about goods, money, work, and in general life beyond the reservation boundaries. Despite the distance between the reservation and Wall Street, the external market also influenced what happened in the trading posts. But traders took whatever Navajos had in exchange for goods, because their own economic survival depended on that of the Navajos, and began more and more to provide them with wage work, either acting as hiring agents for the railroad or farms, or hiring them at the store.

By and large, by the time of World War I, trading on the Navajo Reservation was a distinct occupation. It was usually carried out by men, bolstered by family networks and connections to wholesale houses, strengthened enormously by wives and by cooperation between relatives at different posts. Sometimes trading was one aspect of an enterprise, such as a wholesale business, that engaged in a variety of activities, and whose owner could not be at all posts, and may not have ever worked at a post. These were the "absentee traders" who paid a trader to manage a post. Trading by now had quite a long history, and traders who had done well, been involved in current affairs and business, and made money—Thomas Keams at Keams Canyon, Sam Day and C. N. Cotton at Chinle, Lorenzo Hubbell at Ganado, for example—gave trading a cachet. For the most part, traders of the very early years of the twentieth century were local boys, starting young, beginning with little, building their own post, or patching up and enlarging an older one.

The Days—Sam Day, Sr. and his sons Charles and Sam Jr.—are excellent examples of traders and trading practices at the turn of the century and during the subsequent decades. Sam Day, Sr. came into the country with his wife Anna in the 1870s as a land surveyor of the reservation, worked at Fort Defiance, and became a prominent figure in the small Anglo-American community that lived on and at the southern edge of the reservation. He and his wife homesteaded at what is now St. Michael's, and his three sons, Charley (Charles L. Day), Sammie (Sam E. Day, Jr.), and Willie (William Andrew Day) spent their childhoods in Navajo country. Sam Day, Sr. and his two older sons Charles and Sam Jr. were all involved in trading. They also ranched, raising cattle and sheep, and they bought and sold trading posts, goods, and livestock.

Around 1900 Charles Day bought a post from Billy Meadows near Chinle. His father, Sam Day, Sr., moved up to join him in 1901, and in 1902 they built a large trading post in Canyon de Chelly (much later known as the Thunderbird Ranch). Charles sold the Chinle post a few years later and moved to St. Michael's, near what would become Window Rock, Arizona. There he built a trading post that he ran for some years and, according to his letterhead, dealt in wool, sheep, cattle, Navajo blankets, and silverware, as well as having a garage, supplying gasoline and oil, and doing repairs and welding. Charles Day bought the usual goods for the trading post from Gallup Mercantile Company: 7-foot-long wool sacks (at 34¢ each); butter (27$^{1}/_{2}$¢ a pound); cans of chili, pears, tomatoes; packets of dye (scarlet) and colored yarn (black and especially scarlet); 5¢ cigars; slabs of bacon, sacks of flour, and cases of melons, peaches, and potatoes; Pendleton shawls (fringed) and robes (without fringes) at $6 and $5 each, respectively; and the occasional saddle (at $26) and bolt of cloth.[19]

His business was uneven, a common enough situation for traders. In November 1914, Gallup Mercantile wrote to say they would not load any more of his teams up: "your business has been too irregular to justify us in carrying the account." In March 1915, they noted that "judgement has been entered against you by certain parties" and they must insist on Charles reducing the balance he owed them, some of which he managed to pay through the summer and fall. Charles sold Navajo rugs to a dealer in Phoenix who expressed disappointment, saying that they were more expensive than others of the same grade. In 1915, perhaps to balance accounts, Charles took a partner at the post, a man by the name of J. P. Peterson (we do not learn his first name, nor anything about him). Yet the ebb and flow of business is typical: in December of 1915 Gallup Mercantile wrote him to offer oranges from California and apples from New Mexico. The following year C. N. Cotton and Lorenzo Hubbell, old friends of his father's, urged him to settle his accounts with each of them. The Days were, however, well-off by local standards. Charles Day owned an automobile, uncommon for traders of this time. Indeed, Charles died in 1918 at the age of thirty-nine as a result of injuries from an accident that occurred when he and his father, driving near Chambers, Arizona, went off the road and down an embankment.[20]

Early trading was usually combined with other pursuits. Sam Day, Jr., like his father and older brother, was also a trader though he was rather more versatile (and even less successful). As a very young man, he worked for the railroad, then for Hubbell and Cotton, and later for his father and brother. Sam was constantly out of cash, never able to pay bills. In 1920, he was also a U.S. Deputy Marshal for a time; in 1923, he began to make a series of drawings of Navajo ceremonial sandpaintings to sell to the Fred Harvey Company to put up in the lobby of its hotel, El Navajo, in Gallup. The Harvey Company seemed a promising source of income, and for a year he bargained with them for more and more money for sketches, descriptions of sings and sandpaintings, which he thought he could obtain from his entrée into Navajo culture and his friendship with an aging medicine man. He never made good on his promises. In the end, the medicine man and the Harvey Company all grew suspicious of him. Although he managed to sell several paintings and claimed that he had paid for ceremonies that were providing him with material, Fred Geary of Harvey's broke off connections with him.[21]

The pattern of indebtedness, of lack of money, was not, however, restricted to Sam Day, Jr., and seems prevalent in the trading business and perhaps in business in general during the period from 1914 to 1925. Owner-traders like Sam Day, Sr. bought goods from wholesalers, and supplied goods to clerking traders who managed stores for them, and at each level (the wholesaler, owner-traders) payments were begged for and barely managed. In 1920, a trader at Cross Canyon, apparently in debt to Sam Day, wrote him that "even the notes I held on the business have been forced away from me and as I am absolutely broke, I must protect myself and my family from utter ruination." J. J. Kirk, a wholesaler carrying an account for a clerk of Sam Day's who had died, wrote in 1923: "Can't you send me a check . . . money is quite scarce with me and I'll sure appreciate it."[22]

Say Day's correspondence illustrates the prevalent attitude toward Navajos, from traders, agents, and others. Though Navajos had sheep and jewelry, and were obviously hard workers, the cultural differences produced an arrogance, a superior attitude toward them. Traders, however, sometimes married Navajo women, and almost always stayed on or near the reservation all their lives and learned to temper their attitudes with a certain respect. To be sure, traders had a specific view of Navajo life and spending. Traders who engaged Navajos to work, either for themselves or for the agency or, in the 1930s, the federal government, made sure their wages went toward paying off their credit. But nothing in traders' behavior—at least of those traders who lived among their customers—approached that of one allotting agent, a Mr. Simington, working out near Sunrise Springs, Arizona, in May 1920. His car got stuck in an arroyo. Nearby, a Navajo and his son were working on a road for Maxwell Black, the trader. Simington indicated to the two Navajos, Hasteen Tso and Hasteen Tso Begay, that he wanted them to pull his car out of the sand. Hasteen Tso said "his time was Mr. Black's" and he would therefore have to be paid $2. At this, Simington said "goddamn" and a variety of other swear words, which Tso recognized. He refused his help; as he later said, he would not help a man who swore at him. Eventually, Simington called them back, handed them a slip of paper that he said was a check since he had no cash on him, and they pulled him out.

Hasteen Tso and his son returned to the trading post and handed the piece of paper to Maxwell Black. It was a U.S. government voucher for traveling expenses, on which Simington had written "This Navajo thinks this is a check. It is only my request that you tell him to go to Hell." Black read the paper and told the two Navajo men that it was worthless (we do not know if he told them what it actually said) and suggested that they take their tale to Marshal Sam E. Day, Jr. and get him to do something. Hasteen Tso and his son recorded their separate accounts in a sworn deposition before a witness, and Day wrote to Simington to complain and ask what he was going to do about it.[23]

Day had strained relations with at least one Indian agent, as was typical. On one hand, agents frequently disapproved of traders marrying Navajo women, and were always suspicious of their business practices, and on the other, traders had a deep dislike of regulations. In 1905, a phone line was run from Gallup up to the Franciscan mission school of St. Michael's, and the traders in the area put up some funds to have their own line hung just below it. In 1922, agent Peter Paquette paid Navajos to remove the traders' line, claiming it interfered with the government's own phone line. The animosity between Paquette and Sam E. Day, Jr. was at its height, and Sam Day—who had complained about Paquette at every opportunity—interpreted the action of removing the line as Paquette's revenge.[24]

By the 1910s and 1920s, the reservation, by now enlarged, was filling up with sheep and with families herding them. Distances were great, the people almost invisible in the sandstone outcroppings, forests, and expanses of sagebrush. Journeys were long and unpredictable, yet the land was crisscrossed with sheep and horse trails and dirt roads for wagons and motor vehicles, indicative of travel and use. There were thirty-nine trading posts, tucked away in the recesses of the reservation in 1910, and about eighty in 1918 (demand for wool was high during the First World War). The open, empty landscapes of early photographs of the Southwest are somewhat misleading; in fact, every square mile was used, for grazing or growing, for living and working. This was a land of extremes, of drought and blizzards, of high, dry plateaus and sheltered canyons with running water, of summer thunderstorms that poured water through arroyos, of winter days in which temperatures rose from freezing at dawn to 60 degrees at noon.[25]

In October, when they'd have the Northern Navajo Fair, [in Shiprock] Navajo people would come from as far away as, oh gracious, probably Mexican Water; south, as far as from Newcomb or Naschitti, and it was a six, seven-day trip to get there and attend the fair. . . . I remember the whole area of Shiprock would be just covered with smoke in the evening where they were building their campfires and cooking their supper, and the same way with breakfast. Hundreds of wagons. . . . The heads of one team would be almost in the back end of the other wagon as they journeyed. . . .

They would come, and if the weather was good, they were happy and they really enjoyed themselves. But . . . sometimes the first of October it would be just raining . . . the mud was up to the hubs on the wagons and it just wasn't a fun time. They'd come and the trading post would be just crammed with people coming to get in out of the rain. [Jack Manning, Cline Library interview, March 1998]

Technology began to improve travel and communication throughout the 1920s. Telephone lines continued to go up on the edges (though not the center) of the reservation. By the 1930s, electricity was ubiquitous in towns, but trading posts had generators. The automobile was beginning to appear everywhere. Although rarely owned by Navajos and still infrequently seen on the reservation, it was the trader's boon and main expense, if, indeed, he could afford one at all. Beddow Buick Company Machine and Automobile Shop, established in Gallup by 1924, announced on its headed paper: "Cylinders reground—Pistons fitted—Crank pins reground—Radiators rebuilt—Lathe work our specialty." Freight, however, was still carried by horse-drawn heavy wagons, and Navajo freighters were among other entrepreneurs who hauled all kinds of goods across the reservation, from trading post commodities to pipe and other equipment needed by the developing oil industry in the area around Farmington. Oil was discovered in 1921 on the northeast corner of the reservation, and, as we shall see later, affected reservation life, business, and government.[26]

There were, however, few modern conveniences in life at trading posts in 1924.

We had the store building . . . with a dirt floor. Then it went directly into the little kitchen we had. We had just one room there, where we cooked, ate, and slept, all in that one room. It was also dirt floor.

Had to carry your water from the San Juan River. The store was right up on top of the ridge from the river. When it was really muddy, why, you know how we cleared our water? We'd fill these—there were wooden barrels there when we went down there—the Indians would carry the water up from the river and fill the barrels. We'd take a can of milk and put it in that fifty-gallon water barrel and stir real hard. It just clears all the water up. The sand and dirt all went to the bottom. . . . [Stella Tanner, Cline Library interview, July 1998]

Trading was, above all, a business: it just wasn't like any other business.

Lots of what they called trade slips—probably in today's world it's illegal. They'd bring a rug in that was worth $35. Well, they'd get maybe $3 cash or $5 cash, and then a trade slip for the remainder. And trading out a trade slip was always fun. In twenty minutes you could trade out the $25, and then they were down to the last $3 or $5 and you'd take twice that time to get the last dollars spent because each one of the kids would want a lollipop or a bottle of pop. . . . It took a lot of time to get the last dollars off a trade slip. [Jack Manning, Cline Library interview, March 1998]

The focus was on *Navajo* business, and little attention was paid to anybody else.

Traders, you know, they worked all day long. It was hard work: they opened up in the morning and it was a crash program until they could finally close their doors sometime after dark [in the busy seasons]. . . . Well, when a tourist came along, they took up a lot of time asking questions and wanting to see everything. And while you're talking to one tourist, you could wait on three or four Navajos. A lot of [traders], they held back a lot when they were dealing with outsiders. Later on, as the roads improved, they all got to where they'd like to have a tourist come along, but it took a few years to break them down. [John W. Kennedy, Cline Library interview, December 1998]

A good economy for Navajos meant good business for trading posts also. A resourceful trader could make money, and many did; just as many made nothing, or lost everything. Some went around the reservation working at different trading posts. Trading was a business that was both sedentary and full of travel, depending on season. The trader spent much time waiting for customers—*naalyéhé ya sidahi* is the Navajo phrase for trader, he who sits for the sake of the goods. It wasn't all sitting: repairing buildings or putting up new sheds, loading or unloading merchandise, organizing construction (of buildings or roads) by Navajos, sacking wool, and many tasks of larger or smaller kinds took up the time.

When they first came out here, my dad [Claude Richardson] went to Blue Canyon, he and Hubert from Blue Canyon went and built that store at Kaibito. From Kaibito, there's a government man that told my dad they needed a store at Cameron—a lot of Indians over there, no place to trade, because they couldn't get to Flag[staff] . . . and they gave him permission to go over there. They had to get an Indian to find out where the water was—there's a spring above the store . . . so that's when they built that store, along about 1917.

Those days, there wasn't too much jewelry. Most of the early days was rugs. Had lots of rugs, not much jewelry. They started getting into jewelry . . . in the early twenties, but before that, mostly big belts or beads. They used that more or less just to borrow a little money on till they got their rug made or sold their sheep or lambs or ewes . . . sometimes sell their cow. Whenever the superintendent said they could sell them, that's when the trader could buy them. [Bill Richardson, Cline Library interview, March 1999]

The trading seasons were marked by wool sales in spring and lamb sales in fall. By the mid-1920s, the pattern of activities, of shearing, dipping, and lamb sales was well entrenched. Traders had to herd the sheep they bought a considerable distance to the point of shipping, making sure they had food and water, that they did not get lost, stolen, sick, or dehydrated. Every task required many hands. Navajos were hired. Wives worked.

The men were all—they were the traders. Women were just flunkies! Well, we did whatever had to be done, but the men were the traders. We didn't buy the lambs. But—I bought lambs, and I even bought cows and sheep at Round Rock, when Raymond [Blair, Marilene's husband] wasn't there. I learned! I learned how to do it, but it was hard. There was a time when I was running Round Rock and Raymond was running Rock Point. I had to learn. [Marilene Blair, Cline Library interview, February 1998]

Credit was extended between the two seasons and expected to be paid off twice a year, at roughly six-month intervals. The trader, too, lived on credit, disbursing his own debts to the wholesaler with the wool and sheep, rugs and silver, that he took in trade.[27]

Traders had to be able to understand something of the language, be able to understand behavior in unfamiliar cultural frames, and be able to persuade across two cultures. But at the same time, though they lived in the community and heard Navajo spoken from childhood, they remained apart from Navajo society. As Jack Manning put it, "My dad didn't want my brother, or me, either one, to learn Navajo well enough to understand a sad story. That was his comment." The cultural practices of the Navajos that affected trading were generally known about, paid attention to.

There were challenges, and most traders took them in stride, even enjoyed them.

I'd buy every goat that I could possibly get my hands on. . . . I could buy goats all summer long or all fall long—winter long, for that matter. I've had a corral full of goats in the dead of winter, where if they'd lay down, they'd freeze to the ground, you know. But I could always make a little money on goats—not a whole bunch, but just enough to keep me interested. And so this old man down there at Red Mesa . . . he called me . . . Hasteen Tł'ízí, Mr. Goat! I was the only one on the Reservation that I know of that'd buy a goat. But when he passed on, why then that fun part of it quit. [Jay Foutz, Cline Library interview, August 1998]

And more ordinary challenges.

Money's important to them, but it doesn't last long. . . . If they miss you on the first of the month, nine times out of ten . . . you're not going to get it that month—you'd just as well forget about it, because they had a reason for it, and they're not going to pay you. . . . Most of the time it's that they've had a problem with the family, the family needed money for a medicine man, or school kids. . . . They tell me all the time, "Well, sure, I didn't pay you this month, but where you going? I'm not going anywhere, I'm going to be here. Where are you going? What's your hurry?" So that's their philosophy. [Loyd Foutz, Cline Library interview, August 1998]

And the gambles of business.

I guess my first very pleasant deal was when one year that wool went to a dollar a pound at Teec Nos Pos. I sold my wool at a dollar a pound when it was up to a dollar a pound, and paid off the bank. By spring the people that sold theirs got 25¢ for it, and that was probably my most satisfactory deal. It went to $1.25, and nobody sold, they were waiting for it to go higher. Then it started down. I sold at a dollar, because I couldn't sleep at night, I owed the bank so much money. [Russell Foutz, Cline Library interview, April 1998]

Trading was an entrepreneurial undertaking like, and at the same time quite unlike, any other.

4

⌐·⌐

TRADING IN ARTS AND CRAFTS

I asked Grey Moustache if he would let me take his photograph. He declined, saying: "No I won't let you do that. I don't have any of my turquoise or silver on. People who see it will say, 'Why, that Navajo doesn't have anything at all.' I would feel like a chicken with all its feathers plucked out."

John Adair, 1944: The Navajo and Pueblo Silversmiths, 99

Navajos, on any occasion whatsoever, wore silver and turquoise jewelry of all kinds: bracelets, rings, necklaces, earrings, belts, and brooches. Women wore brooches, necklaces, bracelets, and sewed silver dimes or buttons across the yokes and down the sleeves of their velvet blouses, carrying a weight that indicated wealth and beauty and could be used for trade by cutting off a piece or two if necessary. Men wore concho belts and hat bands, necklaces and bracelets, and sand-cast silver *getohs* (wrist guards). Horse gear, such as headstalls and bridles, was heavily decorated with silver. An older Navajo silversmith, being interviewed in 1938, said: "You don't see many of those today except on pawn racks in the trading posts. At that time [1890s] every Navajo who could afford a silver headstall had one on his horse, because a horse is an extension of the individual—an individual's exclusive possession." Jewelry—silver in particular—gave the wearer style, status, and a distinctive Navajo identity; it was recognized by other

Navajos as indicative of good taste. No matter what the practical aspect of different items, workmanship and aesthetics came into play. Other Navajos acknowledged and prized the skill of certain weavers, basket makers, and silversmiths, and wanted to own their handiwork, or learn from them how to make silver. The origin of Navajo crafts was always something made for their own use, as well as for trade.[1]

In this chapter, I'm going to look at the many different strands of American life and commercial enterprise that led to the popularity of Native American arts and crafts. Traders played an important role in this, but they were not alone, even though they may have thought so, as they looked at rug after rug, talked to weavers, looked at silver jewelry, and worked out how to sell Navajo arts. The UITA was born out of the need to help and protect craftspeople and traders, because the moment crafts became popular they were copied and look-alike objects swamped the market, very much like today. So this chapter will explore influences and commercial trends in American society between about 1900 and 1940. In chapter 5, I'll go back to writing about people.

The traders' involvement in crafts took several years to develop. After Navajos returned from Bosque Redondo, it was some time before weaving returned to its former glory, so much had normal life been shattered and broken. As traders settled into their business, rugs, silver, and baskets were accepted as barter items. The wholesalers who were supplying the traders with goods in exchange for wool began to accept crafts more eagerly as the market for Indian arts and crafts developed. But by then traders were also interested in that market themselves, and entrepreneurial traders bypassed the wholesaler entirely, making a name for themselves as dealers in rugs and, later, silver.

Navajo crafts, and the selling of these crafts, developed in a way that braided together aesthetic and economic interests of outsiders, and old and new ways of life for Navajos. Although such arts are now commonly recognized, known about, exhibited in museums and art galleries, and the skill with which they are made appreciated along with their beauty, this was not always so. An object must be seen in the first place; but more than that, it needs to be understood, and it must have a context that makes appreciation—and purchase—possible. In other words, an object like a Navajo blanket must, if it is to be sold, be put where it can be seen and known, and it must also be given a meaning of some kind. Buyers had to want to own a particular blanket not only because it appealed to their aesthetic sense, but also because it showed how much they knew about

Navajo weaving. Traders played a role, among others, in making Navajo arts and crafts visible, known, and appreciated; more than this, they were responsible for subtly changing them for market and making them available for purchase. Museums, curators, anthropologists, and collectors, and to some extent, traders helped to give Navajo weaving a context, to give the buyers some idea of the life of the weaver, the cultural surroundings of Navajo rugs.

To understand the story of how Navajo weavings and silver came to the marketplace we need to go back in time once more, to a period of American life somewhat like the Dutch mercantile expansion of the seventeenth century. Toward the end of the nineteenth century, America, despite periodic economic depressions, had an economy in which an increasing variety of goods were being made available: practical items and tools, and new goods from factories, things that saved time or increased comfort and convenience, from canned foods to made-up clothes. There were novelty products, the results of ingenuity and developing technology, such as photographs and glass and everyday necessities, such as paper and shoes. Americans who grew rich bought spoils from all over the world—paintings, antiques, parts of ancient buildings. In this cornucopia of goods there began to appear the artifacts, ancient and modern, of Native America. Crafts came from reservations to buyers in places like New York, Philadelphia, and Los Angeles. Traders were the linchpins in this train of goods, and Southwest traders did their utmost to increase business from their own communities and regions.

Toward the end of the nineteenth century the appreciation and purchase of Native American arts and crafts from the Southwest and other areas blossomed. An explosion of exploration, technology, industry, and travel was underway in the United States by 1850. Everyone was involved, in small ways and in large: explorers and immigrant settlers, photographers and well-to-do wanderers, entrepreneurs and industrialists, laborers who built the railroads, teachers, clerks. Travelers brought back tales and objects that hinted at the extraordinary variety of life in the continent; writers spread the word in books, and photographers in pictures; the rich collected artifacts of every kind; the middle classes visited museums and world fairs; and everyone dreamed of traveling, of seeing things for themselves. A quickening technology resulted in the building of railroads and hotels, and made travel easier and comfortable.

Commerce, business, and marketing also thrived on technology. The late 1800s were the years of growth in advertising, magazines, department stores, and mail-order business. Selling through catalogues—such as the well known Sears Roebuck catalogue—was an entirely novel, American way of reaching a larger number of customers widely and unevenly dispersed throughout the country. Some of the traders, C. N. Cotton and Lorenzo Hubbell, for example, took to this method of merchandising, which had already been tapped into by the trade in curios, or curiosities. The curio trade catered to—even created a market for—a fascination with Native American objects, and sold a wide range of items said to be handmade by Indians. This was often true, though the items were specially made and not traditional. The early catalogues of the curio dealers, appearing around 1882–87, gave descriptions about the life of Native Americans that were imaginary and highly erroneous. Mail-order customers nonetheless brought much business through catalogues, and traders adapted their business to this new method.[2]

As commercial life expanded, so did the intellectual curiosity of the nation's inhabitants. John Wesley Powell, for example, was not only an important explorer of the Southwest and the Grand Canyon, he also contributed to knowledge of the West and its Indian people. In 1879, he founded the Bureau of Ethnology (later the Bureau of American Ethnology), part of the Smithsonian Museum, to encourage and support the gathering of knowledge about Indian peoples. Surveys and expeditions focused on Indian life, history, and material culture, the Hyde Exploring Expedition excavated (and traded) in Chaco Canyon, New Mexico, and the Hemenway Expedition brought Frank Hamilton Cushing, as well as Matilda Coxe Stevenson, to Zuni Pueblo. This was the period of museum building: the American Museum of Natural History in New York in 1869, the Brooklyn Museum (then Institute) and the Denver Museum in 1903, and a host of smaller museums were founded in association with universities and academies. All had curators or affiliated anthropologists, such as Franz Boas at the American Museum of Natural History, and Steward Culin at the Brooklyn Museum, whose research and interests in American Indians led to a search in every corner of the continent for the most unusual, or most typical, or most rare, or most beautiful items of Indian cultures.

Indian traders in the Southwest and elsewhere, though they did not recognize it, benefited from museum interest in Indian tribes. It brought recognition and attention to crafts, and gave Navajo traders incentive to trade in them and to influence the work. Traders were often connoisseurs in their own right, and some had their own collections. Curators, as well as private collectors, forged relationships with traders and visited them to see and purchase specific items: C. G. Wallace at Zuni, Lorenzo Hubbell at Ganado, and many lesser-known traders, often became links between collectors, curators, and the local artisans with whom traders worked. But traders were not experts in Navajo life, and it was curators and anthropologists who filled in the background that made Navajo crafts interesting to outsiders. Traders lived close to Navajos, understood their needs, but in those early years most of them maintained a rigid distinction, often marked by clothing—few traders wore cowboy hats in those days—religion—Navajos needed to be converted from "heathen ways"—and language—though men learned enough Navajo to trade, women were discouraged from learning any. Traders appreciated the crafts, not the life; they understood the skills, not the culture.

Exhibits, not only in museums but at the large, popular expositions and world's fairs of the turn of the nineteenth century, were an important means of educating and informing people about Native America. These expositions took place regularly, almost every five years in America's growing cities—Chicago, Saint Louis, San Francisco, San Diego, Portland, to name a few—between 1876 and 1920. People came to see and learn about everything that was going on in America: art, manufacture, styles, innovative technology such as typewriters, electricity, and telephones, and (at many, if not most, exhibits) American Indian life. The fairs were extraordinarily popular: the Chicago World's Columbian Exposition of 1893, whose Indian exhibits were popular, had, for example, 25 million visitors—one-third of the American population of 70 million people. The themes constant in the Native American exhibits of these fairs and expositions were predictable and even patronizing: they stressed the "primitive" and exotic nature of the Indian people, whose culture was thought at this time to be on the verge of disappearing, even though they brought a real appreciation of their material goods. These expositions brought Native American people and artifacts to a broad public, with all the problems of their patronizing perspectives and the creation of stereotypes. Many Pueblo and Navajo people were brought to the fairs to carry on their crafts as people watched, and museum curators and traders were the conduit through which Indian people were involved in fairs.[3]

While expositions brought American Indian crafts to the public view, museums set them in the public eye as items of value. Both fairs and museums helped to explain their context and their history, as well as their manufacture. An appreciative, or at least interested, public grew up around the expositions.[4]

There was also a shift in patterns of selling and buying. While local markets continued to exist, purveyors of Navajo arts and crafts began to look to a collecting elite, and to travelers, who might have money, time, and broader comparative aesthetics, as the ideal purchasers. During the latter part of the nineteenth century, there had been production of inexpensive or non-traditional items, often pottery, some of which had been encouraged, even ordered by merchants and traders, who often claimed the items were "ceremonial." Then as now, this resulted in their eager purchase (although many of these so-called fakes were not only made by Indian craftspeople but were, and remain, interesting in their own right). By 1905, the well-entrenched curio business was focusing on the interest in handicrafts and home decorating. Trains and hotels drew on this interest and encouraged travel and the consumption of Indian crafts. A new market was growing by this time, an increasing number of travelers who wanted reminders of an appealing, if little understood, Indian culture encountered en route.[5]

The arts of the Navajos, especially weaving and silver work, had attracted the attention of traders from the beginning. To begin with, items such as Navajo blankets and jewelry had a practical, as well as a decorative value, and were intended for local use and trade. They were made with skill and beauty because these aspects were always involved in creation. Navajo weavings were well known by at least the eighteenth century, a hundred years before Bosque Redondo. In the late 1700s, weavings constituted part of the trade network with Mexico, a trade that continued with the United States from the mid-nineteenth century. In the beginning, Navajo blankets were made for the Navajos' own purposes and their own use, but their exchange for other items was probably engaged in from very early on with people who lived in the Southwest. Certainly Ute and Pueblo, Spanish and Mexican people had traded with Navajos for their weavings since at least the late 1700s. As basket-weaving (learned from the Paiutes) and silversmithing (learned during the Bosque Redondo period, as well as from Spanish metal workers) developed, these crafts, too, began as items for the Navajos' own use and came to be sought after by other people in trade. The crafts seem always to have had the dual purpose of pleasing the eye and serving the user. Blankets were worn for warmth or used for bedding or under saddles; jewelry, and, in particular, silver jewelry, had many purposes. Brooches, buttons, and pins fastened clothes and boots; buckles fastened belts, bowguards (or *getohs*) protected the wrist of hunters with bows.[6]

Some traders had begun to supply curio dealers in Santa Fe and else-where. Others evolved their own business in Indian arts and crafts in tan-dem with curio dealers, with wholesalers whose off-reservation depots stocked Navajo and other Indian items, and from the 1890s with the Fred Harvey Company's expanding rail and hotel business. But over time, as traders took more rugs and silver in trade, they began to influence the crafts. Artisans in turn devoted their energies more exclusively to their work. In trading outside the Southwest, the very functions of the crafts changed.[7]

Traders like Lorenzo Hubbell, C. N. Cotton, and J. B. Moore sought to make weaving an item of fine quality, in essence recreating the vitality of the earlier trade in blankets. They worked with weavers to adapt the rugs to the tastes of new buyers; they encouraged good weavers and fostered new designs. There were different networks of buying and selling, and entrepreneurial traders found them out or helped create them, making known the availability of Navajo weavings beyond the reservation and its borders. These well known traders don't need introducing, and I shall not attempt to describe weaving styles they promoted, or the specifics of their influences on design and colors that have been well described by others. Rather, I want to sketch their efforts and the business they created.

Lorenzo Hubbell traded at the post that bears his name, in Ganado, from about 1878 to 1930; he built up one of the best known trading "empires," managed in concert with his sons Ramon and Lorenzo Jr. Clinton N. Cotton began in partnership with Hubbell in the 1880s at a post in Chinle, and established a successful wholesale business in Gallup in 1894. Both Cotton and Hubbell separately built up rug businesses through catalogues. Cotton, according to McNitt, was the first to try to appeal to buyers in the east through illustrated catalogues, and in 1897 he employed George Wharton James, an English photographer and writer, to write descriptions for him. He had three categories of rugs, each a differ-ent price: fine rugs, saddle blankets, and thick woven soft shoulder blan-kets or dougies. Cotton mimeographed his catalogues, and, using city directories that he had obtained, mailed them to businesses and buyers in the east.[8]

Both Cotton and Hubbell made changes in the trade in blankets. Around 1880–1900 Germantown yarns—wool from eastern sheep, spun and sometimes dyed in eastern mills—and brightly colored, aniline, dyes were popular with both weavers and buyers. Hubbell (though not Cotton) disapproved of these, and eventually discouraged their use, as well as the use of cotton warps that did not last well. Certain types of dyes began to be avoided at Ganado, especially the bright colors—red, green, black, yellow, white, orange—of "eye-dazzler" blankets, though Hubbell provided red and black dyes, popular among the weavers.[9]

Lorenzo Hubbell encouraged weavers to spend more of their time weaving rugs. An artist, E. A. Burbank, painted copies of older rug designs for Lorenzo Hubbell, paintings that the trader could use to show people who became interested in ordering a rug and to give to weavers when a specific pattern was requested. Weavers (in Ganado and elsewhere), however, never copied each other's designs or reproduced a design they themselves had already woven, and they usually copied the painted designs with subtle variations. Hubbell also began to request very large rugs from weavers, commissioned for the large houses of the wealthy and for Harvey Company hotels.[10]

There were many smaller entrepreneurs who affected weaving. One of these was John B. Moore, who came from Wyoming and bought a trading post in the Chuska Mountains in 1896. He changed its name to Crystal, and from then until he sold it in 1911 devoted his energy to building up trade in fine rugs that incorporated new, complex, and intricate designs. He sent wool from local sheep to eastern woolen mills for cleaning, and had some of it dyed to colors of his own choosing, usually blue and black. When the wool came back, he issued it to the weavers he considered the best, along with undyed colors of gray and brown (the colors for which Crystal is now known came later, under another trader). Moore also created catalogues for his rug business, with his own descriptions. In his 1911 catalogue from Crystal, Moore wrote: "it is also our mission here to buy any and everything the Navajo has to sell . . . [and] to sell him in turn . . . everything, in fact, that he has need for." This was every trader's credo.[11]

A few miles north and east of Crystal were two other traders who encouraged exceptional quality and developed strong rug businesses. One was George Bloomfield, who came from a Mormon family in Ramah, New Mexico, and moved to Toadlena Trading Post in 1912. The other was Ed Davies, another Englishman, who bought the neighboring post of Two Grey Hills in 1912. Bloomfield and Davies worked together to encourage finely spun yarns and quality in weaving. Here, weavers used no dyes, preferring the colors of sheep: black, white, and shades of gray. In this region, on the eastern foot of the Chuska Mountains, quality was spurred on by the instigation in 1909 of the Shiprock Fair, where rugs were exhibited, by W. T. Shelton, then the resident Indian agent.[12]

What traders were doing seems obvious, but the implications are interesting. By encouraging weaving, they focused on something that was already valued by Navajos, and drew on materials and activities firmly centered in the Navajos' own world: sheep, wool, cleaning, spinning, dying, and creating woven designs. Indeed, there was only so much the traders could introduce as innovation: Navajo weavers preferred their own looms and methods of spinning. The major item adopted into the weaver's toolkit was the wool carder, supplied by traders.[13] Traders changed not the craft so much as the role it played: they made weaving a far more central occupation of women who wove skillfully and daughters who were beginning to learn to weave. Originally, weaving was only one among many occupations. A particular woman might prefer to spend more time weaving, perhaps having more relatives who could tend sheep, and become more skillful as a result; others might spend far less time at it. Traders who were interested in weaving and in trading for rugs intensified their interaction with weavers, commenting on their work and requesting new and different styles. They were generous to the best local weavers, who in turn had more to share with relatives and gained status by their ability to support many family members and clan relatives. Traders intensified the economic value of weaving, supporting the strong role of women.

Thus traders, without realizing it, altered work patterns. Because they made weaving economically important, Navajos shifted the focus of their work at the loom, more than it had already shifted within Navajo society, away from use toward trade, toward purchase by people outside the exchange networks of kin, clan, and tribes. Although Navajos continued to use the thickly woven saddle blankets, they gradually ceased to wear their own woven blankets. This change in clothing was also due to the manufacture by Pendleton mills of blankets for the Indian market, the involvement of many more Navajos in the Anglo world, either in school or work, the pressure to wear western clothing, and the fact that such clothes were readily available at trading posts.[14]

The growing appeal of Navajo weaving was acknowledged by the publication, in 1914, of the book *Indian Blankets and Their Makers* by George Wharton James. James, a popular writer, collector, and general man-about-the-Southwest, described the long history of Navajo weaving, explained how far back the quality and design of Navajo weaving went, and quoted many early accounts of manufacture or descriptions of Navajo blankets. It was an indication of the place of Navajo weaving as an item for purchase in the non-Navajo world, and of the links made by travel and tourism between these different worlds. James noted that "four firms, more than any others, . . . stand in close relation to the purchasing public" and contributed to the "rapid improvement" of the art of weaving. In James's opinion these were Fred Harvey and his company, the partnership of Lorenzo Hubbell and C. N. Cotton, J. B. Moore at Crystal, and the Benham (then Burns) Indian Trading Company (which by 1914 was located in Los Angeles). These were, with the exception of Hubbell and Cotton, not trading posts but off-reservation enterprises catering to tourists, as well as well-informed buyers.[16]

In general, traders during the early decades of the twentieth century, even at some smaller posts, began to pay more for better-made blankets, and to refuse to buy, or at least to pay much less for those of lower quality. James notes that "the education in some cases had to be *of the trader* rather than the weaver" and that purchasers themselves were becoming more discriminating. This growth of recognition of quality was a two-way street. Cotton, Hubbell, Moore, and others knew about good weaving and understood its craft. They, and other traders after them, began to make sure that information about Navajo weavings and Navajo life came to the attention of purchasers and collectors. Reservation traders were always as much influenced by their customers' needs as by factors of market preference. However, traders less interested in weaving were pushed—by the market for better weaving, by collectors and museums, by the success of their colleagues—to recognize the difference in quality in what their customers brought them.

As with weaving, so silver also was taken up, traded, and its manufacture altered. Silver, unlike weaving, was a relatively recent Navajo art. While Navajos may have been involved in some metal work before 1864, the working of silver began at Bosque Redondo and developed rapidly in the following years, especially in the area around Fort Defiance. By the 1890s, when Navajos had regained—and increased—their herds, and were again pulling themselves up to a better living, silver jewelry was much sought after by Navajos, as photographs of the period reveal. This was the period in which trading posts began to carry tools for working silver: crucibles, metal-worker's saws, and files that Navajo silversmiths used to file designs in the end of pieces of metal to use for stamping designs on silver. Stamps or punches were used on silver made especially for outside trade—older jewelry, preferred by Navajos, was plain. Silver, like weaving, was originally made for Navajo use and trade among themselves and with

Pueblos, though soldiers in Fort Wingate in the 1880s had apparently commissioned Navajo smiths to make tobacco canteens and other small items. Like weaving, smiths never liked to copy things. Also like weaving, traders took silver in trade, and became increasingly involved in working with and encouraging silversmiths as they had weavers.[17]

Silver jewelry had a high value in Navajo and in trader culture, although for somewhat different reasons. For traders, silver differed from weaving because of the basic value of the metal from which it was made. Navajos used coin silver, at first American coins—dollars, fifty-cent pieces, and quarters—and when the law that prohibited defacing American currency was enforced, Mexican pesos. For Navajos, the jewelry itself was important: they wore it when traveling, visiting, and at ceremonies for style and status. The essential value, for Navajos and for Anglo traders, led to the economic system that developed between Navajos and traders. When Navajos needed to trade between seasons of lambing and shearing, they would pawn a silver piece to the trader to tide them over, redeeming it when they could. Traders added pawnbroking to their range of activities, usually taking silver as pledges, and later accepting other Navajo goods.[18]

By the turn of the century, Navajo silver was getting the attention of— and being influenced by—outside interests, as weaving had before. Herman Schweitzer of the Harvey Company had begun buying pawn from the traders in the 1890s and, when this proved too heavy for tourists, looked for ways to encourage smiths to make jewelry that would sell outside the reservation. He began to supply a trader at Thoreau with silver and turquoise, asking him to request smaller, lighter pieces from silversmiths. The results met his demands, and the Harvey Company began to give other traders raw materials to farm out to the smiths. Mercantile companies in Gallup followed suit. By 1923, some businesses, such as the Kirk Brothers, Gallup traders and wholesalers, advertised on their letterhead "silverware made to order."[19]

By the 1920s, traders were farming out raw materials. They gave silver to silversmiths whose work they liked, and who would work at home and bring the piece back to the trader when it was finished. A few traders recognized that the way in which the silver was made was an inseparable element of the final piece—its creation, its style, its heft and appearance. The creativity of the artisan grew out of the methods of their production: homemade anvils (often stumps of trees and pieces of railroad metal), homemade blowtorches, sets of stamps and hammers, and the surroundings of hogan and family. Bill Stewart, trading at Pine Springs in 1938, noted that "The best way to get good silver made for you is to give out the turquoise and the silver to the smiths and then just forget about them. Don't ask the smiths when they come into the store when they are going to bring in the work. . . . The slower a silversmith is, the better he is." He was one of a small handful of people who understood how silversmithing fitted into Navajo life.[20]

Quality, in the eyes of traders interested in traditional silver work, lay in the weight of silver—heavy, though not as heavy as the oldest pieces—and its designs, stamped with dyes or cast in sandstone molds. Traders had seen the older pieces, both pieces they had purchased and pieces that had been pawned to them, and they encouraged a style that was a blend of old styles and new, that catered to a growing market and that tapped the creativity of the smiths. Silversmiths taught their wives and young sons how to make silver, so that they could help with some of the work. Other relatives would also ask to learn from them, and silversmiths whose work was in demand often had several apprentices.[21]

Tourism fed the competition, often encouraging companies who made lower-priced pieces; not all visitors sought quality or tradition. Yet travelers brought the Southwest attention, generally. The Fred Harvey Company had made a name for itself catering to visitors to the Southwest, building a reputation for service, quality, and style, both drawing on and contributing to the appeal of the West. In 1905, El Tovar, perhaps the jewel of the half dozen Harvey hotels, was opened at the Grand Canyon (not yet a national park). The Harvey Company developed a style of interior decoration that drew from Southwestern Indian cultures: Pueblo pottery, Navajo weaving and sandpainting, murals based on activities, dress, and ceremonies in different cultures. Harvey hotels used the decorative motifs of Southwestern Indians and the idea of "authenticity." The company had formalized Herman Schweitzer's collecting and curio business as the Harvey Company's Indian Department in 1901, directed by John F. Huckel and managed by Herman Schweitzer. Mary Colter, the architect of many Harvey hotels, furnished them with Navajo rugs and silverware, Hopi and other Pueblo pots, and Indian (usually, but not always, Southwestern) murals and motifs. Herman Schweitzer filled the Harvey stores with Southwest Native arts and crafts. At the Grand Canyon, near the El Tovar lodge, a special building, the Hopi house, was built, and Hopi and Navajo craftspeople were hired to make and show their finer pottery, baskets, or weaving. The Harvey Company was undoubtedly an influence on traders: Schweitzer was buying about $25,000 worth of blankets annually from Lorenzo Hubbell. And Schweitzer was picky, rejecting half of what he was offered.[22]

The burst of exposure in exhibits of Indian arts and crafts helped to drive interest, recognition, appreciation—of the crafts, of the Harvey Company's decorative style—just as it helped traders to market Native American crafts and charge good prices for them. Traders, however, were not passive in this enterprise. They were not only middlemen in the exchange of goods for crafts but sought marketing networks and instituted changes in manufacture. As trains and the Fred Harvey Company made travel to the Southwest possible, traders on the Navajo Reservation took a hand in changing not just the production of weaving and silversmithing but the economics of the crafts. They were quick to take the opportunity to bring work, trade, and business to themselves and to their customers.

The demand for Navajo and Pueblo crafts seemed bottomless, and, as a result, other merchants began to manufacture items that copied Southwestern patterns, items that were not designed or made in the traditional way. Companies who competed with the market for Indian silver began to set up small factories, sometimes using Indian labor (not necessarily the same tribe as that advertised) but using machines set up in a warehouse.

The increase in copycat goods was seen by traders not only as a threat but as an affront. Traders' livelihoods, as well as that of their customers, depended on a desire for hand-made Indian artifacts, the real thing as opposed to a copy. In addition, the increase in such fakes took place at the lowest point in the Navajo economy. The depression hit the whole Southwest very hard; poverty in the Pueblos and reservations was extreme. Traders tried to foster an interest in weaving and silversmithing to ensure some income to families, and continued to try to focus on, and educate, the discriminating purchaser on authentic practices. Authenticity was essential to Navajo trade, stemming from an understanding of the crafts, an appreciation of the skill that went into them, and a desire to boost their sales. A few traders, on and off the reservation, set up "bench-work," where Navajos would work on silver at the store, altering the conditions of Navajo life and work. An attempt was being made to pass an Indian arts and crafts bill to protect and promote genuine handiwork. However, it was voted down, due to opposition by some businessmen (and by Schweitzer, who felt it constituted a government monopoly). The inaction of the Indian Service under Commissioner of Indian Affairs

Charles Rhoads did nothing to help the situation, either in Congress or with the situation in the Southwest.[23]

In 1929, William Atherton Du Puy, an author, journalist, and executive assistant to the Secretary of the Interior, visited the Navajo Reservation. While he was there, he suggested to various people—traders, dealers, others in Gallup—that an organization of traders would help to protect Indian crafts. The idea was not new—others had discussed the possibility of such an organization, and the advantages or disadvantages of a private organization by traders, whose interest lay in selling other products, as well as crafts. In 1931, in response to these suggestions and the growing quantity of copycat goods being sold as if they were Indian made, a group of traders met in Gallup, after the Indian Ceremonial. The Gallup All-Indian Ceremonial gatherings had become an annual event from the first decade of the twentieth century—an event that drew more and more people, and at which showing, judging, and selling arts and crafts became a major feature, activities in which traders were always involved. The traders met to discuss how to set up an organization that would coordinate and strengthen their efforts to authenticate their goods and discourage fakes. They hoped to be able to influence standards, and to make these standards known, among traders, government agents, and the public.[24]

So, in 1931, the United Indian Traders Association (UITA) was created, organized "for the perpetuation and protection of handmade Indian Arts and Crafts." Their intention was to foster the arts and crafts of Southwest Indians, and although the association was set up primarily by traders working with the Navajos, traders working with Pueblos could and did become members. Their certificate of incorporation set forth the goal:

> to associate together for their mutual benefit all individuals, partnerships, and corporations living in the territory of the United States and dealing in the handicraft of the American Indians produced according to the traditions and in the manner and circumstances in which such handicraft has been produced in the past.

Membership would consist of "persons engaged in dealing in the products of Indian craftsmanship produced by the Indians in the manner and circumstances in which the Indians have customarily produced such articles."[25]

Clearly, there had been a shift among traders, from exchanging mainly wool and sheep for merchandise, to a specific recognition of the importance of arts and crafts in this exchange. Traders were now actively engaged in influencing and promoting crafts, though in 1931 this did not in any way minimize the central focus of the trading post on wool. They were also influential in insisting to BIA personnel that some government help in protecting arts and crafts (to some extent, their business) was needed.[26]

Despite the traders' roots as isolated, individualistic, even peripatetic small merchants, not particularly fond of rules, regulations, formal proceedings, or any kind of organization, many of them supported the UITA. The directors (there were seven) had to be traders with at least ten years of experience dealing with Indian customers. The president was a respected trader, Bert I. Staples, who had been involved in breeding sheep with Navajos interested in improving herds, searching for breeds that would raise the quality of both meat and wool. The vice president was R. C. Master, from a trading post in Zuni; Tobe Turpen and C. N. Cotton, both Gallup traders, were secretary and treasurer, respectively. The first directors named were traders on and around the Navajo reservation: L. L. Sabin (Fort Defiance Trading Post), C. G. Wallace (Zuni Trading Post), J. M. Drolet (Tohatchi Trading Post), Ramon Hubbell (Hubbell's Trading Post in Ganado), Lloyd Ambrose (Thoreau), Bruce M. Barnard (Barnard's Trading Post in Shiprock), and Mike Kirk (Manuelito Trading Post). The UITA set up a place of business in Gallup, from which the Association sold raw materials for crafts, as well as the crafts themselves.[27]

The manufacture and promotion of crafts falsely labeled as "Indian" continued, however. Despite complaints from all quarters, Commissioner Rhoads did nothing to provide a remedy. In 1932 the Federal Trade Commission (FTC) began hearings on a firm in Chicago accused of shipping weavings and jewelry claimed to be Indian made, but, manufactured in mills or factories. The case was based on the Act of 1914 that covered interstate commerce, and the final ruling ordered the company not to use the words "Indian" or "Navajo." The FTC marched on to fight other companies, carrying out proceedings against the Maisel Trading Post Company in Albuquerque and in Gallup, New Mexico, for selling jewelry manufactured by Indian laborers using mechanical equipment under the supervision of non-Indians, but calling it Indian-made (implying traditional Indian work). The Maisel Company ignored the ruling against them, and the FTC struggled through the courts, attempting to require the company to state clearly that its goods were not Indian made. The case lasted until 1935, and despite its best efforts, the FTC's attempts came to nothing: the court of appeals accepted Maisel's obfuscating wording.[28]

Because the livelihood of Southwestern Indian people was at stake, the Indian Service was the appropriate government department to become concerned about copies and deterioration of quality and prices. In 1933, John Collier was appointed Commissioner of Indian Affairs under Harold Ickes, Secretary of the Interior; both men began reforms to try to protect and restore Indian life. Ickes began to institute action to ask for a ruling that National Parks could only sell handmade Indian crafts. In 1939, the Educational Division of the Indian Service began to set up craft projects at BIA schools. Ambrose Roanhorse, a silversmith, was hired to teach the craft at Santa Fe Indian School around 1937. In 1939, he went to the Wingate Vocational High School in Fort Wingate as director of the Wingate Guild, to stimulate employment and craft production.[29]

Collier fought to create an Indian Arts and Crafts Board as the government's primary attempt to help develop and market Indian crafts. The United States Congress, after two failed attempts, passed a bill in 1935 creating the Board to boost the Indian economy through the work of artisans, although it was recognized that this alone was not enough. The following year the staff of the Indian Arts and Crafts Board set up standards for silver work, and in 1937 began the use of a government stamp as a means of authenticating the manufacture and quality of silver, pieces, and a tag for the same purpose for weavings.

In 1936, a year after the creation of the Indian Arts and Crafts Board, Rene d'Harnoncourt was hired as assistant manager under Louis West. He had been involved in the arts in Europe, Mexico, and America, and his interest in, and activities toward, Native American craft production was influential in stimulating interest and trade. In June 1937, d'Harnoncourt replaced West as general manager and began a series of endeavors aimed at marketing Indian crafts. He was concerned, of course, with all Indian crafts, but his efforts relating to the Southwest were relevant to jewelry: he commissioned John Adair, a young anthropologist, to do a survey of southwestern silver work in 1940, and in 1941, he instituted the Navajo Arts and Crafts Guild under the aegis of the Indian Arts and Crafts Board. Adair had done research on silversmiths in 1938; he interviewed many traders, as well as Navajos, revealing their interest in the history of Navajo crafts: older traders like J. W. Bennett, who had traded at Houck in 1882, and Robert Prewitt, coming to Farmington in 1883, remembered details of old silver, recalled that they had noticed smiths beginning to use turquoise in bracelets and rings during these years.[30]

There were, however, problems, despite the intent to improve quality and sales. The Arts and Crafts Board was a bureaucracy that could not move swiftly, in work or on decisions. For example, the original standard for weavings had been the weight of wool; by now, traders knew that quality depended on virtually everything but the weight, yet the Board could not decide whether to change this standard. In order to stamp silver, Board officers had to examine each piece before judging it eligible for marking with its stamp (which read "U.S. Navajo" or "U.S. Zuni," and included a number indicating the trading post or Indian school where the piece had been made), a slow and cumbersome system. In addition, the silver standards turned out to be a mixed blessing, resulting in prices so high that it hurt the sales of authentic Indian silver, at a time when buyers were affected by the 1937 fall-off in the economic recovery. By 1943, the Board had stopped stamping silver, but the idea of having some form of authentication—both for quality and to ensure that the manufacture was by Indians using traditional means—did not disappear, and was taken up later, as we shall see, by the UITA.[31]

But it was d'Harnoncourt's exhibits that were arguably most influential on the market. In 1939, he set up the Indian exhibit at the Golden Gate Exposition in San Francisco—to which as many as 1.5 million visitors came. In 1941, he was responsible for creating the exhibit "Indian Art of the United States" at the Museum of Modern Art in New York City, "one of the most provocative and acclaimed exhibitions in the then-young life of that powerful institution." The exhibit took up the entire museum, and the intent was to show objects made by Native Americans, whether from the past or the present, as art, stylistically relevant to the most modern of paintings and sculptures. These exhibits not only continued the tradition of bringing Indian life to the public's attention, they were aesthetically powerful views of Indian life and Indian crafts set in the context of their own cultures and also in the context of art—American, and particularly modern, art.[32]

The actions of the government, through the Indian Service, were not successful in controlling competition to Indian crafts. The UITA, determined to try to ensure quality and authenticity, took up a more focused, and local, approach. In 1946, the officers attempted to draw up better standards for crafts, specifically for silver work that was then under heavy competition from machine-made jewelry of inferior quality. Standards involved how pieces were made, the equipment used to make them, and the way in which decoration was put on the pieces—hand-stamped, for example, not machine-made. Silver jewelry was required to have "workmanship, substantially that expected in good hand craftsmanship," weight that ensured sound construction, and typical Navajo or Pueblo designs.[33]

In addition, the Association developed a system of stamps and marks, similar to those the Indian Arts and Crafts Board had instituted earlier, for the sale of pieces. The stamp (an arrowhead) was licensed to UITA member traders who sold a substantial quantity of hand-made silver purchased directly from Navajo or Pueblo silversmiths. Each trader who paid an annual fee for membership was assigned a specific number, and the UITA had to approve their use of the UITA stamp. Once traders acquired the stamp, they could mark the silver jewelry they bought from Navajos with a tag containing the UITA stamp and their own number. They were responsible, at that point, for the quality and authenticity of the craftsmanship and the piece. The division of the labor among traders made it more practical than the earlier government stamping system. The UITA tag was in use for several years, although not all traders used it.

The exhibits of Rene d'Harnoncourt and the work of the Indian Arts and Crafts Board had a broad effect on the public interest, and on the effort to seek standards for crafts from all Indian tribes. Traders and the UITA had an effect more specifically on the quality of Navajo silver work and rugs, though competition with false goods continued. D'Harnoncourt had pulled Indian artifacts into the world of art, which commanded a different respect—especially in the Southwest—and a new view of Indian creations. Both Rene d'Harnoncourt and traders had a concern for authenticity, which they believed ensured quality, as well as bringing a better price.

Navajo jewelry, however, is staunchly Navajo, worn and appreciated by Navajo people.

My mom loves jewelry, she always has to have a pin on her shirt. Even when she's around the house, she always has a beautiful pin to wear on her shirt. When she goes somewhere to sell her rug or goes to the store or to a ceremony, she'll put on a necklace and bracelets. When I was growing up . . . she'd give me jewelry . . . the way she introduced jewelry to me, it just stayed with me for years. I knew that she loved those pieces and she wanted me to wear them, and it was just a tradition for us to have jewelry. [Colina Yazzie, Cline Library interview, January 2000]

Traders were uniquely placed between the larger American society with its expanding world of artists, buyers, banks, and goods, and the smaller Navajo society with its complex of sheep, weaving, silversmithing, and indigenous traditions. Traders had an entrée to both societies, and though their knowledge of each was specific and narrow, this entrée created their way of life. Their position on the edge of Navajo and Anglo society gave them a crucial role—or roles: merchant, pawnbroker and banker, economic advisor, culture broker, and arts and crafts dealer.

World War II broke the depression, and traders and Navajos alike went off to serve their country. Upon their return to the Southwest, to their families and their work, they hoped for peace and prosperity. In 1930, the Federal Trade Commission, Indian agents, traders, and Navajos were all on the same side, linked by similar perspectives about Navajo work and its relation to the market. By 1970, all these players—Navajos, traders, Indian agents, the FTC, and the Navajo Tribe itself—had changed philosophy, direction, and positions.

1. Near Tolchaco. 1904. A building typical of early posts; note wattle and daub, more easily assembled than stone. NAU.PH.413.1330, Philip Johnston Collection.

2. Chilchinbeto Trading Post, interior. No date, probably late 1920s. Note pawn hanging from ceiling and rug on scales. NAU.PH.413.719, Philip Johnston Collection.

3. Cedar Springs Store. 1913. A solid, well-built post, reflecting the fact that trade is settling down. NAU.PH.658.106, Leo Crane Collection.

4. Kayenta Trading Post, interior. Circa 1920. Note variety of tools and horseshoes on back wall. NAU.PH.412.2.86, Warren Collection.

5. Loius [*sic*] and Biyal [Yazzie, Navajo freighters]. 1924. Navajo freighters delivered goods and equipment all over the reservation. NAU.PH.226.27, Florence Barker Collection.

6. Oil rig, Navajo man with horse. 1927. Oil discovery led to a new Navajo tribal government. NAU.PH.413.523, Philip Johnston Collection.

7. Rough Rock Trading Post. 1930. A later post was built, in the same style, half a mile away; it is still in operation. NAU.PH.658.970, Leo Crane Collection.

8. Tuba City Trading Post, exterior. 1932. Babbitt Brothers bought and rebuilt the store in 1905. NAU.PH.413.692, Philip Johnston Collection.

9. Tuba City Trading Post, interior. 1932. NAU.PH.413.696, Philip Johnston Collection.

10. Shonto, sheep. 1932. One entry to Shonto Canyon and the trading post was the sand dune in the background, now a paved road. NAU.PH.413.675, Philip Johnston Collection.

11. Shonto Trading Post, interior. 1932. Shelves contain a limited inventory even for the period: baked beans, coffee, cornflakes, cornstarch, and baking powder. NAU.PH.413.691, Philip Johnston Collection.

12. Garcia's trading post at Chinle. 1932. Note the gas pump. NAU.PH.95.48.667, McKee Collection.

13. Sacks of wool at Cameron (Trading Post). 1935. An empty wool sack was 7 feet long. NAU.PH.95.48.985, McKee Collection.

14. Jot Stiles with Navajo goat herders. No date. NAU.PH.99.54.116, Mary May Bailey Collection.

15. Truck loaded with sacks of wool, Lukachukai. 1947. Traders and their wives did much of their own freighting by the 1930s. NAU.PH.98.71.3, Kennedy Collection.

16.
Elijah Blair
(and unidenti-
fied assistants)
putting in
gas pump
(Mexican
Water Trading
Post). 1950.
NAU.PH.98.20.3,
Blair
Collection.

17. Claude and Alver Caler unloading Roscoe McGee's truck (Mexican
Water Trading Post). 1950. Relatives and visitors were all put to work
at a trading post. NAU.PH.98.20.2.36, Blair Collection.

18. Ron and Don Kennedy, in front of Red Rock Trading Post. 1951. Note the new style gas pump, a sign of change. NAU.PH.98.71.32, Kennedy Collection.

19. Tocito Trading Post. 1955. Bessie (holding rug) and Melvin McGee. Trading out a rug; note traditional stove, shelving. NAU.PH.98.21.27, Herring Collection.

20. Elijah Blair weighing a lamb at Mexican Water Trading Post. Circa 1950. NAU.PH.98.20.2.49, Blair Collection.

21. Joe Tanner weighing sheep (at Navajo Shopping Center). 1964. This was a decade of few changes. NAU Photo, J. B. Tanner Collection.

22. Navajo Shopping Center, exterior, Gamerco, New Mexico. 1959. This was one of the very first self-service, cash only, trading posts. NAU Photo, J. B. Tanner Collection.

23. Navajo Shopping Center, Gamerco. Circa 1960. Left to right, Don, J. B., and Bob Tanner. NAU Photo, J. B. Tanner Collection.

24. Sanders, Cedar Point (Trading Post). 1962. Bruce Burnham bought this off-reservation store, which later burned down. NAU Photo, Fronske Collection.

25. Cameron Trading Post. 1963. On a major route to the Grand Canyon, the post had an extensive tourist trade. NAU.PH.85.3.153.35, Fronske Collection.

26. Dinnebito Trading Post. 1970s. (Left to right: Tina Sheperd, Johnson Lee). By the late 1960s, posts employed Navajo store managers, buyers, and bookkeepers; the Tribe began to insist on it. NAU.PH.98.20.4.51, Blair Collection.

27. Dinnebito Trading Post, Gladys Shepherd in produce and meat departments. 1970s. Modern version of the trading post. NAU.PH.98.20.4.58, Blair Collection.

28. Highway sign. 1979. Inscription House Trading Post is six miles away; it was one of a few posts still buying sheep. Willow Roberts Photo, Chaco Archives.

29. Kayenta Trading Post. 1979. Then owned by Brad and Carolyn Blair, a thriving post in a growing community. Willow Roberts photo, Chaco Archives.

30. The road past Inscription House Trading Post. 1979. Navajo Mountain Trading Post is about 36 miles farther. Willow Roberts photo, Chaco Archives.

31.
Remains of
Castle Butte
Trading Post.
1997. One of
many recent
trading post ruins.
NAU.PH.99.54.458,
Mary May Bailey
Collection.

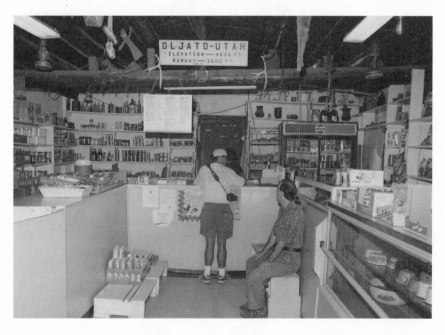

32. Oljato Trading Post, bull-pen style trading area. 1999. Oljato is run as a
combination historic site and tourist attraction and a local store.
NAU.PH.99.53.3.25, UITA Collection.

33. Tuba Trading Post, interior. 1999. This long-time Babbitt post, now a
National Historic site, was bought by the Navajo Nation in November
2000. NAU.PH.99.53.1.225, UITA Collection.

5

⅃·Ꮮ

THE WAR YEARS ON THE RESERVATION

World War II changed Navajo life forever. . . . From the fabled Navajo Codetalkers to those who left home to find work in war-related industries, to all who remained but later heard, shared, and wondered about the wartime experiences, the war represented nothing less than a major turning point in Navajo history. Their world and the American world could never be the same.

Peter Iverson, 1981: The Navajo Nation, 47

The Second World War marked a watershed in the lives of Navajos. Robert Young noted that changes brought by the war were "so broad and deep that they shook the traditional pattern of living to its very foundations." But two things preceded and contributed to the changes brought about by the Second World War: an acceptance of time-saving, desirable, new goods, and the disruption of traditional economy (and the end of even the hope of prosperity) by the Stock Reduction Program. Peterson Zah, Navajo Tribal Chairman from 1982–86, pointed out that the reason why the Second World War was so fundamentally influential was that Navajos went into the outside world and saw it for themselves.

Many of our Navajo people went out of the Navajo Reservation to serve this country during the war. So they had contacts. My father is a good

101

example. He went into the service, and he saw what kind of society is out there, because he rode the train between Los Angeles and San Francisco so many times when he was stationed in San Diego. And so he saw for himself the way life is out there. A lot of Navajos did the same thing. [Peterson Zah interview, Cline Library and author, March 1999]

By implication, they saw that life was different, easier, more prosperous. When they came back to the reservation after the war, they were more critical, and they found conditions harder to accept.[1]

Peterson Zah's father spoke and read English fluently. After his return from the service, he would read and translate letters sent to his neighbors from their relatives.

He had a great sense of responsibility towards his people. . . . He would deliver the mail . . . he always had them open the letter, and then they gave him the letter and he would read it to them in Navajo, he would interpret from English right into Navajo words.

And nine times out of ten, those Navajo ladies would say, "We want you to write back to this person for us." And my dad would sit there and the ladies would tell him what to say, and so he would write back to the people. Most of these letters that I remember as a young boy were letters that came from young men that were in the service during the war. And I remember him reading to his own brothers and sisters what kind of war was going on, what happened at night. . . . The letters would say something like, "I don't know if I'll return home, but I'm just telling you the way life is here when you're in the service. They would describe the food that they would eat, and the long walks that they had to take, and how they got thirsty, let's say on one trip, and how one of their buddies would get killed. . . . And I remember some elderly Navajo women would cry as my father would read the letters to them. [Peterson Zah, Cline Library and author interview, March 1999]

Navajos who served in World War II served everywhere: Stateside, Europe, and the Pacific, dealing with challenges that ranged from learning to cope with seasickness to walking among the dead. They faced the horrors of war, proud of their discipline, their skill in shooting, their ability to get along with men from all over the States.

When Navajos returned home it was "like heaven." But there were enormous challenges: readjusting to normal life, to the community, and to the question of how to earn a living. Their families held traditional, Blessing Way ceremonies to safeguard and ensure their son's, brother's, or husband's reentry into Navajo life.

> I walked up to the brush hogans. I came right to the door and stopped there. Then my grandmother and everybody was there. They recognized me. They all jumped up and shook hands with me. They had tents around the brush hogans. I went inside the tent. There was lots of food and I ate all I wanted to. I just stayed there.

The veteran telling his story at this point "pulled his cap down over his eyes, but it did not hide the fact that his eyes were full of tears." A Blessing Way ceremony had been arranged by his grandmother: "I was figuring that I needed it, too." It was, however, still difficult for him to adjust.[2]

And while some veterans felt they needed ceremonies, others resisted, and felt uncertain, edgy, unable to come home from the war, or to talk about it, or to settle down.

> Everything looks different to me. Hogan was kind of different. I was in houses all the time. We lived in Quonset huts. . . . In the navy I used to talk English all the time. . . . I can't get used to talking Navaho [sic].

And another said, "When I ride a horse, I almost fall off. . . . Long ways off going to town . . . not much to do around. Not like the army. Just sit[ing] around kind of gets tiresome." And, like returning soldiers everywhere, the old lifestyle jarred with the new experiences, and drinking helped them to forget the feeling of dislocation, as well as the memories of war.[3]

Before the Second World War, life was expected to be hard. Peterson Zah, for example, grew up in a family that bridged the old ways and the new. He was of the Kii'a'ani clan, born for the Tahchii'ni, and his family lived in Keams Canyon, in the more southern part of the reservation, near the Hopi Mesas. His grandmother had livestock, his grandfather was a carpenter by trade, and also mined coal in Keams Canyon, a small mine set up by the BIA. His grandfather had built a house and furniture—Anglo-style—with his own hands. Zah's parents and his uncles and aunts lived in the more traditional hogan; the children went to school in Winslow or Payson, and one member of the family worked in Payson. Zah had the traditional duties of a child.

My parents were responsible for letting the sheep out in the morning. And then while that sheep corral was being opened, I was always having my breakfast. Once they got two, three miles up the canyon, then it was my job to follow the sheep. No questions asked, no argument—that was your duty. And the other thing was, that when you came home, there was always wood to be chopped, wood to be gathered. . . . You don't go to bed without any wood inside the hogan, for example. You always had to have that, because it gets cold—particularly in the wintertime. The animals had to go out and graze, and they had to be tended to from day to day. [Peterson Zah, Cline Library and author's interview, March 1999]

Traders—they, too, had been called up for military service—also returned to the reservation, back to the heart of things. Trading posts were still vital elements of Navajo life. The way in which trading posts operated in 1930 was maintained through the war years and for some years thereafter with few changes. Trading posts were best staffed by two people, and wives became crucial to the operation, partners in the work, as well as companions. Women, like their trader husbands, had to be able to cope with the isolation, cultural, medical, and geographical, as well as the physical demands, of the post. Managers and assistants were also needed, and the post-war years found many traders eager for a relief, and many young men found work.

Trading posts were still small buildings, still maintained the bull-pen style counters with all the goods behind them, each item brought to the customer one by one. Though by now most stores had generators for electricity, only a few had coolers for dairy or meat in the store, and none had freezers. The outbuildings, barns and corrals, of course, remained.

At Mexican Water [Trading Post, in 1949] we had ample room. The stove there in the kitchen was a combination of propane and coal, so it heated with the coal and heated the hot water in the reservoir, and then you had the propane burners on the other side, which was very convenient. We had a propane-operated refrigerator. It was all very nice, until the wind quit blowing and the windmill quit going around, and sometimes we'd run out of water. If we knew it ahead of time, we drew water and saved it . . . sometimes in the winter I even melted snow. [Claudia Blair, Cline Library interview, February 1998]

Traders kept simpler records in those days, adapting bookkeeping methods from whatever they had learned in high school or been shown to do by another trader: they kept a book recording pawn; they kept balance sheets. And there was the McCaskey Register for individual accounts.

We called them charge pads. You just listed the individual's purchases for the day, and this sort of stuff. And you just kept a continuous record of this, and the item was written down and priced out. These were then your receivables. And they were kept in what we called a McCaskey Register, and each individual had his own slot [by letter of the alphabet]. These [sheets from the charge pads] were torn out and put in this register, and they were continuously updated all the time. So if the need be, you could go through and get your receivables daily, if you wanted to do that much. Normally, we didn't. We took our inventories twice a year, once in the spring and once in the fall, to determine what our condition was. [Jay Springer, Cline Library interview, December 1998]

Traders learned to trade, in the long run, by doing it, picking up skills by observation but mostly by working for another trader. This ad hoc apprenticeship, all there was in the way of training, included much moving from post to post, learning the methods of different traders and the needs of each community.

A trader who learned his trading in the pre- and immediately post-war years is Walter Scribner. During the depression, Walter, a teenager who needed to supplement his family's income, went to work for Stokes Carson at his trading post southeast of Farmington. Walter worked in a couple of small stores, then around 1938 went to work for Mildred Heflin, Carson's daughter, and her husband Reuben at Oljato Trading Post on the border of Arizona and Utah. Walter quickly recognized that each community was unique, and that communities differed in their combination of new and old ways of life. At Oljato he found a very traditional lifestyle still in place. Even the language was slightly different, different Navajo words, older forms, not at all like those he had encountered southeast of Farmington.

By 1938, traders were not so much the harbinger of novel goods, though they continued to be culture-brokers, mediators of Anglo-American ways. The automobile was by now a more common sight, though paved roads were not; visitors, who might buy rugs and silver, were more frequent. There were a few telephones, and a few propane-run refrigerators; everyone had radios (there was a program from Window Rock, which Walter Scribner's customers at Oljato would come to the store to listen to); and communication by letter, especially from Navajo children away at school, was very common. Traders were useful, and some were well-liked, well-respected, and fun to tease. By now they were accepted features in the more traditional Navajo universe. The exchange of goods in isolation from the outside world was just beginning to erode.

One time Reuben [Heflin] decided to put a new roof on the store there [Oljato Trading Post] . . . this box car roof on there. Well, in the process there were some Navajos around there criticizing, they didn't know whether that would be any good or not, that might leak. I was saying, well at Carson's we had them, they lasted twenty years. You put board over them and about that much dirt, and it was cool and it didn't leak. All this in Navajo. There was an old shaggy-looking fellow there who I wouldn't have thought spoke a word of English. He said, "You failed to take into consideration the differences in climate and soil." In perfect English. They fool you; they like jokes, always poking fun at you. [Walter Scribner, interview by the author, November 1979]

Two years after World War II, material life on the Navajo Reservation was at a low point. Navajos had changed steadily, but conditions had not changed enough. Navajo men and women who had served in the military or worked in munitions and other industries desperate for workers during the boom years of the war were now unemployed. On the reservation, there were few jobs, and overgrazing, stock reduction, and controls on the grazing of herds made traditional life of herding and agriculture far less productive than before. The government began to look at a policy of termination of the special tribal relationship to reservations and relocation of tribal members to cities and jobs. Off the reservation, Navajos began to find that they did not always have sufficient education or training to compete for available work.

To add to the difficulties, the winter of 1947–48 was unusually hard, and fierce blizzards hit the Southwest. The Red Cross and many private, public, and federal agencies responded with food, clothes, and emergency aid to Navajos, who were in an especially critical situation. News stories brought public attention, and numerous reports on the Navajo Reservation appeared: in 1946, by Elizabeth Clark, by A. L. Wathen in 1947, by the Navajo Agency in 1947 on the subject of welfare, by the Secretary of the Interior in 1947 on measures for long-range rehabilitation, by Max Drefkoff in 1948 on industrial potential and economic revival, and on trading posts in 1949. The attention brought some remedies. Federal funds were provided in 1948 for welfare and a program of employment.[4]

Also in 1948, Navajos and other Native Americans in Arizona and New Mexico finally got the right to vote, a right obtained by Indian people by federal law in 1924, but denied them in those states. In 1947, Sam Ahkeah, chairman of the Navajo Tribe, hired a tribal attorney, Norman Littell. Littell's mandate was to work on land claims following the 1946 Indian Claims Act, but he and his staff were active in many other aspects of tribal government and reservation life, and had considerable input in the activities and development of tribal politics, resources, and legal claims.[5]

Changes slowly filtered across the reservation against this backdrop. Navajos began to rely on wage work more and more, supplemented by the moderate welfare programs of the times. For many people, the work they could get was that of unskilled labor. Those who were educated and lived near border towns or communities like Fort Defiance or Shiprock could get jobs with the BIA. Some young people began to get work in Phoenix or Albuquerque, or even in cities in more distant states. Those living in the reservation interior depended on traders, who not only hired men and women to work at the post but continued to act as labor exchanges for other work, such as the time-honored railroad jobs and agricultural labor.

> The trading posts . . . is where everybody came, not only to trade or sell their product—whatever they had—but they also came there to socialize. So everything that happened in this community, say, of a radius of twenty miles or so, this was the hub, and it all came into the trading post, and everybody met there, things were done. And you dealt, whether or not she had a rug to sell or to barter with, or they had an account already established with the trader previous to you, they would bring in their rugs to pay the account. Or they would sell a cow. [Elijah Blair, Cline Library interview, February 1998]

The seasons of trading remained the same.

> If it was in wool season when they were shearing the sheep, then they would bring the wool in. Or lamb season, they would bring lambs in. Or if they ran out of food, they would bring a lamb in, so the trader would always trade the lamb for merchandise. They would need flour and things that they didn't have, like flour, lard, baking powder, sugar, salt, stuff like this. Those were big staple items for the Navajo. . . .

That was the biggest thing that we did, we took care of every need that the Navajo had.... Whatever they needed, whatever type of merchandise, we stocked it; if we didn't have it, we got it for them. And any products that they produced, whether it was farm products, livestock they raised, piñon nuts that they gathered if there was a piñon crop that year, rugs, saddle blankets, anything that they had, we furnished a market for it.

We bought goat and sheep hides, and he'd bring those in, and he would bring it up and stack it on the counter. We would weigh it back in the wool room and then we would pay them, or sometimes you would trade them, depending on their choice. That didn't come to a lot of money, lots of times you would just pay them if you had the money to do it.... He always had the option, "Did you want to trade it out, or did you want us to pay you?" Many stores may not have had money, but I usually had enough money that we gave them the option. Lots of times they had no place to spend money other than there at the trading post, so lots of times they'd just say, "Well, give me a sack of flour...."

This was the hub. The social hub, actually, was the trading post. [Elijah Blair, Cline Library interview, February 1998]

Peterson Zah described going to the trading post as a social event, as well as a practical one, and small children wanted to go along with their family. Zah remembered going with his parents and grandparents to Keams Canyon Trading Post in about 1945, when they traded their wool and bought groceries.

I was always put at the end of the wagon, way at the back. As we were driv- ing to the trading post and coming back from the trading post, you just had to listen to conversations that go on.... So it was beginning to be kind of like a daily conversation about what new was happening in the community, and then over at the Keams Canyon BIA Agency. So it was one experience that to this day I would really cherish.... And when you're a little kid, you were to be seen and not heard, and so they always put me in the back of the wagon. It was a lot of fun. It brings back a lot of good memories. They would shear the sheep and pack the wool into one big huge bag. I remember how big those bags were. When you filled them up, that's one wagon full, so we would have to take that one bag over to Keams Canyon.

But back home at the camp, we would have maybe five of those. So that meant five trips down to Keams Canyon. And they got some cash for the wool. And then on occasion, the trader would just make a note, they would say, "Well, we weighed the wool, and it weighed this much, and they are so much per pound. We will just make you a little note" that says, for example, twenty-five dollars, let's say. And then they [Zah's parents and grandparents] would get groceries—usually flour, potatoes, coffee, tea, some canned goods. And they would buy the groceries up to the level of the note that they got from the trader. And that's how they dealt with the traders. . . .

And then another time they would get the sheep skins and the goat skins. We took that in, and I remember they cost something like fifty cents or a quarter. So you took four sheep skins in to get a dollar. When we butchered a sheep or a goat, we'd save all the hide and the wool. You build it up during the year, in the springtime you took it all in, and that was traded with the traders at the trading posts. [Peterson Zah, interview by Cline Library and the author, March 1999]

However, there was little difference between this description of trading, circa 1945, to a description of trading at the end of the 1950s.

When I was a small child, I remember we only had wagons with a team of horses, and being that we lived about twenty-five, thirty miles west of the nearest trading post, Dinnebito Trading Post, it took at least a whole day to travel there and back. . . . Wool would be sacked, and they would put it on the wagons and they would take it. And there the wool was sold. Back in those days, a couple of bags of wool will buy you a lot of the stuff. That was the way it was.

When a sheep is butchered, the skin is saved. It is stretched and pinned down on the ground to dry. After it dries, it's all rolled up so at times you might have nine, ten, eleven sheepskins all rolled up. These were even taken to the trading posts to be sold. And a couple of these sheepskins, that was my spending money, because I did a lot of herding sheep. . . .

Sheep was our ticket. This was like dollar signs, if we had about fifty head of sheep there, we were secure, we knew that we could make things work. So fifty head of sheep was a good herd, back in those days. . . . And we looked at people and you sort of determined in your mind, "They're a lot richer than I am, because they have about a hundred head more than we do." Yeah, sheep was very important to us, it was our ticket to the store. . . .

The necessities of life, it seems like, is always there: shovels and tools and hoes, something that made your job a lot easier. . . . And that's what the trading post was to us, is a convenience for us. Everything that we need, it seems like it's there. It's always something you look forward to. And, of course, as little children, we'd cry because the wagon is leaving, we want to go . . . most of the Navajo kids will be shy. Boys and girls, they're both shy. They have this mother here, and, of course, the mother wears the long skirt and you could see the little kids hiding behind the mother's skirt like this, and looking at the trader. [Paul Begay, Cline Library interview, February 1998]

Descriptions of the past often preserve the traditional, blur the changes because, often, we don't notice their beginnings. Traders have similar memories of trading in these years. So much had stayed the same, the same goods were in demand, the same people came in. They felt that they were part of the community, providing services, earning a living for themselves and their customers.

It was mostly what we would call the local people. A lot of people would come in to buy groceries, sell baskets, buy baskets, sell their rugs, sell sheep, sell cattle, sell horses—I can remember when the tribe was paying ten cents a pound for horses to get them off the range, they were probably only worth a nickel a pound.

It [trading post business] was primarily credit. In those days, I can remember welfare checks were around thirty dollars. . . . Can you imagine getting along on thirty dollars a month? I mean, that would be pretty tough. Of course, I think pop was probably fifteen cents then, but that still doesn't relate to what you can live on. [Bill Malone, Cline Library interview, August 1998]

Traders went to work with the weavers, the makers of jewelry, baskets, and later on, pottery. These post-war years preceded a new burst of interest in Indian artisans—that would come in the late 1960s—and traders worked hard to encourage quality, introducing certain types of patterns or color combinations that often produced new regional styles, sometimes supplying them with materials. Navajo weavers of the 1950s tended to weave saddle blankets, simpler, smaller rugs popular *as* saddle blankets; perhaps they wanted to keep their outlay low, perhaps they did not want to risk a larger, more complex rug without assurance that it would be accepted and adequately paid for by the trader.

[The trader] appreciated the weaving, he appreciated what went into it, so he tried to direct—not exactly direct it, but encourage weaving—and other art, but weaving is a big thing, for the Navajos the biggest thing. You just tried to improve it by talking to the people. And you know the Navajos were so receptive, the weavers were, of good traders who were interested in what they do because they knew that when they made it good, that they would be better off. [Elijah Blair, Cline Library interview, February 1998]

Russell Foutz was one of those who liked weaving and built up a business in it, working mostly out of Teec Nos Pos Trading Post. After the war, he introduced commercially spun wool to his weavers.

I had some rugs woven out of it; I even had one of the weavers split it [this yarn] and weave it . . . and I just put it in the Gallup Ceremonial. "I don't know what category this rug should go in. You can put it in whatever category that it goes in." So they put it in the category of the hand-spun Navajo weavings and gave it the blue prize of hand-ply weaves. Well, . . . I took the ribbon off of it.

So I thought, "Well, if the judges can't even tell the difference in these rugs, and these old rugs are worth a lot of money, why wouldn't the new rugs be worth just as much money as the old ones whether they were commercial [yarn] or not?" So whether it was a good thing or a bad thing . . . I introduced the commercial one-ply wool on the reservation that all the rugs are made out of now, except maybe one percent. [Russell Foutz, Cline Library interview, April 1998]

Foutz held rug contests, which he had judged by tribal authorities, giving good jewelry to the prize winners.

We would always buy a little girl's first rug. We always did that to encourage them, and there is some men that got to be good weavers. . . . James Sherman went blind and even though he couldn't finish a rug, he would get it halfway finished and we'd buy his unfinished rug. . . .

Weavings and rugs was my first love. I started my first collection before I was married. Now the main things I put back was I was real interested in sandpainting rugs. So the rugs that I saved mainly was the rugs that was woven from the red sheep. The reddish sheep was the color, by the time they carded it out, was the color of the sand. I knew this color could never be reproduced because the reddish sheep was going out of existence. . . . [6]

A sandpainting rug is a copy of a sandpainting they do in a ceremony . . . you're not supposed to weave one of those rugs, you'll go blind if you do. I remember the first rug I got, the first sandpainting rug I bought, it was at Gallegos[7], and I had made arrangements to buy that rug for a certain price. And when it was finished, the deal was made.

About two weeks later she [the weaver] came back and said that I had to give her another $200 because she was going blind from weaving that rug, and she would have to hire a medicine man to give her a ceremony. So I had to give her another $200. [Russell Foutz, Cline Library interview, April 1998]

Foutz sold these rugs to different places, to the Fred Harvey Company, his biggest customer, to the national parks, and to dealers. He would go on what he called a rug trip around the Southwest and beyond, showing and selling, as traders who deal with crafts still do today, though the circuit is a little different.

The appearance of changelessness is misleading. Traditional behavior had begun to shift. The taboo on contact between mother-in-law and son-in-law had disappeared, and although the restrictions and taboos surrounding death were persistent, there were some new burial practices also. Although only a very few families in the 1950s had vehicles or access to them, radios were very popular—there were Navajo language programs in 1953—and in places where radio signals were weak, people went to friends or the trading post with better reception. There was an improvement in health services, and a new acceptance of Anglo-American doctors, clinics that, encouraged in places by medicine men, now drew on modern, as well as traditional, healing practices. The Public Health Service took over Indian health care from the BIA in 1955, and Annie Wauneka, an influential Tribal Council woman, led a vigorous campaign to eradicate tuberculosis, a serious health problem among the Navajos. Now, when Navajos became ill, they began to visit doctors and clinics (hospitals were built at Shiprock and Gallup, clinics at Chinle, Kayenta, Many Farms, and Tohatchi), as well as going to traditional diagnosticians and healers.[8]

Years later, Joe (Joseph Elwood) Tanner (whom we met in Chapter 1) was working with *National Geographic* on an article to do with wool and culture, with the Navajo chosen as the people from the U.S. whose lives were most involved with wool. Tanner suggested people to interview.

I wanted them to go out and talk to Annie Wauneka, Chee Dodge's daughter. We got to Annie Wauneka's about four o'clock in the afternoon, and, of course, the first thing she says is, "Well, what in the world do you want to talk to me about wool for? I've told my people from the very beginning, 'get those sheep hides out of the hogans, that's what's bringing all the disease.' I'm the champion of getting rid of disease on the reservation, and disease was those hides that my people were sleeping on, on the floor." But then we got past that, and we had a great session. [Joe Tanner, Cline Library interview, March 1999].

Most Navajos still did not speak much English, though by the mid-1950s there was an increasing need to speak at least a little. People began to recognize that education would improve their work opportunities. Many supported the idea of education in general for their children, although they continued to keep some children back to help at home and to take up traditional occupations. But the schools on the reservation were limited, or irregular, in places even non-existent, and people had widely varied access (as well as attitudes) to education. At Aneth, Utah, in the mid-1950s, for example, no child had completed eighth grade—there was a school there, but it only covered first and second grades—and only four percent of the families sent all their children to school. In contrast, Navajo families living around Mexican Springs, or other communities close to schools, sent almost half of their children to school and kept them there. Navajos interviewed about their work and general economic and educational situations in 1953 acknowledged that their life was changing fast, but said that they still followed "the Navajo way." Navajo extended families still relied on the combination of products from their small herds, their fields. They still drew on the varied skills of family members: some herded, others wove or made jewelry for trade and sale, some earned money in border towns or even further away, some received pension or unemployment checks. Each individual was connected to a broad, loose network of kin and clan relatives, and everyone would be asked for help with transportation for hauling water and wood, with herding and farming, with goods, both modern and traditional, and cash. It was very difficult to refuse.[9]

The 1950s were years of enormous change and modernization, visible and invisible. Oil and gas drilling and exploration continued and a search for uranium began; new fuels that in turn fueled new technology, new lifestyles, new economies. These years brought a slow prosperity throughout America in general, and a steady growth of a cash-based economy on the Navajo Reservation, a growth that helped to foster political development of the tribe. Income was hard to gauge, but it grew slowly; average individual income on the reservation was $80.00 in 1946, $290 in 1952, and $520 in 1960 (reflecting income from livestock, farming, crafts, wages, and welfare, though the relative proportion each source changed through the years). As prospectors tapped the hidden resources of oil, gas, coal, and uranium, royalties began to increase the Navajo tribal budget. Tribal Council members decided not to distribute this money to individuals, a per capita distribution, as many tribes did when they obtained tribal funds. Rather, they funded a broad series of important programs: electrification on the reservation, college scholarships and education in general, the building of community centers, clothing for school children, later on they funded a Tribal Works program. The Tribe also funded the building of more Chapter houses, the local political organizations.[10]

Prosperity led to better education and more jobs. Cash became more common, but it was still a novelty and fitted uneasily into the pattern of trading and buying. The depression era had begun the slow trend to social programs and social welfare checks, continued by World War II veterans benefits. Unemployment checks came to Navajos from the Railroad Retirement Board (a federal program), when men were laid off. There were, however, no banks on the reservation, no means of cashing a check unless people had the means to travel to a border town. Checks became another commodity, an item to barter to the trading post, exchanged like sheep, wool, rugs, and silver for groceries and goods. Traders took the checks, signed or thumbprinted by their customers, and they extended credit to families or individuals they knew would receive checks as they had to those they knew had livestock or weavings.

Traders down the years tried to create income out of the very cultural situation in which they existed, to bring in outside money to benefit their customers and themselves. Not all traders were successful at it. Indeed, by 1940, many traders had settled for running a small enterprise in which expenses and profits were low, which tried to bring just what Navajo customers needed (and no more), bringing their knowledge of the Navajo economy and traditions to bring the right goods, to help out, fit in, and make a small living. The word for "No" was "*dooda*," and traditional trader advice was to "put everything on your shelf here that the Navajo wants, and then learn to say '*dooda*.' That means, 'You can't have it.'" Saying "*dooda*"—refusing to give extra credit, or not buying a rug or other item—had to be done, however, with finesse, without offending customers or causing them to lose face with their neighbors. That caution restricted spending, kept credit in check, and also maintained a traditional outlook and a limited consumption of "outside" novelties, goods, and products.[11]

> Some traders knew how to say "no" without offending their customers. Other traders didn't know how to, and they would offend people in denying them something on credit. So some trading posts had all their dry goods and everything hidden in boxes on the shelf. The trader knew what was in the box, but the customer didn't necessarily know. [Bruce Burnham, interview with the author, July 1998]

A trading post was very much like the general store of the nineteenth century but had some interesting differences. Not only did the trading post involve itself in many unique transactions that were not like the old general store, but it operated in a cross-cultural context that provided a very different environment. The post was subject to risks and insecurities unlike any general store. Traders did not own any of the land or buildings, their accounts were "largely unsecured."[12]

> I went to the First State Bank in Gallup and borrowed the money to buy [Fort Wingate Trading Post] and made a deal. Then I went back to California and resigned my commission and left the Marines and went to Fort Wingate and took over the trading post January 1, 1946. In doing so, I became postmaster, that went along with it. That was the first time I'd ever run a trading post. . . . I was there forty-six years. . . .
>
> It was strictly credit, very little cash. We gave credit to the working people for thirty days, and we gave credit to the stock people for a six-month period of time. We'd give credit up until the time wool came on, and they got paid for the wool. Then another six-month period, during the time that the lambs came on. And that was hard, because I had lots of money on credit. At one time, I had $30,000 to $40,000 worth of credit out to the Navajos. And most of them were very good about paying. Later on, when the automobiles came along, and I began to sell cars, the credit business was much tougher after that. [Paul D. Merrill, Cline Library interview, January 2000]

In the 1950s, both traders and Navajos were dependent on loans and credit.

> We would run $20,000 or $30,000 worth of receivables. As I say, it was

ongoing. We cleaned up pretty good in the spring and in the fall, but other than that, everything was just on paper. [Jay Springer, Cline Library interview, December 1998]

Navajos sometimes still secured credit by pledges, usually silver or turquoise jewelry that was more important than money, especially the heavy, traditionally made heirloom silver. Traders took these heirlooms in pawn, as well as for credit security, as visible, tangible assets similar to a bank account, accepted in both cultures. Nor was jewelry the only pawn item—shawls, boots, a saddle, and more modern items: a radio, a good watch—but it was the most frequent, exchanged for goods or small amounts of cash, redeemed for cash, then often pawned again later on. This was a Navajo trading tradition. In the past, Navajos did not deal much with money, which had been in every way meaningless to them unless it was literally hammered into jewelry or turned into goods. Now, money was needed more, and was becoming more familiar. Anglos had, then and now, symbolic and institutional meanings centered on money, and its use, as well as its meanings, have been incorporated into everyday life over centuries. Pure barter is buried in the past of western societies; money, the idea of profit and loss, was new to Navajos. Economic and personal values of each society all came into play in trading: Anglo-American ideas of thrift, the honoring of debts, the nature of profit, Navajo ideas of reciprocity, economic cooperation among relatives, and taking care of present needs rather than the unclear future.

The trading post began to change a little, also, its business based more essentially on money value, though there was still little cash, so that trade in, for example, sheep was in terms of market prices. Markups on goods varied—lowest on basic foodstuffs, like flour, lower on necessities than on desirable items. The stores saw some changes in style and equipment—traders built new additions or even new stores, using cement block and boards, and bought equipment like larger power generators, coolers, refrigerated shelving units, new cash registers.

One novel store, however, was opened in 1957, in Gallup: the Navajo Shopping Center, started by J. B. Tanner, Joe (Joseph Elwood) and two other Tanner brothers, his parents, Stella and Chunky Tanner, and Don Tanner, an uncle. The Navajo Shopping Center, built in a Quonset hut, was a cash-only self-service supermarket but one that bought, as well as sold and dealt in all the traditional Navajo commodities: livestock, rugs, piñons, whatever Navajos had to sell.

We made a supermarket-type [store] in this Quonset building. And then we built steps up to the scales over in the livestock building in the back, and put a vault on each side, one for the bookkeepers on one side and pawn on the other, and then put in homemade shelving. . . .

Uncle Don . . . said, "Well, it's going to take quite a bit to stock this. This is a big store." I said, "Well, it'll take $30,000 at least." That was a lot of merchandise back then. [J. B. Tanner, Cline Library interview, August 1998]

The Tanners bought sheep, rugs, and jewelry for cash, and sold their goods for cash; it was a very large brokering operation.

In the grocery department, we would butcher our own sheep, right there at the facility. There wasn't any government law then. . . . We would bring thirty head of sheep down at a time, into a little corral just outside. Here's the meat case in the store. The back door was this corral where these sheep were. I struck a deal with the Navajo ladies that would come and butcher: they got to keep the insides and the head, I'd bring the mutton in, and I had days there that when I was running the meat department, when we first started, where I would cut and wrap and sell a hundred head of sheep in one busy Saturday, with no help. . . .

I remember days in Navajo Shopping Center that I would have as many as thirty women standing in line, all day long, bringing their rugs up to sell to me. Paying cash. We paid cash for everything. [Joe Tanner, Cline Library interview, March 1999]

Despite the fact that it did not last long as a Tanner operation, the Navajo Shopping Center was a departure from trading post tradition that marked a new phase: self-service trading posts.[13]

Traders themselves changed more slowly. In general, traders of the post-war period were traditional and hesitant to alter anything; that is, those of the older generation—their sons and daughters were the ones who changed. The communities they served were also traditional and seemed unchanging. Traders felt that their system matched the way the community worked. An anthropologist, William Y. Adams, who went to work for a year as manager at Shonto Trading Post (he had worked there on and off since 1951) wrote a description of a trading post in the late 1950s. His book describes the trader-Navajo economic exchange and the role of the trader in the community, concluding that traders, once a force for change, now played a conservative role, preserving traditional culture, and were anachronisms in Navajo life.[14]

Adams, who had grown up on the Navajo Reservation, criticized traders heavily, through observing the insecurities of their situation. He described the trader as a paternalistic authority figure, whose relationship to his customers constituted a "territorial monopoly," and his methods "credit saturation"—in other words, the trader extended enough credit to his customers that they had no income left to spend money elsewhere. He also noted that the annual net profit of Shonto Trading Post, between 1950 and 1957, "varied from a profit of $20,000 to a loss of nearly $10,000."[15]

Adams was also, elsewhere, critical of Navajo economics, noting that Navajo grazing practices were "inefficient," their utilization of welfare more "fully developed." Navajo economic demands, he thought, were easily satisfied: "Making a living has not been a matter of traditional and collective concern to the Navajos." He commented that the trader fitted into Navajo culture:

> Shonto Trading Post as a functioning institution is in closer harmony with the conditions of Navaho life, and better integrated into it, than with the conditions of modern American life, even in the Southwest.

But this fit, Adams thought, was itself a problem, holding back the development of a modern Navajo economy. His book was published in 1963, at a time when young, educated Navajos, growing critical of reservation life and its institutions, were looking for ways and means to alter that life and its structure, and Adams's criticism of trading provided them with ideas.[16]

At the Tribal level, there was enormous development of the apparatus of governing the Navajo nation. Reforms and reorganization of election procedures, tribal courts, and Chapter representation through selection of delegates to the nominating conventions all took place during the 1950s. In 1951, the first election following procedural reform, Paul Jones was elected tribal chairman. He was an articulate, experienced, bilingual veteran of World War I, and he and his running mate, Scott Preston, brother of Peterson Zah's father and a medicine man from the Western reservation, presented a combination of the modern and the traditional that reflected precisely the mood among Navajo voters. The passage by Congress of a law (Public Law 280) granting states the ability to institute jurisdiction over reservations encouraged the Navajo tribal government to reorganize and improve their court system. Such reform was essential to ensure that the tribal courts would be able to rule responsibly and justly on civil actions, to avoid the states of Arizona, New Mexico, or Utah instituting state jurisdiction in such cases, taking Navajos into a state court where there would be no Navajo jurors and little understanding of Navajo culture. The Navajo tribe was responsible for the enforcement of tribal regulations; the federal government for the offenses listed in the Major Crimes Act and its amendments. During a period in which termination and relocation was the approach of the federal government in Washington, the political structure and sophistication of the Navajo tribe grew. The 1950s seem to be perceived as the "golden" years for the Navajos, the years in which they came to political and national maturity.[17]

Relations over the counter between trader and customer were among the most consistent and long-term of any between Navajo and Anglo, and reflected, on both sides, the trader's continuity in the Navajo community, and the friendships, frustrations, understandings, and misunderstandings that accompanied this cross-cultural commerce—as well as the paternalistic attitudes and even superior approach of some traders. This relationship is hinted at in names. Navajos gave everyone "nicknames"—in reality, just a name that they could call a person by, since it was not right to tell your real Navajo name nor for others to use it. Traders, too, were given names—usually something to do with their appearance—but with implications that might or might not be fully explained. The Navajo language is an extraordinarily complex and subtle one, and Navajo conversations are full of wordplay, puns, and double meanings, and teasing was often a carefully worded criticism. Stokes Carson, trader for many years at Inscription House, was called Baa Hojooba'i, which meant Old Poor man, since he always said, when he refused to give credit or buy a rug, "I'm too poor—Baa Hojoobá'í." Since Navajos perceived traders as rich—they owned a store full of goods, and to have such goods was wealth—this name was surely used in irony. Other trader names were descriptive. Jewel McGee's name was 'Ashkii ditł'o—Hairy Boy, "seeing all this hair on my chest and my arms."

Many names had to do with ears. Elijah Blair came out to the Southwest from Kentucky, and, following his two elder brothers, Raymond and Brad Blair, went into trading, beginning at Toadlena. In 1949, he went to manage Mexican Water on his own, and earned the name Jaa'i, round ears, or Jaa'i Yazzie, little round ears.

I was hired to go out and manage [Mexican Water Trading Post] with

Claudia [his wife]. From Shiprock, it was eighty miles west, on a dirt road. It isn't the present-day Mexican Water, that's a new store; the old Mexican Water is three miles north of there. . . .

When we got there, the next morning I get up and there's a new wagon sitting out front. I go to the door and I figure, "Well, that's the store's wagon." But there was an old fellow there, a Navajo fellow that kept coming up and talking to me, and he kept pointing at that wagon—he had his horse, he wanted to haul it off. And I kept saying, "Where's the money?" So this went on all day long. At noon he'd come back in, wanting to haul off the wagon. Well, I wouldn't let him have it, because he wouldn't pay me for it. This went on for about three days, every day the same thing. And my brother Brad was at Red Mesa, he and Carolyn. And Brad and Carolyn came down one night, and this old guy—we always had a guest hogan at the trading post, for customers when they came, and they stayed in there, we even furnished coffee and the staples for them to stay in there—so he just camped there. . . .

So Brad came down—he had been there about two years longer than I had, he came, I think, in '45—and so when [the Navajo] saw Brad, he was really happy because he knew that Brad could speak Navajo. So he got up and he started talking to Brad. Well, come to find out, he had bought the wagon from the previous owner, and he had already paid for the wagon.

You know, a Navajo is the most tolerant person in the world, the most accepting person in the world, and he finally said, "Your ears are just round and nothing goes in!" And that's when they first started calling me Jaa'i, or Jaa'i Yazzie. [Elijah Blair, Cline Library interview, February 1998]

The name stuck, and followed him to his next stores, Aneth Trading Post, then Dinnebito. In the meantime, Elijah learned to speak Navajo.

After the first couple of years, you learn to speak fairly well what we call "Indian trading Navajo." You learned the words and stuff like this. But to really learn to speak . . . you learned to speak body language, and that's the first thing you learned. You learned by watching them, what the feel was, and then you learned to speak orally. And after you learned to be able to communicate in that way, then you had to learn what I refer to as "speaking the culture." Until you can really speak the culture—or "understand" is probably the better word, after that you can speak the language. . . . But I was twenty years old when I started, so that makes a difference. [Elijah Blair, Cline Library interview, February 1998]

Trading was still a local business, though there are always a few newcomers from outside the Southwest. It still required some specific knowledge of the Southwest, the Navajos, and their language, culture, and economics, as well as work and the economy beyond the reservation. Traders don't go far, when they retire, and often meet old friends from their trading past, customers who greet them by their Navajo names, and it delights them.

Words, however, are two-edged swords. There is an old saying that sticks and stones may break your bones, but words will never hurt you. It is not so; no words ever stung like Navajo words when they are chosen to hurt. Navajos are careful, their manners, interactions, and etiquette more precise than in most societies. Language is a tool, a weapon, in prayer a mediator of the powers of the universe. Navajos think highly of eloquence and wit, and enjoy a well-turned phrase, a clever implication. Stories and words are important, in everyday life, as well as in prayer, and much meaning is carried by epithets and phrases. In the mid-1960s, Navajos gave traders the worst epithets of all: *bithatso*, stingy and mean, *bina'adlo'*, a cheater.

There was a guy in here . . . real nice guy, he's talking about being a silversmith, and I realized I didn't know him. We were talking in Navajo and English, too, back and forth, and I said, "Where are you from?" He said, "I'm from out at Inscription House." I said, "Oh, you knew Baa Hojoobá'í," which was the name they called Stokes Carson. Stokes Carson [the trader at Inscription House Trading Post from 1954 to 1974] was in this country forever. When I said "You knew Baa Hojoobá'í," he said, "He cheated!" First thing he said! "He cheated!" And then he switched to Navajo and he said, "Stingy-tight-crooked-cheater." And he first said "*bithatso*" and then "he cheated." I said—I didn't offend him—see, I knew Stokes, I knew the whole family, and I said, "Well, what do you mean he cheated?" He said, "He stayed out there all of those years, and he never gave nothing back and he finally died. There's no way he could get all that stuff into that box with him." So that made him crooked, because he took more than he needed, he became the capitalist.

To me that was the best story about capitalism versus socialism. The only difference in collectivism and socialism is where the control is vested—in the state or in the culture itself, which is much more demanding. . . . This guy said, "He cheated." I know the Carson family: they were good. And Stokes, he was a trader, he made money. But you don't make money—the Navajo interprets this as, You make money off of us. You actually got more from us than you needed, because when you left, you couldn't take it with you, you couldn't get it in that box. So this makes you crooked. . . . [Elijah Blair, Cline Library interview, February 1998]

Traders who had spent years doing business on the reservation, who thought they had contributed—in Anglo American terms—to Navajos' well-being and economic life, who felt that they had appreciated the Navajo way of life and even helped to sustain it, were accused of cheating, of being mean. Those who prided themselves on honesty, on working hard to bring prosperity to Navajos, were cut to the quick. This situation grew out of the events of the 1960s, during which the traders and their activities were investigated (by Navajo students, federal agencies, and Navajo legal service lawyers), criticized by the media, brought into court regarding pawn and credit, and required to attend a series of public hearings by the Federal Trade Commission. Traders were put under the gun for the way they ran trading posts, from practices of credit and pawn to hiring, and accused of putting the Navajos into "economic bondage." Why and how that happened is the focus of the second part of this book.[18]

PART TWO

THE END OF AN ERA

6

⅃・L

CASH MONEY

The injection of cash on the reservation was something we really didn't
start dealing with until the mid-60s. . . . The old trader's philosophy was
"sell them what they need, not what they want" and that came over just
fine as long as you were the only place to get it. Pretty soon, after [Navajo]
people were away they learned to like some of the other fruits and vegeta-
bles, and Hamburger Helper . . . Hamburger Helper, boy, now that was
something you'd never seen at a trading post.

Bruce Burnham, interview with the author, July 1998

The business of trading in the post-war reservation was neither quite like
old-time trading nor, by all accounts, quite like business as it was known
in the streets of any city, the crossroads of even the smallest community,
in America. Indian trading, though it shared the same profit basis as the
corner drugstore, was a mixture of retail sales and cross-cultural services,
a curious combination of two different economies, Anglo-American and
Navajo, which had evolved over time. The late 1960s saw social changes
that were completely unrecognized in the 1950s. The economy was shifting like blown sand, spinning on what traders called "cash money." *Money*
had slowly penetrated the reservation as a mode of value over the past
sixty years; now *cash* money was beginning to make an appearance.
Checks were familiar, but currency, hard cash, was still a novelty in 1960.

Bruce Burnham remembered when the idea of having money in the cash register was new, when a trader—in this case Brad Blair—making change for a twenty dollar bill had to raid his children's piggy banks.

Checks didn't seem to be money, and they were bartered just like commodities, sustaining an old tradition. The trading system was a mixture of commodity barter and cash profit—a common pattern in cross-cultural trade. Traders introduced capitalism, but cash wasn't really part of the system until the mid-1960s.

The Navajo economy can be roughly divided into phases. The first phase came before 1864 (when Navajos were taken down to Fort Sumner), during which independent groups of Navajos hunted, farmed a little, traded small amounts of goods with other groups, raised sheep, and on occasion raided; it was raiding and husbandry that brought their main resources.

The second phase followed the Treaty of 1868 and lasted roughly until the depression of 1929. This period was one in which the Navajo people turned livestock husbandry and agriculture, combined with trade, into a successful way of living. Their success came from resourcefulness, hard work, and skill. Most importantly, sheep and wool were valuable in the dominant economy, and were brought to this market by middlemen traders. Navajo families produced commodities (some of them raw materials) valued in the American markets, which brought them wealth through trading. There was a strong ethos of reciprocity and sharing, which did not prevent the rise of wealthy Navajos and larger stock owners. This period of prosperity, whose economic high point came around 1890, did not last long. Reliant as Navajos were upon the industrial economy for their barter, they were subject also to the cycles of economic depression that marked this period in America, punctuated by brief moments of demand, such as that when wool was bought up at the beginning of World War I.

By 1930, the slow descent into a basic, hand-to-mouth subsistence was intensified by overgrazing. The reservation had filled up with sheep (and people), and sheep herding became less productive in terms of the external economy. Competition with non-Navajo stockmen outside the reservation, scarcity of land, the growing disparity of Navajo and Anglo herding practices, and the Stock Reduction Program of 1935, led to a collapse of the herding way of life. Stock reduction was a punishing and forceful interruption of an indigenous and, in its own terms, a successful economy. Indeed, sheep economy was, like the dominant economy, aimed at growth: more sheep, more individual wealth, controlled by family and kin groups.

There were far fewer opportunities for any family to rise above subsistence. Wage labor became more important. New practices and breeds were introduced by both BIA agents and traders, both of whom had an interest in making sure the Navajos survived economically. This was a period of poverty, as Navajos struggled to survive in a new economic situation.[1]

Following stock reduction, there is a fourth phase of Navajo economy, from about 1940 to about 1960. The herds were decimated, and thus the wealth, the structure of work, and the source of trade (and meat) of family groups. During this period new programs of federal support and wage labor were brought in for the rampant poverty and hunger that now existed. At the same time, oil and resources of the reservation were beginning to contribute to the development of Navajo tribal government, funded by and directing mining royalties. This resource depended on both outside technology and outside demand. The Navajo economy was itself in a slow process of conversion from the self-sufficiency of families, a communal approach to labor, to a broader tribal economy that included a strong program of support for education.

By the 1960s, another phase of Navajo economy was beginning. Sheep were no longer the crucial center of Navajo economy. They remained symbolic and useful ties to an older, traditional life. Cattle slowly became more important, and the nature of herding shifted as federal aid programs were brought to the reservation. To qualify for welfare checks, individuals needed to divest themselves of livestock. Many younger people were not interested in herding, and had no experience or skills in it. By 1970, there were many families with few or no sheep, and money was becoming the new commodity. Wage work was now essential, and provided some—but not all—of the income for a family. The Navajo Tribe provided many programs for training and working, funded by some of the Great Society programs of the Johnson administration. Many younger Navajos successfully combined new skills, new approaches, and new kinds of jobs while retaining respect and continuity with traditions.

This shift, these changes in political economy, came with a price, a widening split between traditional and modern Navajo life. There was also an increasing drift toward, and focus on poverty, not only in fact but psychologically. Hard work had never been shunned by Navajos as long as it could be productive, but too often such work could not bring the old satisfactions—let alone subsistence. Navajos, more visible to the outside society, were constantly viewed as poverty-stricken even when this did not mean either starvation or deprivation—though this existed. Poverty existed as a label, a terrible identity. Navajos themselves wanted more: more goods, more comfort, more ability to go abroad, to earn salaries. The acceptance of the comfort of goods is the only easy part of assimilation, of accommodation to the new social arrangement that new goods trail behind them.

The Navajo Reservation population had been rapidly growing, from approximately 69,167 in 1950 to 79,587 in 1960. By 1960, Navajo society was varied and complex, different from region to region, community to community. There was, of course, no "typical" Navajo: there were Navajos with roots in a shared past, with a shared philosophical and ceremonial tradition, and quite different (and influential) geographical roots, who now looked toward a modern way of living and of being Navajo that incorporated a wide range of new ideas. Navajo people continued their old ceremonies, and also took up different forms of Christianity or the Native American Church, gave voice to an array of political opinions, new ambitions, and hopes for their children, all while retaining many traditional values, strengths, and beliefs. A Navajo woman elder said:

> My opinion is that traditional education and Anglo education are similar in many ways. Both teach a student to be independent, to have self-respect, to know the facts of life and so on. . . .
>
> We elders . . . have an important job. We try to teach our children what we know and have it passed on to their children. . . . Our Navajo children need to have good manners and self-respect, as well as respect for others. Parents must reason with their children so that they will understand that father and mother have the upper hand. Parents must not shy away and let their children tell them what to do.[2]

In 1962, Raymond Nakai was elected chairman in the tribal government election. He worked hard to bring factories and other industrial concerns to the reservation. As money and programs flowed from the tribal government to individuals and communities, the Tribal Council began to gain people's attention. Traditional leadership, found in respected elders, or certain individuals who took responsibility for specific activities, coexisted with the introduction of new forms of a wider tribal leadership, such as elected positions, the structure of the Tribal Council, and a growing bureaucracy. This mix of old and new might itself be seen as a Navajo way—even a tradition—of blending ancient and modern.

At this period, young people were, as before, subject to their parents' management of resources. For example, at Shonto in the northwestern, somewhat remote, area of the reservation, Grace Brown of the To dich'i- i'nii Clan, born for Bit'ahnii Diné, described her growing up. She went to school locally for three years, then went away to school for one year.

> I wanted to go back, but when I came home at the end of the year, my mom—she was very traditional—said, "Why don't I keep you around here." So I only went that far [in school]. I didn't go back again. Then I stayed home with my parents. I herded sheep and I kept house for my parents. [Grace Brown, interview with the author, June 1999]

Grace, as a good Navajo daughter, made her own decision to follow her parents' wishes.

Individuals owned certain goods, such things as jewelry, clothes, saddles, and horses; wagons were jointly used, though they might be individually owned. Networks of relatives provided a mix of resources: those who herded, others who were silversmiths or weavers, some who worked on the railroad, at the trading post, or in modern jobs in Window Rock or off the reservation. In addition to exchanges with the outside world, there was a less visible economy of community exchange, barter, gifts, and payments, for, among other things, transportation, jewelry, and ceremonies. When individuals earned money they could spend it if they chose, but they were supposed to share it, also—anyone in the family could ask for things, and while there was any money left, the earner could not deny them, though he or she might decide whose needs within the family circle came first.[3]

Wages, welfare payments, and credit at the trading post were, of course, part of the structure of the family economy. It was a system both successful and at odds with the dominant society. Traders extended credit to an individual, but that individual was the head of a household, or had dependents, and the trader had to know exactly who could, or could not, be allowed to purchase on the account. Traders might give a good weaver, for example, an account for her and her family and also an account for her own use. Extended family members could be included, and individuals could be specifically excluded, by request of the account holder, from using the account.

> I would say that the role of the trader in the community was almost family-like, inasmuch as you had a responsibility to take care of your customer. You had a responsibility of making sure they ate year-round. . . .

A good trader always knew within ten dollars of what every customer owed. And you knew that they would have ten, twelve bags of wool, or you knew that they would have seventy-five or eighty head of lambs to sell. So you knew what their capacity was to pay their bill. . . . [Bruce Burnham, Cline Library interview, July 1998]

This changed with the arrival of cash in the 1960s.

When there came a lot of welfare assistance on the Reservation, the trader's cash flow really changed. Before, there were many days where we didn't see a dollar in the cash register in cash, and yet we did a volume of business that day. But as that cash flow increased, to where there was money on the Reservation, and your customer had some money to spend, you weren't quite as prone to keep your thumb on a customer and not let them buy something. [Bruce Burnham, Cline Library interview, July 1998]

Traders, too, had their own economic system by which they were bound: the costs and practices of wholesale and retail, of profit and loss, and of the payment of bills and salaries. They were also in a unusual business situation.

Because of their special legal status the assets of Navahos [sic] and other reservation Indians are not subject to lien or attachment of any kind, so that the trader, unlike the general storekeeper, cannot deal in notes or crop mortgages, and has no legal recourse of any kind in case of default. Except in the case of pawn, trading post accounts receivable are entirely unsecured.[4]

Trading-post prices were high, and had always been high, partly as a result of the credit situation. Traders, too, ran on credit: the wholesaler extended six months of credit to a trading post, and rarely gave price breaks. A salesman for Henry Hilson's wholesale company in Albuquerque, Bob Bolton, began traveling around the reservation in 1963, showing goods and taking orders, and became familiar with the traders.

You didn't drive between the stores in just a few minutes. It might take you an hour, hour and a half to get from one store to another one. But the people [traders] were very friendly, and most of them were very lonesome. And when you got to the store, you had a lot of conversation and catching up . . . you would spend the evening with them, and usually work the store after supper . . . and then the next morning get up and go on about your business. . . .

When I first started going out there it was very difficult to get some of the traders trained to pay their bills on a monthly basis, because they wanted to pay for the merchandise when they sold their wool or sold their lambs or sold the piñons or sold their cattle. And they gave credit on those sheep and on those lambs and on that wool. And they didn't get paid until they brought in the wool and sold the wool. Then they wanted to pay their bills at this time. I remember Henry Hilson, I heard him say a couple of times that he told customers, "I have carried you longer than your mother carried you!" because they'd owed him money for longer than nine months. [Bob Bolton, Cline Library interview, December 1998]

The mid-1960s was the period in which traders, after the success of the short-lived Navajo Shopping Center in Gallup, began to convert trading posts to self-service operations, doing away with the old bull-pens and putting in "gondolas," or checkout counters with a cash register. Camille Garcia at Chinle Trading Post was one of the first of the older generation of on-reservation traders to put in self-service shelving. Others followed.

It was such a diversified store—I mean, you had everything. I got the idea that we ought to open it up as much as possible . . . so me and Camille Garcia from Chinle, I think he and I were the only ones that finally opened up our grocery side of the stores. We put gondolas [modern checkout counters] in, and we had our groceries and made it sort of a self-service deal. [Joe Danoff, Cline Library interview, January 2000]

Clarence Wheeler, trading at Greasewood store in the early 1960s, remembered that he modernized his store reluctantly. The trading post had bull-pen style counters, and a few years after he bought it self-service checkout counters were coming into fashion. At first he was resistant to this change.

We'd had some trouble with the butane tank and some gas was escaping. Somebody didn't tighten the valve. And I was out there taking care of that and I told them "we're not going to change the store." . . . [Gas] was escaping and it was dangerous, and finally I got it shut off. By the time I shut it off, I went in and I told him [his manager] I wasn't going to do this.

He said, "It's too late, we already started." They [his manager, Bill Laubel] had started tearing out the counters and everything. . . .

So we went ahead and put in our self-service. And it worked out real good, it was a lot better . . . rather than the old counter-type service, why, we reconstructed and put in another vault, and added on to it, and it was nice. And it really brought us business. [Clarence Wheeler, Cline Library interview, March 1998]

The credit situation began to change for traders, and they, too, had to pay in thirty days. A group of traders began to buy goods from Associated Grocers, and had to put down a deposit with them, larger than their orders. Joe Danoff claims responsibility for encouraging traders to change to Associated Grocers.

I was really concerned about the prices we were having to pay for the commodities we were buying. So I took it on myself to make contact with Associated Grocers, and they talked favorably about it but said, "to come out there on that reservation was a lot of traveling for just one [trader]." So I personally went out and tried to get clients for them [on the reservation]. . . . You know you had to put up a deposit of so much money. But that opened up a big deal for us traders because we were getting merchandise at really better prices. [Joe Danoff, Cline Library interview, January 2000]

Younger traders took to self-service eagerly. The new generation of traders was growing up and going into business, and it was a generation that had traveled around, seen other ways, other worlds, and in coming home to the reservation brought back new ideas to combine with the old ways. Lavoy McGee, Jewel McGee's son, went to Brigham Young University and graduated in agricultural sciences. After a short time during which he worked for the Forest Service, he, too, went into trading like his father, and went to work in 1965 at Red Mesa Trading Post, in the northern Arizona portion of the reservation. Lavoy was interested in livestock, which had by the 1960s begun to revive, and much of his trade continued to be in sheep and cattle.

That country used to be quite remote. You'd leave Shiprock and head out towards Northern Arizona, and you're out in the boonies. But just recently, a highway [Highway 160] had been built out through that country, and just a few years prior to us buying an interest out there, they had moved the old trading post [Red Mesa] up onto the highway. So by the time I got there, it was a fairly modern building, and it was a self-service store, so it wasn't like the old-type stores. . . .

A lot of them had pickups and still a lot of them used wagons and horses. Everybody didn't have a pickup, but it seemed like every family seemed to have access to one and got around pretty good.

Our market there was for the Indians; we were there to serve Indian needs. Even though the highway was there, and the tourists were starting to use the highway a lot, and it was a popular tourist road, still we were an Indian trading post and we supplied all their general needs, from groceries and mutton, to dry goods, hardware, feed, gasoline. [Lavoy McGee, Cline Library interview, March 1998]

The late 1950s saw mining for mineral resources take off, bringing royalty money to the Tribe, as well as to a few individuals in off-reservation allotments. Much of the development of the Navajo tribal government and the subsequent modernization programs related to oil, gas, coal, and uranium discovered on the reservation. Utah Mining and Construction contracted with the Tribe to mine coal in 1957, and in conjunction with the Arizona Public Service Companies developed the Four Corners Power Plant, which opened in 1962. The New Mexico Public Service and Tucson Gas and Electric companies built another plant across the San Juan River (though it was on public land, and soon ceased to buy Navajo coal); the Salt River Project obtained Tribal permission for a generating plant near Page, Arizona, in 1968. The Pittsburgh-Midway Coal Company obtained a lease for right to mine coal near Window Rock in 1964, and Peabody Coal Company obtained rights for mining on Black Mesa in 1966; the coal was primarily strip-mined. Uranium was found after the Second World War, and by the 1970s was being mined and milled on the reservation, primarily at Shiprock, Mexican Hat, and Tuba City.[5]

Troy and Edith Kennedy, trading at Red Rock Trading Post in partnership with Jewel McGee, were in the middle of the mining area, and the demands of the community kept the store busy.

We stayed open most of the time till six o'clock every day. When the uranium started, we'd close for a little while and open back up. We stayed open lots of times until nine o'clock, because they didn't get out of the uranium mines till late. And Jewel and Troy would have to cash their checks. They'd bring their checks in for us to cash.

It was big business, that uranium, when it was going on—vanadium trucks were coming out and hauling it into Shiprock to the smelter there. Kerr McGee had this big smelter at Shiprock or whatever they call that, where they took the uranium and vanadium, separate it, ship it out. We would stay open during those years until late at night. [Edith Kennedy, Cline Library interview, March 1998]

Work in the mines brought good wages, contributing to the purchase of pickup trucks and other modern goods, although the Red Rock traders still kept busy buying silver, rugs, wool, and sheep.

Navajos who earned money spent money. They built more comfortable houses—new hogans, sometimes Anglo style square houses—bought house trailers, sheep, cattle, jewelry, as well as pickup trucks, and held ceremonies—Blessing Way, Enemy Way Ceremonies, and the winter Fire Dances—for healing and feasting.

Navajos were critical of the way trading worked, of the fact that goods and services were not extended by the trader in the same manner as among Navajos. Navajo family and clan members shared goods and services, and could request help and groceries in return, later or in a different form. There was some resentment, and much misunderstanding, of the business of trading: traders were seen as rich, in Navajo terms, because they owned all the goods in the store. Traders were accepted as community members, who, though they were outsiders, put down roots and stayed. Because they seemed to understand so much of Navajo life, Navajos thought they ought to behave the way the people themselves did, sharing and exchanging wealth.

Paul Begay, whom we met in previous chapters, when asked what Navajos expected from the trader, how they thought about the trader's business, said that many people did not understand that the trader was there to make money. They did not grasp the idea that, in a store, goods were sold for more than the trader paid for them. But because the trading post's goods made life easier, the food on the shelves was food that kept, that did not have to be eaten quickly before it spoiled, people came to rely on the store.

The trader . . . he's got food that will last a long time, as opposed to if you butchered a sheep, you divided it up among all these different hogans that you call your group of family living together. . . . It's sort of consumed within a short period of time. . . . And the more and more stuff began to go into the trading posts, more and more we began to go over there. They kept coming up with more new stuff. So in a lot of Navajo people's minds, I think that the Navajo people think they were being ripped off in many ways by the trader. But then again, they also understand that they can't do without the trader, because then it seems like they're not advancing with the changing times.

There was always a little animosity, there's always a little anger set towards the trader. But then it's also understood we cannot live without the trader also. . . . And so that's why even the person that got mad at the trader will always be back over there again about a week later—not necessarily to apologize, but he's going to go back over there because he needs this place to also be there. [Paul Begay, Cline Library interview, February 1998]

This attitude was one that had echoed through the decades. A glance back to Tribal Council discussions in 1948, continued in 1953, the year traders were granted twenty-five-year leases, will give a better understanding of relations between traders and Navajos, and how those relations related to the business of trading.

On March 20, 1948, the Navajo Tribal Council passed a resolution on trading: the Council would regulate prices, charge a tax on gross sales (a form of rental of trading posts), and generally bring trading under tribal control. Traders protested this resolution in Congress, through the UITA, claiming that it would "place an impossible burden on them," make business difficult, and eliminate credit to Navajo customers. Although the Tribal Council's resolution was not approved by the Commissioner of Indian Affairs—because, in his view, it was in conflict with the Bureau's mandate by the constitution to regulate trading—it did have several results. The Commissioner of Indian Affairs was confirmed in having the sole right to regulate Indian trading. However, the right of the Navajo Tribe to "withhold its consent to the use of tribal land for business purposes 'for any reason deemed by the council to be sufficient'" was upheld. The BIA responded to this failed resolution by carrying out another survey of trading posts to investigate possible problems and improvements, despite the reluctance of the Tribal Council, whose members felt that they had made their opinions clear and no inquiry was necessary.[6]

So, in 1948, Bonney Youngblood, Experiment Station Administrator of the U.S. Department of Agriculture, who had already made an extensive trading post survey in 1934, planned a new survey. The Navajo Tribal Council selected Zhealy Tso, the Council's Vice Chairman, to observe the work. The UITA also selected a representative from their Executive Board, A. H. Lee, to assist. Staff members of the Indian Service, Horace Boardman, Robert Cole, Arthur Hubbard, and Robert Young, carried out the survey under the direction of Moris S. Burge, who wrote the final report.[7]

Twenty-six trading posts, 30 percent of the 102 stores licensed to operate on the Navajo Reservation, and three Navajo owned stores (included for comparison) were surveyed in the fall of 1948. The findings illustrated the economics and business practices of trading posts. For the year 1947, the total amount of goods sold for 21 posts came to approximately $1,650,000. The average gross profit margin, before deducting expenses and salaries, was 24.5 percent. Five stores had higher profit margins (between 34 percent and 56 percent), and several had such low profit margins that it seemed unlikely that they were making enough money to survive. One post showed no profit at all. But Burge noted that it was

> difficult to reconcile figures on gross markup or profit with the markups shown by the price schedules. The gross profit would, of course, be influenced by the profit or loss on the resale of products purchased by traders from Navajos, especially lambs and wool, but even this does not fully explain the discrepancies.[8]

Surveyors commented that prices at trading posts were high, and Burge argued that this could not be explained by the cost of freight. Rather, he said, "The credit risk assumed by the trader has a more important influence on prices." Credit practices varied: some traders charged interest (from 10 percent to 25 percent), others did not, but their prices were higher. Traders advanced credit based not on the customer's ability to pay but on the need of the Navajo individual or family, criticized by Burge as a "haphazard" and unbusinesslike practice. Burge pointed out that Navajos who paid their debts were "carrying those who default on their payments" and suggested that traders instead advance loans, charge interest, and take on mortgages and liens as security.[9]

The report mentioned considerable variations in operating expenses. Burge concluded, the wide variation in methods of bookkeeping, the paucity of records kept by some traders, and inconsistencies apparent in some cases would make any but the most generalized conclusions dangerous.[10]

To further confuse the economic picture, trading posts provided many "non-commercial"—that is, free—services such as mail, transportation (to hospital, work, and meetings), they let community members draw water from their wells, provided employment services, and gave financial and even domestic counseling. Burge suggested that the need for such services would eventually disappear as communities developed and took over these activities.[11]

Burge noted that traders were reluctant to invest in improvements, uncertain of their tenure. Navajo tribal officials, though they wanted better facilities, were reluctant to consider long leases because it limited their ability to control the trader. He reported that Navajos in general wanted more stores, and the Tribal Council members believed that "the more stores there are on the reservation, the greater the competition, and, therefore, the lower the prices." The Council had grasped a basic capitalist theme. However, Burge stated firmly that "this is . . . not a fact" citing the isolated communities, the need for a certain volume of business. In his opinion, trading posts needed to operate more efficiently, at a higher volume—and in relative absence of competition—in order to bring goods to Navajos at the lowest possible prices. He recommended that the Tribal Council take care to issue only a limited number of leases within a certain area.[12]

The description of Navajo-owned trading posts and cooperatives (in 1948 there were three community stores, at Piñon, Red Lake, and Many Farms) included in the survey was not a bright one. The report noted that these stores lacked capital and experience, and the owners and managers were subject to pressures from family and community to share the goods rather than sell them. Burge commented that this would also change over time. Prices at such stores were comparable to Anglo-run trading posts.[13]

The report appeared in 1949, but the Tribal Council continued to raise problems of traders and need for trading post regulation. When traders bought sheep and lambs, they had to feed them and drive them to the railroad loading point, depleting Navajo grazing both around the post and on the reservation lands they crossed. Some traders (about sixteen) never paid dues to the tribe (at this point, dues were one quarter of one percent). The tribal attorney sought the assistance of the UITA with problems, only to find that this voluntary organization had no ability to enforce anything. And finally the question of checks came up:

> He [the trader] holds the checks for months and months and there are people coming in there asking for them. The people write a note to the trader asking him to give their check to a certain party, but they will not do it. They make the person come in and get it themselves. When they do come, he forces them to spend the check and sometimes, they still have some money coming and they will not give them cash. They give them a credit bill.[14]

Council members discussed the complaints of Navajo customers that if they took the check in cash, they received less than if they took it in credit or in half cash, half credit. From the traders' perspective, this meant they gave slightly more than face value if the check was traded out rather than cashed. "We are not talking about all the traders," Howard Gorman said, "but there are some who are unscrupulous, unfair, and crooked, and taking advantage of our poor people." Council members noted that complaints related as much to nearby, off-reservation traders (not subject to regulations) as to those located on the reservation. And so the Tribal Council sent a plea—to the BIA director, Alan Harper, to the lawyers, to the UITA—to get matters in hand, to regulate traders on these matters.[15]

The trading regulations in force at this point dated to 1940. The trader could not raise livestock (or co-own livestock with Navajos) on the reservation, could not permit gambling in the trading post, could not trade in antiquities, sell imitation Indian crafts, or trade on Sundays. Traders had to be bonded in the amount of $10,000, had to confine their trading to the "licensed premises," keep those premises sanitary, obtain and keep current a three-year license at a cost of $25 a year. Moneys went to the BIA agent, "to be expended by him in the enforcement of the regulations." They might accept pawn or pledges to secure accounts, had to give a written receipt with the pawn date, a description of the article, the amount loaned, and the market value agreed upon, and they were liable for loss or theft of any such items. Pawn could become trader property only if it had not been redeemed in 12 months. Traders could extend credit at their own risk, they were to give receipts for articles they bought from Indians, and they must pay all government checks in cash, merchandise, or credit (at the option of the customer) to the full value of the check.[16]

The regulations were, in fact, weakly enforced. They also reflected the

Bureau's determination to acculturate tribes, including a prohibition against donating "any money or goods to the performance of any Indian dance or ceremony," ignored by every trader who chose to contribute to sings or who gave the masked Ye'ii dancers food when they came to the store.[17]

The Tribe agreed to grant traders twenty-five-year leases, in return for which they paid 1½ percent of gross sales. Neither the Tribe nor the traders were enthusiastic about these leases—the traders were unhappy about paying this minimal rent—but they were, in fact, one of the most positive things to happen. Leases secured around 1953 would last until around 1978. The tribe earned rent, and the traders had tenure. The Tribe now had some control over the leasing of land for trading posts, and community members had some say in who worked at the post. Many traders began to invest in their store, installing refrigerators and other new equipment, repairing buildings, and generally settled down to business with a sense of long-term security.

Trader attitudes had come up in the discussion, and the point was made clearly by Jimmy Largo, "They have treated us like that when we had no voice of our own and now that we have a voice, let us use it." This new, strong voice of the Navajo Tribal Council might be said to express opinions not just about traders but, in general, about those who dominated their lives—traders being the most available, and representative, figures. The twenty-five-year leases came with a purpose behind them, that of the Tribal Council members' determination to know, as Howard Gorman put it, "how to do business with white men."[18]

Trading became more business-like. Now traders were businessmen who, buying goods wholesale and selling them retail, sought—indeed needed—to make a profit, to pay the store's bills, the percentage due to the Tribe, and the basic repairs on or even expansions to the trading post buildings. Trading posts were now more like other American businesses, in which economics and culture rested on the foundations of capitalism: working for wages, trying to build up capital or savings in money, doing business in which profit was essential. The symbols and ideals that tied together economics and ways of living were as strongly based in this specific cultural economy as that of the Navajos. Profit paid the store employees, the expenses of travel and delivery, and their own salary. If a trader was ambitious, he or she could expand, seek to sell more rugs and silver in larger markets at higher prices, diversify, swallow deficits in other parts of the business, hire more people, put more capital aside—in general, make more money. Profit also meant that the trader could extend services to customers and be generous to the community, and these services were an important part of the trading exchange. The trading post also had to negotiate within the community economic complex, and the trader, more especially if he and his wife got to know the community well and understand the practices, had to work out his and her own accommodation to the system. Some traders felt they could do good business and still make decisions that would not be considered "good business practice" elsewhere.

> We buy just about everything we can, including very rough stuff . . . we don't just buy the best, we try to buy everybody's. . . .
>
> We have clientele that can spend different levels of money. But you need to support all the weavers, not just the best, or there eventually won't be any best. There has to be the whole supporting cast of people with different levels of skill in order to produce the finest. [Les Wilson, Cline Library interview, March 1999]

However, profit was a concept that did not travel over the cultural boundaries, and traders knew it.

> A lot of them don't even know I get paid. A lot of them really are surprised when I say, "Well, I gotta get paid." They look at you like, "You get paid?! You've got a store here! What do you get paid for?" They really look at it in that respect. You got a store, you don't need paying. That's the way it is. [Lloyd Foutz, Beclahbito Trading Post; Cline Library interview, August 12, 1998]

In the late 1960s, more "progressive" trading posts began to develop, and an entrepreneurial trader, very different to the old style trading posts and the trader who sold just what the community needed and no more. These were the stores that changed from behind-the-counter to self-service stores, stocked a wider variety of food, and increased their dry goods departments. These were the traders who had switched to Associated Grocers, which carried a much bigger inventory, now paid their bills weekly on top of placing a deposit larger than an average weekly purchase.[20]

This was a revision of the entire trading operation. Some traders took a gamble on Navajo ability to buy and trade in this cash economy, and made changes. They no longer abided by the old trader vision that families and communities ought not to be encouraged to spend beyond their means, and that traders were responsible for assisting customers to budget for the year. The careful fifties had metamorphosed into the spending sixties, fueled by President Johnson's War on Poverty programs, as well as an economy—and a society—charged by the war on Vietnam.

Trading posts like Dinnebito, Elijah Blair's store high up on Black Mesa in the Hopi-Navajo Joint Use Area, or Shiprock Trading Post, owned by Ed Foutz, or Tuba City Trading Post, a Babbitt post, stores in growing communities, were examples of this revision.

> I remember, we had a pretty big discussion on what we were going to sell when we remodeled [Dinnebito]. . . . So I got the grocery book out and, well, you only sold yellow cake and chocolate cake before. Well, we put applesauce cake in there or, you know, spice cake. We put in white, yellow, brown—every kind of cake mix there was. We started selling canned frosting. [Bruce Burnham, interview with the author, July 1998]

Two factors contributed to making a trading post of the late 1960s and early 1970s successful. One, already discussed, was the influx of cash among Navajos, and along with cash, growing consumer desires and knowledge. The other was the popularity of Southwestern Indian arts and crafts, rugs and pottery, baskets and silver. Livestock was still a thriving business, as well as crafts. Traders worked, as traders had done in past decades, with weavers and silversmiths, especially with the renewed interest in Navajo jewelry. There was often a division of labor between a trader and a manager, or brothers in business, one focusing on livestock, the other on crafts. Many traders were inspired with the idea of making the trading post a thriving economic center of the community, bringing new ideas and new goods to the store, and doing a good business while providing services. Ed Foutz was the trader at Shiprock Trading Post around 1969, when business in livestock and weaving was doing well.[21]

> My great love was the arts and crafts. I was fortunate enough to find a manager . . . and his love was livestock. And so we took that store together and probably had more fun at that period, a ten- to fifteen-year period. . . . We would ship [the wool] to Johannesburg, to France and England. . . . And it just got to be where we were doing—we had what I call every door in that

trading post working at full-bore: the livestock, the arts and crafts, and the front door with groceries. [Ed Foutz, interview with the author, September 1998]

Pawn also continued to be one of the trader's services in 1968 as it had been in 1868. Paul Begay remembered his mother and father and his grandfather pawning in the 1960s.

There was times when you needed to do it. Just because you had a hundred head of sheep didn't mean that you had sheep to sell. . . . It seems like it's not necessary at this time to sell the sheep. Save it for later.

So let's say, for instance, in the middle of the summer, May, June, why would the Navajo sell five head of sheep when he could save it and use it? Not sell until August so he can buy the kids' clothes to go back to school. So in the meantime they resort to their jewelry, a set of beads, a concho belt, a bracelet. They could pawn it for fifteen, twenty dollars. Growing up, I remember watching Mom and Dad do that. They would take off their bracelet, not sell it, but pawn it. And they would get some money— fifteen, twenty dollars maybe . . . that's a lot of money—you could buy a lot of stuff. [Paul Begay, Cline Library interview, February 1998]

For traders, the shift to a new consumerism meant a shift in attitude.

We had to convert from a system of denying the customer what they wanted, to displaying it and merchandising it. So it was a totally, totally different philosophy in trading. . . .

It's hard to say "no" in Navajo. When that lady comes in and says "*Shiyaaz*" it means "my son.". . . And you don't want to offend them, partly because they owe you so much already, partly just because of respect for them, out of your feelings for them. You don't want them to feel humiliated. So, you know, it's a balancing act that you're doing all the time. [Bruce Burnham, interview with the author, July 1998]

Innovation in the trading posts stimulated interest in new items, driving the customers' desire for cash income, but bringing with it the problem of credit extension and payment of debts. Traders still tried to match the credit allowance of a family to the amount of the checks he or his wife knew the family received from welfare and other checks. Welfare money contributed a steady flow of income, and traders were helping families obtain welfare checks before the state services came out onto the reservation in the 1960s.

In the mid-60s, I know in Arizona they sent caseworkers out to the trading post. These are caseworkers that weren't familiar with Navajos, they didn't speak Navajo—those came later—but the early bunch came out and they would use the trader to interpret. Well, the deal was that if an individual owned 500 head of sheep, they weren't eligible for welfare. So what they would basically tell us to tell our customer, or their future welfare recipient, was if they would transfer their grazing lease and ownership of sheep to a daughter or somebody, then they would be qualified for welfare. If they would divest themselves of their wealth, they would be eligible for $260 a month—that's just a figure I'm pulling out of the air, but they would be eligible for this welfare assistance. . . .

Well, $260 a month in cash was equivalent to a $1,500 livestock account in the store. That's a pretty good-sized livestock account, someone that had $1,500 worth of wool that came in and paid twice a year, either $1,500 worth of lambs or $1,500 worth of wool. This was the equivalent of what this lady was going to get just for divesting herself of this herd of sheep. And from a pure standpoint of economics, that was the thing to do. I didn't know a Navajo that got rid of their livestock, they only transferred the ownership over to a relative, usually a daughter, and so that doubled their resources. [Bruce Burnham, Cline Library interview, July 1998]

Traders never really approved of welfare, though it brought cash to their store.

They would get a check, and they would end up there in your store with this check, and there was no bank, so then we cashed all the checks for them. So we either extended credit towards those checks, or when they cashed a check they would turn around and buy whatever they wanted. The greatest thing in the world to a retailer is having someone sitting in your store, trying to throw money at you; and that's exactly what they were doing. [Elijah Blair, Cline Library interview, February 1998]

Still, traders felt that welfare deprived people of independence, that the wealth in cash did not add to the family resources, but altered them, and in the process altered the Navajo subsistence and relationships. Could you compare such different livelihoods, such different economic systems?

Everything that counted in the Navajo cultural economy was sheep, grazing permit, and tied to that was independence. And a pride of being independent and self-sufficient. Here was a lady that was one of the wealthier ladies in our community by Navajo standards. She probably had an earned income of less than $4,000 a year—so she was considered [by the outside society] to be living in this poverty level. [Bruce Burnham, interview with the author, July 1998]

Sheep were on the way out, and though crafts were highly prized and sought after, they were the only part of the Navajo traditional life that was being encouraged by outside business. Traders saw the effects on traditional life and regretted them, as many of their customers did also, but these where whirlwind years.

The trader and customer faced each other across a counter—Jay Springer described those old high bull-pen counters of early decades as fenced with chicken wire to prevent goods from disappearing—that was symbolic of the differences of manners, values, and philosophy, of each side interpreting the other in their own terms. When progressive traders of the late 1960s changed to self-service shelving and checkout counters, it was a change in more than architecture and design. The old relationship between traders and Navajos changed. That relationship had included generosity and interest in the community, and a kind of authority to managed budgets for families—now seen as paternalism. But at times the relationship had also included meanness, anger, and bullying, reflecting the larger society's terrible flaws and patronizing attitudes, as well as the frustration and bitterness of those so treated, and the long memories that made the four years at Hwéeldi seem like yesterday. But the lines between old and new trading habits were not so clear-cut, either. Many old style traders understood their customers well, and had lived their entire lives in the same community, knowing families from generation to generation, as unchanging as their customers were. By the same token, the newer trading practices, whether by newcomers who came into trading from outside the Southwest or younger members of trading families, were different: these were traders running a business.[22]

Evelyn Jensen was born on Black Mesa near Kayenta, Bit'ahnii clan, born for To 'ahani, and grew up both on and off the reservation, and she herself, after working in banking, became a trader at the tiny Oljato Trading Post. She remembered noticing the change in traders through the 1970s.

After going through school and then after high school in the seventies, I guess, it seemed to me that there was a different set of traders, they had different values. It was more like they were after, I guess, making money. So the new traders that came along weren't as understanding, or not as caring about the people. . . .

A trader that is very well concerned about the people, you know, he will go out of his way to do things for them. Whereas, a trader that is just there for the monetary gains, I think that he's rude to people, and he doesn't spend too much time with them, and he doesn't engage in community activities. [Evelyn Jensen, Cline Library interview, February 1998]

Joe Danoff, at Ganado, said, "It was difficult to keep [customers] within the limits of the checks . . . sooner or later, the trader was going to lose on that account. We knew it, I knew it, they all knew it." From the trader's point of view, business was risky. As they renovated stores, many took a more businesslike approach.

When I went up to Ganado [in 1957], I went up to run a business. I didn't know what kind of business we were going to have, or what we were going to do. . . .

We did take pawn, and even that I kept to a minimum, because I used to go out to these trading posts, and my god, they had fortunes in their vaults, of pawn that they'd held for years and years. Well, the old traders did that, they held that pawn forever. And I was too much of a businessperson to say, "Hey, this is not making me any money." So I wanted that pawn to turn over, and I would push that pretty hard. And when it came due and they didn't redeem it, it went out in the showcase and I sold it. [Joe Danoff, Cline Library interview, January 2000]

Business was brisk in the 1960s and 1970s, and trading posts needed all the help they could get, behind the counter, at the gas pump, with cleaning up in the store and counting cash, stocking shelves and checking the warehouse, writing up the orders, keeping the books, working with the customers, the crafts, the accounts, and the sheep. Most stores needed additional clerks and managers, and hired community members. Marie Lee began working at Aneth Trading Post, for Elijah Blair, in 1960. She had herded sheep as a child, then went to school. Her father traded wool: "That's what he raised us on, that wool, and working a little bit, and planted corn . . . fourteen of us."

One time my dad came home, he says, "that trader wants you to work for him." I didn't know him at that time. I tried to decide if I'm going to work for him or not. So he came over here one time. We lived in a small hogan. . . . I just slid under the bed. My dad was sitting on the bed, so I lay in there. I told him, tell him I'm not here, I'm just gone to herd sheep down the river, tell him." . . . The next day I was trying to decide to work or not. Took me all day . . . then I went down there . . . that's when I started working, April 6, 1960. [Marie Lee, Cline Library interview, July 1999]

Marie worked at Aneth for five years, then went to Dinnebito in 1965, after Blair bought the lease there. She liked it: "I like the place, Dinnebito. My second home, to me, was over there."

I used to be behind the counter when I was over there. Everything's behind the counter, they fixed that up . . . they put a checkout stand in front and groceries on the shelf. The customers like it that way, so they don't have to stand in line, "gimme that," and "gimme that." And then waiting for their turn. . . .

When I was in Dinnebito, I did a lot—paid bills and count money. And then I used to do the quarterly report, too. [Marie Lee, Cline Library interview, July 1999]

Grace Brown described how her career at Shonto Trading Post began.

Dale [Walker, then managing the Shonto store] says "I'll train you to work in the store." I said, I don't know how. . . . He showed me how to wait on customers, how to do the cash register, how to be a sales clerk. So I tried, and he said, "You're doing pretty good." That's how I started. . . . I was shy with customers at first. But it was pretty interesting. My father worked there, too, he was janitor. Then Raymond [who became her husband] was working there, too. After about six months, my parents—the way it used to be with parents, they said you had to be married, they arranged it and we were married. . . .

Then I had Jeanette [her daughter] and I was working here at the store. We bought a vehicle in 1969, that was our first vehicle. People came in wagons, just all wagons lined up outside the store. They rode horses then, too. . . .

When I first started in the store, it was all behind the counter, you had to get everything for the customers. . . . Walker was working on the wall, he took down that wall. He says it's going to be self-service. Everyone was surprised. They liked it. It was better than waiting in line—people had to wait, when you helped everyone. One at a time, you had to do it, so everyone had to wait for their turn. They all came in to see how it was. . . .

The older people were really surprised. They had to go round for themselves. It was a change, they had to get used to it. They had been used to having the service, somebody getting everything for them, bringing it to them. [Grace Brown, interview with the author, June 1999]

Grace's husband worked at Black Mesa, at the Peabody Coal Mine, for twenty years, while she worked at the store, and their daughter went to school in Shonto. After several years at the post, Grace became the dry goods manager.

I asked all the customers, what did they like. Then I talked to the salesmen, I asked if they carried those things. We had it all: jackets, shoes, pants, ladies' clothes, lots of fabrics. . . .

They used to come out, different salesmen, they came out—for boots, jackets, we used to get it from Texas. And then the clothes, regular clothing, we used to get it from Hilson Company, from Albuquerque. . . . Fabric, we used to get it from Ledbetter, they used to get it from Chicago. We ordered it through Phoenix, and they would get it from Chicago. [Grace Brown, interview with the author, June 1999]

By the late 1960s, more Navajos began to seek and use cash for things the traders did not sell, such as pickup trucks, furniture, medicine, incidentals of college education for which the tribe now provided scholarships, as well as trading post bills. As tribal work programs (coming through the Office of Navajo Economic Opportunity) and welfare checks brought money to Navajos in the reservation communities, many traders doubled their efforts to make their business successful. They thought that credit was necessary, though it was often taken for granted, and when cash came in, payment of old bills at the community trading post seemed to be low in priority. Traders moving from one post to another inherited credit debts that were never honored.[19]

But the other thing that came with that pickup truck was freedom of movement. And so they always had a neighbor or someone that was willing to put a tank of gas in their truck and haul them to Flagstaff or to Farmington or to Gallup or to Page. And so, boy, here the pickup's going fifty-five miles an hour, whoosh, past the front of the trading post, heading for town! That's where things really changed. All of a sudden we had to start competing with town. [Bruce Burnham, Cline Library interview, July 1998]

7

⅃·L

RADICAL CHANGE ON THE RESERVATION

The trader system was a bad system. There was a trade-off: all Americans get the benefit of free competition except the Indians, and the trade-off was that they were supposed to get extra scrupulous people, because they were all vetted by the federal government. In fact, they got the same people that everybody else gets, and they didn't have the presumed benefit of competition. So they had a monopoly situation.

Eric Treisman, interview with the author, November 1999

Traders—white men and women—were, for better or worse, part of Navajo society, part of Navajo communities. It's crucial to understand this: it's the reason why Navajos criticized them, why they said they were stingy and selfish—*bithatso*—and cheaters—*bina'adlo'*. They were part of the community, and perhaps the thinking was, they ought to behave more like Navajos. For these reasons, many of the changes in Navajo society surfaced in the trading posts and were worked out in that arena. For the next several pages, I'm going to leave the story of trading in order to describe some of the events of the 1960s and 1970s on the reservation, to make clear why and how traders were affected.

Raymond Nakai's chairmanship of the Navajo Tribe lasted until 1970, steering the tribe through a time of development and challenges. The work of the 1950s, by Annie Wauneka in supporting improved health care and clinics, and by the Council in creating scholarship programs, as well as setting up a judicial branch of its government and a tribal court system, meant that in the late 1960s Navajos both on and off the reservation grew up in a society very different from that in which their parents were raised. Peterson Zah points out that service in World War II created a new awareness on the reservation that intensified in the 1960s.

> The Navajo people were kept on that reservation . . . we just stayed there, we didn't know the outside world. We didn't know the good things that were happening out there. So all of a sudden two things happened. One of them was that many of our Navajo people went out . . . to serve this country during the war [World War II], so they had contacts.
>
> The second thing that started happening was the scholarship program kicked into place. Paul Jones [Tribal chairman from 1955 to 1963] and Scott Preston [vice chairman during the same period] had allocated $10 million for the Navajo scholarship program. . . . So then more Navajo kids started going out, getting their college education. They saw with their own eyes the kind of life that exists out there. They came back into the Navajo [Nation], then as a result, they started saying, "Hey, we have this situation here." And as a result of those two things, a lot of Navajos were beginning to question some of the activities of the traders. [Peterson Zah, Cline Library and author's interview, March 1999]

Navajos had more choices: in economic matters, in education, religion, and lifestyle, and in material goods. As a result, Navajo society was becoming more diverse, more complex, more than ever a mix and a recombination of old and new.

Throughout the 1960s and into the 1970s, young people in America, pushed by anxiety and outrage over the Vietnam War, began to become more active politically and to try reform society. Younger Navajos and other Native Americans were also involved in this kind of activism, fueled by an economy that, among other things, put unaccustomed money in the pockets of the young and the poor. Native American activism, however, focused not on the Vietnam War, in which many of them fought, but on the problems and issues of reservation life and tribal government, the dominance of Anglo rules and BIA bureaucracy. Their attitudes were marked by a new resistance to and anger about centuries-long economic dependence and cultural suppression. Much has been written about the 1960s; here I will take up only those details that relate to the Navajo Reservation and trading.

Raymond Nakai, as he had promised during his campaign, attended to two popular issues on the reservation, that of bringing an end to enforced grazing regulations and to harassment of the Native American Church. He was instrumental in attracting industry to the reservation, and with the consent of the Tribal Council contributed tribal funds toward buildings and infrastructure for businesses willing to invest in on-reservation plants. Nakai did not always see eye-to-eye with Norman Littell, the Tribal General Counsel, who was becoming more and more unpopular in the Council and among Navajo people at large, though he had done much to bring them to their current strength. Indeed, strong differences of opinion and of action marked the 1960s, not only between Nakai and Littell, but between Nakai and Tribal Council members, and between heads of tribal government divisions and, indeed, between members of tribal departments. Growth of the tribal government, the rise of new leaders and of bureaucracy, came at the price of increased factionalism and power struggles. These conflicts severely tested the Navajo political system.[1]

During the Nakai administration, traders and commercial enterprises (as well as school boards and health services) were challenged informally by educated and politically active young people, both Navajo and non-Navajo, and formally by lawsuits set in motion by a new organization, Dinébeiina Nahiilna Be Agaditahe Incorporated, known simply as DNA, which was created in 1967. Legal action on the Navajo Reservation became intense in this period, illustrating new national movements, as well as tensions within the Navajo tribe. The DNA, staffed by Anglo lawyers and Navajo tribal court advocates, was a program that tried to change economic patterns on the reservation, to help develop an indigenous economy, and in particular to create a more competitive business situation and do away with the trading post "system." DNA lawyers believed traders held unwarranted power over the cooperative and essentially socialistic Navajo way of life, and they tried to institute new ways, such as Navajo trading cooperatives and Navajo-run organizations and services. DNA was also, as its name indicated, part of an effort to improve living situations of Navajo people. The resulting changes were dramatic.[2]

In 1965, the Navajo government had created a new agency, the Office of Navajo Economic Opportunity (ONEO) funded by the Office of Economic Opportunity (OEO) in Washington, D.C., as part of President Johnson's War on Poverty. ONEO staff, almost all of whom were Navajo, directed or created programs intended to make it possible for Navajos to live and work on the reservation, rather than seeking jobs outside it. The goal of every ONEO program was to create work or at least sustain life on the reservation, a sharp change from the New Deal programs of John Collier and the 1950s relocation policy. Collier had encouraged tribes to become self-governing and had provided economic benefits to those living a traditional life on the reservation, that is, a way of life no longer considered economically viable by the larger society. In the 1950s, the BIA, as part of the government's relocation policy, fostered a program of extensive "acculturation" and began to terminate trust relations between tribes and the U.S. government. Indians were encouraged to relocate from their reservations to towns and cities so they could earn a living and, ultimately, change from Indian to more generic American ways of life. Now Peter MacDonald, ONEO's Director, set in motion programs of education and employment that would keep Navajo people at home and provide them with an income.[3]

Legal assistance was one of the programs folded into ONEO. A legal aid service had been set up by the Tribal Council in 1958 to assist the increasing number of Navajos who needed the services of an attorney and were without the means to afford it. The demand was heavy, but there was essentially only one lawyer available from the Tribal Attorney's office to provide legal services: Norman Littell compared the situation to an attempt to build the Glen Canyon Dam with two men and two shovels. In 1966, ONEO instituted a new tribal legal services program, called at first the Office of Navajo Economic Opportunity Legal Aid and Defender Society, and then renamed Dinébeiina Nahiilna Be Agaditahe Incorporated.[4]

DNA was planned and set up by Theodore R. Mitchell, a lawyer, a graduate of Harvard Law School, and an Arizona Mormon, and Taylor McKenzie, a highly respected Navajo doctor and a graduate of Baylor medical school. McKenzie, who in 1965 went to work for the Public Health Service and in 1970 became director of the Shiprock unit of the Public Health System, was a pioneer in obtaining better services, services run by or more responsive to Navajos. Mitchell had worked for the Navajo Tribal Legal Aid Service in 1965–66, and it was during this period that, together with McKenzie and Raymond Nakai, he had begun to plan the DNA service. Ted Mitchell had an agenda and a vision for DNA: he saw economic reform as vital to the future of the Navajos. Indeed, the name Dinébeiina Nahiilna Be Agaditahe—given by John Rockbridge, an older Navajo who was one of the original board members and a strong supporter of Ted Mitchell—translates as "Lawyers who contribute to the Economic Revitalization of the People." Its name was indicative of its purpose, to be not merely a poverty law program, but a center for economic and social reform.[5]

In December 1966, ONEO hired Ted Mitchell, then working in Phoenix for the OEO's regional office for legal services, to set up the program. DNA began in February 1967, with Mitchell as Director. The Board of Directors consisted of two members from each of the five Navajo agencies (including Dr. McKenzie), as well as Chapter representatives. Chairman Nakai at first saw the DNA service as a possible way to improve living standards and health and to solve land and other disputes, but Nakai and Mitchell did not long remain in agreement. Mitchell was described by those who knew him well as brilliant, idealistic, charismatic, visionary, afraid of nothing and no one. He was a conceptualizer, driven by philosophy and a sense of the need for justice for Native Americans that grew in part from his knowledge of the situation in border towns around the Navajo Reservation. He was also contentious, strong-willed, unwilling to brook opposition, and contrary; he tended to create relationships marked by either strong loyalty or deep enmity. The majority of the DNA Board of Directors supported him, as did virtually all the lawyers and court advocates who worked for DNA—particularly Peterson Zah and Leo Havens, the Navajo leaders at DNA, and lawyers in the Law Reform Unit, whose commitment and professional respect he never lost. He had, however, incurred the wrath of Annie Wauneka from early on, and the opposition of Raymond Nakai from shortly after the inception of the DNA program.[6]

DNA was born of need—the earlier legal aid program had been swamped with cases, and DNA staff estimated a caseload of nearly 19,000 people in its first year and a half—but it was raised in conflict. As a tribal legal service funded through OEO in Washington, the DNA program was similar to other poverty law services that had been set up in 1966 in OEO's battle to eradicate poverty itself. DNA was a poverty law program, like others, based on the work of idealistic lawyers; Ted Mitchell, its director, however, had a distinct social agenda. The main office at Window Rock had a special unit, the Law Reform unit, and that unit's lawyers sought cases that would further the DNA's mission of revitalizing Navajo economic life and tackling problems related to poverty, a mission of radical change that challenged the status quo with a new and politically charged vision.[7]

Harmony was as scarce on the reservation in those years as it was else-where in American society, but if there was a center of tribal conflict, it was the DNA program, its director, and its activities. The large Navajo tribe was organizationally complex, and had its own distinct social structure and political differences, always cross-cut by the dominant bureaucracy of the Bureau of Indian Affairs and constrained by the ultimate power of the U.S. Congress. Many of the DNA actions ran into conflict with the Navajo Tribal Council during the Nakai administration. Mitchell and others thought the tribal government was too much influenced by, and support-ive of, the BIA. The opposition to DNA by the Tribe's leading figures is thus hardly surprising. Many of the DNA staff, especially Navajos involved with the program, not only hoped their activities could create a new and more equal relationship between the tribe and the federal government, but also sought to provide a way for Navajos to call their own government to account.[8]

One of Mitchell's first actions was to employ Leo Havens, who had a degree in sociology, as a Navajo legal aide. Havens in turn recruited Peterson Zah, who was then training VISTA volunteers at Arizona State University, in Phoenix. Mitchell, Havens, and Zah together hired and planned the training of tribal court advocates who could work in tribal courts though they were not lawyers. Havens was to be involved in work-ing with communities and the Tribal Council; Zah was to help Navajo people who were appearing in court. In addition, both men assisted Mitchell in a search for promising young law school graduates at elite pri-vate universities such as Harvard, Columbia, New York University, Princeton, Stanford, Yale. Service with DNA would not be well paid, nor would it further the ambitions of up-and-coming lawyers. Rather, in these years of war and idealism, Peterson Zah compared it to the work of VISTA volunteers or the Peace Corps.

> Experienced lawyers were already into their work, and they had families. It was pretty hard to move somebody that has a house in Phoenix, for example, to move up to Window Rock. . . . So we decided to go after the young ones at law school. [Peterson Zah, Cline Library and author's inter-view, March 1999]

Zah, in particular, took on the job of recruitment. He combed the universities for candidates, interviewing and keeping files on promising students in their second or third year, telling them he could offer not money, but culture, beautiful landscape, and something worthwhile to do.

> My pitch to them was that, "You're never ever going to experience any other things as exciting as DNA. Yes, we don't have any money, we can't pay you much. But we have a Tribal Court system here that we're trying to develop. There *is* a Navajo sense of justice. We *do* have our own views about what we mean by due process of law, which may be different than the Anglos' concept of due process of law. And your job is to weigh those when you're handling these cases." [Peterson Zah, Cline Library and author's interview, March 1999]

When he was interviewing candidates, Zah described the scenery, his people's way of life, and the cultural aspects, but most of all he focused on the importance of the work. "You'll always remember DNA," he said he told them; "you'll always remember what you did immediately after law school."

> What we're trying to do nationwide for American Indians is that we're trying to enhance tribal sovereignty. . . . We need to take some good cases to the Supreme Court where we can prove our points about tribal sovereignty and how those are really, really important to the Indian people. [Peterson Zah, Cline Library and author's interview, March 1999]

The appeal was irresistible. Idealistic, liberal, activist lawyers, both women and men, recently graduated from Ivy League universities and facing possible service in Vietnam, committed themselves to DNA, and they did indeed remember those years as the high point of their careers. They were at the gates of battle—not in Vietnam, but on the Navajo Reservation, hoping to be involved with legal reform for a Native American tribe struggling with the issue of how to exist, economically and socially, within the larger society. Those who joined DNA believed that legal services could improve Navajo society, its system of justice, provide help for the needy and underprivileged that would help to eradicate poverty, and they hoped their legal training and skills would make contributions where they were most needed.[9]

The young lawyers who went to Window Rock, Chinle, Crownpoint, Fort Defiance, Tuba City, or Shiprock—DNA had offices in the communities where there was a Navajo BIA agency office—did not claim to know anything about Native Americans or Navajo society. Some had taken a course in anthropology, or on being accepted by DNA, signed up for one, or read *The Navajo* by Clyde Kluckhohn and Dorothea Leighton. At this time Native American law was in its infancy; it was not taught, so few publications on or about it were available. Later on, DNA ran a series of short seminars to educate their lawyers on Navajo life. Part of the challenge was precisely the unfamiliarity of the life they began to lead. The reservation offered some surprises.[10]

> I was involved in groups in New York that were looking for radical change. And it was the '60s, and I was affected by the war, I felt it was a waste of human life, both American and Vietnamese. . . . And, when I came out to the Navajo Reservation, I guess I expected to see people who would be up in arms about all that, and, of course, what I found was quite the contrary. People were very patriotic. People who were there, many of them were going to the war or else had gone and were supportive of the American values. . . . And it was quite a lesson for me, that the real lives of people were different from the politics I was experiencing. [Paul Biderman, interview with the author, December 1998]

DNA hired eighteen lawyers and sixteen Navajo Tribal Court advocates by 1968. The new lawyers, a few of whom were selected to work in the Law Reform Unit, went to work immediately upon their arrival: the caseloads were large, and they had little help. However, they were introduced to Navajo life by their clients, and spent time with them, often in their homes, their communities, and at ceremonies. By 1969, DNA was in the midst of a confrontation, as Ted Mitchell ran into serious opposition from Annie Wauneka, Raymond Nakai, and some of the Tribal Council. Mitchell was neither hesitant to do battle nor tactful in his strategies, and he and the DNA attorneys ran headlong into some of the major forces on the reservation: the BIA, the Public Health Service, the public school system, and the Navajo Tribal Council, as well as Peter MacDonald and ONEO. Mac-Donald was then Director of ONEO, and sought to have some control of DNA, though he supported it and later on helped to ensure its funding.[11]

There were also differences among the DNA lawyers, not all of whom were radicals. A few opposed Mitchell's leadership, others disagreed with some of his decisions or his style.

> It was something like a royal court, filled with intrigue. Ted Mitchell was

glamorous—there's no other word for it. . . . And he set the program up and he got the grant, and he went around and he hired a bunch of people, and from before the time they went to the reservation, they were plotting against him. [Eric Treisman, interview with the author, November 1999][12]

But except for this small group of dissenters, among DNA lawyers there was agreement in general on Mitchell's philosophy.

His overall approach to the reform that DNA set out to do was sound. . . . I think that he properly understood the Navajo tribal government was the handmaiden of the BIA, and unless its structure and organization could be changed, it would never succeed in truly creating self-government for the Navajo people. [Michael Gross, interview with the author, October 1999][13]

In addition to the opposition of Wauneka and Nakai, Mitchell had begun to alienate many Anglos, on and off the reservation, including political figures such as Senator Barry Goldwater. Councilwoman Wauneka, who vigorously upheld traditional life and scorned federal programs, and Chairman Nakai, who believed in federal aid, economic development, and change, were political rivals, but opposition to Mitchell was the single issue on which they saw eye-to-eye. This antagonism brought about a controversy that led to Mitchell's exclusion from the reservation and eventually his resignation.

The flash point of this confrontation took place in the Tribal Council chambers in July 1968. Duard Barnes, Acting Associate Solicitor on Indian Affairs, had come from Washington, D.C., to explain the recently enacted Indian Civil Rights Act. In the course of his presentation, which was being translated into Navajo, Mrs. Wauneka asked if this new law contravened their 1868 Treaty that allowed the Navajo Council to remove anyone they chose from the reservation. The solicitor said he would need to know who she had in mind; Mrs. Wauneka said, no one in particular. Mitchell, who was in the audience, laughed. He later described it to Michael Gross, a DNA lawyer who had just arrived from Yale to work in the Law Reform Unit, as "a huge embarrassed guffaw" since he thought (rightly, as it turned out) that if she had anyone in mind for exclusion from the reservation, it would be he.[14]

The next day Mitchell went back to the Council, taking with him Michael Gross, whose recollection of the incident follows.

We were sitting there about an hour, listening to the description of the law, everything being translated back and forth, English to Navajo, Navajo to English, . . . when some Councilman . . . got up, and walked majestically around the room to get to Annie Wauneka, who was sitting way in the front. . . . And she looks up, and looks back over her shoulder straight back at us. And then she gets up—she was a large woman, easily six feet, and comes back to us. . . . [Mitchell] says, I'm sorry, Mrs. Wauneka, I think we'll go, and begins to get up. And then she says, you're not going to laugh at me again, Ted Mitchell. And with this part of her hand she struck him on the cheek. . . . She continued to pound him on the back five or six more times. The place erupts—total, complete bedlam. [Michael Gross, interview with the author, October 1999]

As a result of the laugh, which was an insult to Mrs. Wauneka, and the ensuing disruption of the meeting, the Tribal Council voted on August 8th, 1968, to permanently exclude Mitchell from the reservation, and he was led off by Navajo police officers. However, this by no means ended Mitchell's direction of DNA, which he continued from Gallup, just outside the reservation boundary. Nor was it the end of the tribal government's struggle with Mitchell, who immediately initiated a protracted legal battle against Raymond Nakai and the Tribe, suing them for $10,000; tribal sovereignty was not one of Mitchell's goals. Supported by the Navajo Board of Directors of DNA, Mitchell argued in his lawsuit that the Tribe could only exclude other *Indians* from the reservation. Nakai, Wauneka, and the Tribal Council were powerless to stop Mitchell's activities or his lawsuit. Eventually, members of Arizona's congressional delegation entered the opposition against Mitchell. Senator Barry Goldwater wrote to Shriver, Director of OEO, and Arizona congressman Sam Steiger wrote to DNA, both complaining about the controversial nature and the cost of this program.[15]

By 1969, Mitchell's confrontational activities endangered DNA's application for renewed funding. In March, the Tribal Council, led by Nakai, voted against releasing funds from ONEO, directed by Peter MacDonald, for the program, and suggested (as had Goldwater) that a new legal services organization be created. However, the program was kept going by a grant from ONEO in Window Rock and one from OEO in Washington. Mitchell was the eye of the storm: in April the Tribal Council voted 38 to 16 to remove him as director, while the DNA Board voted 12 to 3 to retain him. DNA was closely identified with Mitchell, though the program, as well as its director, had many critics. And, according to Eric Treisman, a graduate of Stanford working at DNA's Crownpoint office, many supporters:

> Nakai got the Tribal Executive Committee, which was his hand-picked bunch to pass a resolution against Mitchell. But . . . he couldn't get all ten to vote against him. . . . So you can't say the tribe was opposed to DNA. Navajos have an attitude, and they wouldn't go out of their way to help a Bilaagana [white person], but they wouldn't go out of their way not to help. But if you were stuck in a ditch, and you yelled "DNA" they'd stop, they'd haul you out, take you to a party. They liked us: "Oh you saved my life; Oh, you got my daughter's license back." [Eric Treisman, interview with the author, October 1999][16]

However, in February 1970—in the first months of the new Tribal administration of Peter MacDonald—Mitchell resigned. His resignation was reluctantly accepted by the Board of DNA, and Leo Havens became the new director of DNA. Mitchell continued to work as a regular DNA lawyer, but some months later went to Micronesia to direct another OEO funded legal service, taking a handful of DNA lawyers with him. Havens, though expected to be a pawn of Mitchell, proved to be his own man.[17]

Despite the turmoil around them, DNA lawyers (with the exception of those in the Law Reform Unit) went to the different offices spread across the reservation and got on with cases. The work consisted of legal assistance to hundreds of individual Navajos, with problems that ranged from repossessed vehicles to bankruptcy, divorce, custody, adoption and paternity suits, and many other situations. Caseloads included the general range of misdemeanor and other petty criminal cases, family law, consumer cases to do with debts and garnished wages, welfare, and other benefits. There were various complaints about traders, especially in relation to pawn, handled by some but not all of the lawyers. In the DNA newsletter, *DNA in Action*, of December 30, 1969, the editor lists all the types of cases handled by their lawyers. Problems with traders included indebtedness other than pawn, pawn or pledge, receipt of public assistance or other checks, keeping of or access to records, combination in restraint of trade, and "other problems with traders."[18]

The practice of law on the reservation presented many challenges. There was little in the way of established court procedure on the reservation at this time.

At that time there not only wasn't a Navajo Bar Association, there really wasn't an established rules of civil procedure. . . . I remember going into court on what I thought was an uncontested divorce case. My client was a woman, she was quite Anglicized, not a traditional Navajo woman. And we wound up losing . . . because the husband got up on the stand and said that he really wished his wife would come back, and he still loved her, and it was difficult to figure out what the issues were. It was a real conflict of cultures, of the Navajo view and the Anglo view, a very technical view, of whether or not the courts should grant a divorce to this couple. And the judge said, I think this couple still love each other, this man still loves this woman, and I'm going to deny the couple the divorce. [Bruce Herr, interview with the author, October 1998]

His client was extremely upset about the situation, got another lawyer, this time in Window Rock, took her case to the Navajo Court of Appeals, and the judgment was reversed. This was a time of development in Navajo court procedures, for which the Tribe began to provide funds and training.[19]

Many DNA cases grew out of misunderstandings and ignorance of modern economic life, with its advertising, its easy credit, its promises of material wealth. Navajos could now purchase vehicles, that most desired and useful new commodity, on the installment plan. Navajos had had experience with credit accounts and pawn at the trading posts, but the inexorable deadlines and the idea of repossession were utterly unfamiliar—traders had been lenient in comparison. When Navajos were late with monthly payments to the auto dealers and furniture and department stores opening in Gallup and Farmington, the goods were repossessed. Few people could understand that they still owed money *after* repossession, that they had to pay for items they no longer owned. Debts and money problems constituted a large number of DNA's cases. Lawyers found that non-payment was indicative of cultural differences relating to work, money, and debts. The question of time was one problem—traders had accommodated to a more Navajo-oriented timing and bills were due in seasons of lambing and shearing—but the necessity of continuing to hold a job in order to continue to make car payments was not a cultural norm. DNA lawyers, in addition to much other work, began presentations on consumer affairs to help inform Navajos about such requirements, and to clarify their rights and opportunities.

At the same time, the lawyers in the Law Reform Unit sought out cases to set precedents, to make case law, to create change. It was, as Peterson Zah put it, "the most exciting time."

> DNA during that period handled some of the most interesting cases coming out of Indian country. And it was those cases that developed American Indian law for everybody across the nation. McClanahan vs. Arizona Tax Commission is only one of them. Rosalind McClanahan came to me, personally, and complained about what the State Tax Commission was doing to her, levying her income on the Navajo Reservation. So we took that case and we developed it, and ran all the way with it, through the United States Supreme Court. [Peterson Zah, Cline Library and author's interview, March 1999].[20]

DNA tried to improve the system of justice within the Navajo national government. Some communities of 200 voters had one delegate to the Tribal Council, while others, with as many as 8,000 people, also had only one delegate to represent them. Zah and other Navajos instigated legal action for better representation, as a result of which the Tribal Council was reapportioned. Zah commented on his parents' different attitudes about his activities.

> I remember being with my mother and with my father at one of those times, and my mother was really discouraging me, not to get involved in that kind of thing. My father, on the other hand, was glad. He said "It's about time. That's why you went to school. . . . If there's a wrong here . . . your job is to correct that situation." I remember him saying that. [Peterson Zah, Cline Library and author's interview, March 1999]

The overall work of the DNA lawyers involved a variety of cases that related broadly to the rapid infiltration of new economic practices and the need to improve Navajo institutions. In addition, DNA lawyers carried out a program of education and information about law and consumer education. They were, in effect, a force for acculturation and change—like non-Navajo government agents, missionaries, traders, and teachers, before them—with a new style but similar results.

The range of DNA activities was broad and drew considerable input from the younger Navajo leaders working for DNA, as well as for other ONEO programs. In turn, DNA gave these leaders institutional support and organizational resources. News and information was spread through a small newsletter, *Dine Baa Hani*. DNA staff supported and helped create grassroots organizations for rights and radical new approaches, pursuing welfare benefits and general assistance payments that Navajos were often unaware that they qualified for. They organized meetings to explain welfare rights and the food stamp program, and discuss problems relating to the BIA, Tribal and State Welfare agencies, and traders.

From the beginning, Ted Mitchell's own agenda specifically targeted trading posts. He took a stand against traders, and encouraged this perspective among those hired to work for DNA. He encouraged the lawyers in the Law Reform unit to look for case law that could tackle the trading post problems. His goal, explicit according to at least one lawyer who worked with him and implicit in his actions and influence, was specifically to break the power of the traders, whom he saw as having an economic monopoly over Navajos that allowed for no indigenous business development. Mitchell articulated this position in the spring of 1968, when he appeared in a CBS TV documentary, *The Forgotten Americans*, in which he charged the traders with exploiting Navajos.[21]

DNA lawyers in the branch offices did not, on the whole, seek out cases—they dealt with the cases people brought to them. Many shared Mitchell's view of the trading post system. Although some recognized the social agenda inherent in their work for DNA, others did not, or only in the broad sense of bringing justice to the Navajos. Most of the lawyers were intent simply on providing services that built up Navajo-owned operations, increased their income, and strengthened their abilities to make demands and give input. Robert Hilgendorf, a DNA lawyer hired in late summer of 1969 who worked in the Chinle office in the center of the reservation, said that he had no social agenda, that the lawyers were not there to be social engineers. He recognized that Mitchell had a specific agenda, but other lawyers dealt with whatever complaints people brought. He himself, as a lawyer, took whatever cases came through the door. Clients brought complaints; the DNA lawyers responded to them.

> You have to recognize that Navajos were in a dependent status, in relationship to every agency, service, every outside agency. They didn't vote in State elections, they didn't really have any representation in Congress, they didn't have any economic power, they didn't own their own land, they didn't have alternatives to go shopping in different places on the reservation. . . .
>
> I'm sure they even said DNA lawyers were colonialists in a sense; we're

coming out and telling them what they should do . . . and there's a little bit of truth to all of that. All the colonialists were putting their judgment ahead of the Navajos'. I suppose if there was an agenda, it was simply that the Navajos were going to have lawyers take on the colonial system . . . you had the Law Reform Unit doing that kind of stuff. We [DNA lawyers in local offices] were just dealing with the front lines, what would come up. [Robert Hilgendorf, interview with the author, October 1999]

Many complaints, he said, were related to trading, problems to do with pawn, credit, and the cashing of checks. Certainly the Chinle office was a center of anti-trader activities.

The fact is that it's the company store—that would be the model. People work for a certain company, and they get their room and board . . . so when their check comes in they've got to pay back the company.

We've already seen that problems had been raised in discussion in the Navajo Tribal Council meeting in January 1953. Resentment was building up against the traders for a variety of reasons but also partly against the very idea of profit. Problems in 1953 included complaints about traders taking advantage of the poor and the elderly, not listing prices on the items, selling inferior goods. Traders were said to be overcharging customers, or adding to bills (in some cases by padding, in other cases by charging an exorbitant interest for loans and credit); they were said to avoid giving cash and insisted that customers take payment (for sheep and wool, or on checks) in trade.[22]

These problems foreshadowed later issues, but there was a tone of bitterness to these earlier discussions.

We know the traders have formed an Association and they met to discuss problems of the Association. I wonder if they discuss ways and means to get the best of the Navajo people. When we [Navajo Tribal Council, or Navajo Chapters] meet we are discussing problems that would be beneficial to our people; how they can be well cared for in various areas. Those are some of the things we talk about. We do not think about taking advantage of anyone, and I wonder if that is the way they do, because of the complaints that have been made about them. They go with the white people and are looked upon by them as respected businessmen, namely, traders with the Navajo people . . . when they return back to the Navajo people, they still persist in doing those things that are not right in behalf of our people.[23]

Navajos knew traders who did the right thing, provided receipts, and handed over checks, but council members knew other traders who said, in a phrase repeated by several in the council, "This is my post, and what are you going to do about it?" Clearly, certain trader attitudes were creating frustration and anger.[24]

The generalized distrust of the idea of profit and the growing resistance to patronizing attitudes show that the tide had shifted. Many Navajos no longer looked to the trading post to help them with work, goods, ideas, and the other unfamiliar facets of the larger culture. Now their own sons and daughters gave them information. The groundswell of feeling against traders grew into a tidal wave.

In 1967, with the advent of DNA, Navajos found a way to turn these complaints about traders into action. Mitchell's comments in the 1968 CBS documentary about trader exploitation of Navajos renewed Tribal Council attention to trading posts. Not to be outdone by Mitchell, Edmund O. Kahn, associate attorney for the Tribe, drafted a resolution to close all trading posts that employed non-Navajos in their stores without Tribal approval. The Tribal Advisory Committee passed this proposal unanimously. Kahn told a *Navajo Times* reporter that he had been working on the problem of business leases for some time, since before Mitchell's appearance on CBS.[25]

One of the major complaints the DNA lawyers heard in the late 1960s was that, because Navajos often used the trading post as a postal address—the trading post usually included the community post office—the traders always knew when their customers received a check. Zah commented that the traders

> based on the complaints, would always know which letter contained a check inside. And the trader would put that check into a different box, and would leave all of the other mail in the box for the people to come and check. . . . So an individual would ask to see if the mail is there. Then they would look at that other pile, and they would look through it. And the trader worked in such a way that he always got his money back from that individual. The individuals were saying that "the trader should not hide the check from me," or "they should not open my mail." [Peterson Zah, Cline Library and author's interview, March 1999]

Trading posts had been active in getting post offices set up—none had existed in these communities before. All mail came to the trading post. Stores had pigeon hole boxes, by letter of the alphabet, into which the trader put each person's mail, and anyone could come and pick it up. But this meant anybody could pick up the mail, anyone at all, and checks—or any official looking envelope—were put aside so that the individual, and only that individual, could get it. Every trader will tell you, it is not very difficult to tell if an envelope has a check in it, and as postal officials they felt it was their legal responsibility to make sure that a check was only received by the person to whom it was addressed. In their role as business-people, they also felt that bills should be paid out of the income checks provided.

Other complaints made in the 1960s: too little fresh food or meat that was spoiled for lack of proper ventilation and refrigeration, scales were rigged; and traders, in their role as railroad agents, would only seek out those Navajos who owed them money when the railroad would call for laborers. Finally, there were problems with pawn.

> When you pawned something at the trading posts, you were paying such a high, high interest rate on those pawned articles, that nowhere else in the country do you go to a pawn broker, for example, and pawn an article at such a high rate as the trader would charge. . . . When the pawn became dead was always an issue. The traders, as we understand it, through the complaints that were coming to our office, if there is some good valuable squash blossom, the trader worked in such a way, kept their records in such a way, that it became a dead pawn immediately. [Peterson Zah, Cline Library and author's interview, March 1999]

In other words, Navajos accused traders of selling their good, old pawn jewelry too soon, to make more money from the sale of the silver than from the interest on the pawn. Money from that sale, Navajos complained, ought to go to the owner of the jewelry not to the trader/pawnbroker.

Early in March 1969, Joseph Shirley, at the Chinle DNA office, wrote to a trader, Raymond Blair at Round Rock Trading Post, concerning a complaint from a client. The details illustrate the nature of pawn problems and the responses of Navajo customers, DNA lawyers, and traders. Shirley wrote that his client said he had pawned a bracelet in September 1967, and that the trader was now asking for the balance owed ($55) plus payment of his grocery bill ($110) before giving him a bracelet back, a replacement bracelet since the original pawn piece had been lost. Shirley wrote to Blair and pointed out that he was violating federal regulation 252.16 of title 25: failing to include the agreed-to market value on the pawn ticket; the ticket showed inaccurate amounts owed, did not state the description of the pawn piece, and also did not show the amount due clearly; finally, if the pawn was dead (i.e., past the payment period), where was the written notice to his client showing the cancellation of the debt? Shirley said he hoped that Blair would like to settle the matter "without legal controversy" since he could be subject to revocation of his license and forfeiture of all or part of his trading post bond, noting "by raising these statutory violations, I am not making an idle threat."[26]

Blair wrote back to Shirley that the piece had indeed been pawned on September 18, 1967, that nothing had been paid on it, and it had been put on display as dead pawn in April 1968. The client had come in during July 1968 to make a $15 payment, which Blair pointed out was less than the 25 percent required by regulations to hold the pawn. However, Blair had then discovered that the bracelet had been lost, and had told his clerk to let the customer know that he could have a new bracelet to replace the old one if he would pay his debt and some of his account. He wrote to the customer at the same time.[27]

A few days later, Blair wrote again to Shirley to inform him that his client had come into the store, had agreed to pay his $55 debt and part of his grocery account, and that Blair had in return agreed to give him another bracelet, for which the customer had signed a receipt.

> I am sorry this happened. I never like to lose anything that belongs to a customer. Neither do we like to sell their pawn and will hold it as long as we think they are making any effort at all to redeem it. If traders took advantage of the clauses in the regulations allowing them to display the pawn for one month and then notify the customer that his indebtedness was canceled and then sell the pawn, there would be nothing left to be pawned on the reservation.[28]

In June of 1969, the Trading Committee of the Tribal Council published a request to the traders in the *Navajo Times*, reminding them that they had to abide by the trading regulations: leases and licenses could be terminated if they violated the rules. The article pointed out three problem areas: traders should not charge state sales taxes; they had to cash all checks tendered by Navajos in full, and could not hold any part back for payment of their accounts; and there could be no thirty-day deadlines on pawn. The committee outlined the pawn regulations. A written receipt was required, showing the transaction date, a description of the pawn piece, the amount loaned against it, and the "true market value." Pawn had to be held for at least six months, unless the owner of the pawn had paid at least 25 percent of the amount within five months of the pawn date, in which case the piece should be held for another two months. For every additional payment of 25 percent of the amount due on the piece, it had to be held for another two months. If the time—either eight months from the date of the receipt, or two months from the last payment if that payment brought the amount up to 25 percent, 50 percent, or 75 percent of the loan—had elapsed with no payments, the piece had to be conspicuously displayed for thirty days. After that time it could be declared dead pawn and sold. Finally, at the end of the article, the Trading Committee noted that "It seems strange that businesses outside the Navajo Nation often have sales, when they are over-stocked or when a special selling season has passed." Navajos, too, wanted sales.[29]

In July 1969, a new federal law was passed, called the Truth in Lending Act, which set forth strict requirements for revealing interest rates, specifying dates for payment and extension. The law, which as it turned out was complex and not entirely clear or easy to interpret, was of particular relevance to traders, whose business included loans, credit extension, and pawn. Graham Holmes, Area Director of the BIA, wrote a memo on July 15 to everyone with a business lease on the Navajo Reservation.

> Re: Truth in Lending Act effective July 1, 1969.
> Please advise this office how you propose to comply with it? Will you submit written information to customers showing charges, if any, for credit? Re pawn: what type of statements do you furnish customers? Does this show the purpose for which credit was given, the amount of credit and charges?

He asked for a response before July 31st. Ike Merry, Secretary of the UITA, wrote back to Holmes that

> the Truth in Lending bill requirements are likely to be very confusing to specialized merchants like traders who deal in so much credit and under conditions that vary so much from the usual practices of American business.

He asked if the BIA would be able to interpret the regulations as they applied to traders. "The Association," wrote Merry, "expresses the hope it can turn to your office for both assistance and understanding in implementing the law's requirements."[30]

Throughout 1969 legal activism—including cases addressing police brutality on the reservation, school board composition, and social welfare and the rights of Navajos to receive it, as well as cases against traders—had more effect than the Vietnam War on the reservation, though many Navajos were engaged in active combat, and it was a rare issue of the weekly Navajo Times in this year that did not have a front page obituary. But the war was not the issue for Navajos. Like other tribes, they were interested in civil rights. The National Indian Youth Council was formed in 1961 in the wake of the southern civil rights movement. San Francisco became the center of several activist groups including Indians of All Tribes, the American Indian Movement, and United Native Americans. Indians of All Tribes (incorporated in 1969) in particular brought public attention to the anger, resentment, and passion for change among young, radical Indian people by occupying the island of Alcatraz, in San Francisco Bay, on November 20, 1969, and holding it for nineteen months. The long occupation reminded Americans that past treatment of Indians was not forgotten, and that bitter memories and current conditions were leading to a cry for increased recognition and independence.[31]

The Navajo Reservation had its own activists. Gallup briefly became a focal point for politically active Navajo students, with its many pawn shops, numerous bars, and frequent deaths or arrests of Navajos as a result of drunkenness, as well as its treatment of Navajos in jail. Navajos began to be more and more outspoken against exploitation, mistreatment, and the general tone of Indian-White relations. At the Gallup Ceremonials in 1969 they tried to distribute leaflets entitled "When Our Grandfathers Carried Guns." Ordered to stop this distribution by city officials, the young demonstrators promptly took the case to district court, with DNA assistance.

But activism was not widespread on the reservation. The differences among communities, regions, and generations, and the many varieties of experience and opinions made Navajo society complex. Window Rock was not a focus of attention. There were changes, but communities continued their traditional round of activities. Cecilia Yazzie remembered the years when Annie Wauneka was councilwoman.

The Navajo people seemed to be very happy for her and they used to call her the "mother" of the reservation. She did a lot of things for the Navajo people and she did a good job. But . . . the people never really paid attention to what was going on in Window Rock. . . . It was quiet, and they never used to talk about it. . . .

At that time all these programs were just starting out, too. . . . The Navajo people had livestock, wagons, and their fields. The people were stronger, they built their own homes, hauled their own posts, and everything was from scrap. Now people depend on all these different assistance programs they have available. [Cecilia Yazzie, interview by her daughter, June 1999]

As a teenager in the mid-1950s, Mrs. Yazzie worked at a trading post in Pine Springs, and shopped there a few years later when she was married. It was close by, and that was the deciding factor—wagons were the main mode of transportation in her area until the early 1970s.

I paid for my groceries with cash if I had cash, and sometimes I paid with credit. . . . I usually made rugs to pay off my bill and I worked for the traders. . . . Traders were good about credit and they understood how people would pay off their credit bill and they knew how long it would take for the women to complete their rugs. [Cecilia Yazzie, interview by her daughter, June 1999]

Her parents had pawned; she, too, pawned, first at the trading post, then later in Gallup, for small amounts—$5, $10, $20. Traders were cooperative, she said; and the trading posts operated the same everywhere, she thought.

In the summer of 1969, several Navajos created a nonprofit group, Southwestern Indian Development Inc. (SID), with an office in Window Rock. SID was led by Charley John (a counselor at the DNA Shiprock office) and Peterson Zah (director of education of DNA), who were president and executive director, respectively; others on the Board included John Lewis, Lorene Bennett (who was involved with ONEO and DNA), Bahe Billy, Gordon Denipah, Gloria Emerson (a Harvard graduate who had worked for ONEO's Head Start program), Ben Hanley (counselor at DNA Tuba City office—he became the first Navajo lawyer), and Norman Ration (counselor at the DNA Crownpoint office). Southwestern Indian Development was funded by a grant from the United Scholarship Service of Denver, Colorado, and was assisted and encouraged by DNA lawyers. SID's first action was to carry out a survey of trader activities. Investigators, mostly Navajo students, went across the reservation to visit trading posts and examine the goods, prices, and general conditions of the stores. In particular, they examined the trading posts of Greasewood, Beclahbitoh, Ashcroft's (in Fort Defiance), Fleming Begay Company (in Chinle), Rough Rock, Rock Point, Piñon, Low Mountain, Red Rock, Toadlena, Brink's (between Gallup and Shiprock), Shiprock, Steamboat, Cross Canyon, and Wide Ruins. They compared prices, inspected the premises, the refrigeration, the goods, asked to put on the trader's scales an item whose weight they knew—a fifty-pound bag of flour, for example—and interviewed the trader. Traders were more irritated than worried, and they did not take the SID surveyors very seriously.

In August 1969, Ted Mitchell filed a suit in the U.S. district court: John Rockbridge and Henry Zah vs. Graham Holmes, Area Director, BIA, Walter J. Hickel, Secretary of the Interior, and Louis R. Bruce, Commissioner of Indian Affairs, to force the Bureau of Indian Affairs to regulate traders. The lawsuit stated the facts of trading, referring to the "trading post system" and to William Y. Adams's "excellent study in the 1950's" of Shonto Trading Post, which the statement drew on. Traders, the suit claimed, had a geographical monopoly over Navajo custom and resources

> and this monopoly combines with his superior functionability in the Anglo culture to give him great power over the Navajos. . . . Indeed, the trader managed to keep most Navajos in a kind of economic bondage—he is the "company store" to which they have been forced to sell their soul.

Mitchell's argument was that the BIA had failed in its duty to enforce trader regulations, and that the federal district court should "enjoin him to execute it."[32]

The case was part of a cluster of actions against traders, mostly by DNA lawyers and staff, during 1969: a memo from the Trading Committee of the Navajo Tribe in May, sharply reminding traders of the regulations; the memo from Graham Holmes of the BIA in July, asking for traders' responses to the new Truth in Lending Act; the trading post survey and inspection of the premises by students during the summer; and finally Mitchell's mandamus suit to the BIA in August. Traders woke to the recognition that they were under attack.

Officers of the UITA were already aware of this. Earlier in the year, Ike Merry, UITA secretary, had got hold of a copy of a report titled "Question: May a Trader be a special claims agent for the United States Railroad

Retirement Board?" written up by Richard Reichard, of the DNA Law Reform Unit. In it, he suggested that it was illegal for traders to also be railroad claims agents. Merry sent a copy of the report out to all the UITA directors with a cover letter: "It is patently a special and slated pleading based on undocumented charges about the status of the trader in relation to his Navajo customers."[33]

The Association had always been a useful source of information relating to arts and crafts, costs, livestock, silver, and wool, and federal and tribal trading regulations. UITA had, as we have seen, secured a source of silver for Navajo smiths during World War II. It gave the traders a voice, sometimes on behalf of the Navajos, as in the Stock Reduction Program, sometimes on their own behalf, as in 1953 Tribal Council meetings regarding traders, though, in fact, traders also acted independently in such affairs. In January, UITA officers had hired Charles Tansey, of the firm of Tansey, Roseborough, Roberts, and Gerding in Farmington, to act as secretary and to give legal opinions. The UITA had just formally separated from the Gallup Ceremonial, and the officers recognized that the duties of secretary—sending out dues and notices—were onerous for a busy trader without assistance. Tansey agreed to take over these duties, and to carry out the "usual work" of an association attorney: drawing up papers, giving opinions on problems arising out of federal, state, or tribal governments. His responsibility included reviewing leases, which traders considered to be the major problem ahead, as the end of twenty-five year lease period, negotiated in 1953, drew closer.[34]

Traders were especially concerned about the Tribe's new lease form, which had been drafted without the normal discussion with traders, and which Tansey noted was quite detrimental to traders. In June, Ike Merry wrote to Tansey about the new lending law:

> the specific application of the new Truth in Lending law can not only be confusing but certainly will open the door for every possible harassment of reservation traders by individuals and agencies that already carry it on as a matter of policy.

He also began to try to arrange for experts to present information on the new law to UITA members at meetings in Flagstaff, Gallup, and Farmington; as he pointed out, "without such information, traders will find it difficult to comply with its technical requirements even though acting in good faith, and may find themselves in trouble over violations."[35]

This is precisely what happened. Truth in Lending problems escalated over the following year, as the DNA discovered in the law a tool to use against traders. Mitchell had told—or at the least, motivated—the cadre of DNA lawyers to seek out creative legal means to try to rein in the traders: they had succeeded.

8

⅃·L

TARGET—TRADERS

Navajo trade is the only retail business in modern America in which the customer is always wrong. "If you don't like it, you can go to the store across the street" jokes the trader. . . . In major disputes regarding trading, it is the trader who is usually right; the customer wrong—for the trader is a white man, and trading is a white man's game.

Southwest Indian Development, Inc.:
Traders on the Navajo Reservation, n/d., 7

By 1970, the atmosphere on the Navajo Reservation was electric. Window Rock was the center of activity: new funding flowed through ONEO, the Office of Navajo Economic Opportunity, for new programs. These included a variety of initiatives into all aspects of Navajo life: Head Start, a novel na-tionwide preschool program; a summer youth program; a Home Improve-ment Training program; a Migrant and Agricultural Placement program; and a host of others in health, alcohol treatment, and recreation. The tra-ditional community with which traders worked seemed unchanging, yet sons and daughters were growing up to become new leaders. Their families had thought education—that is, learning gained outside the home and the culture—was important; the Tribe had shared this view. Navajos, sent to university on tribal scholarships, brought their skills and their dreams home to the reservation, and were hired in administrative positions.

Navajos snapped up the jobs and training opportunities offered. Suddenly, there was work on the reservation, of all kinds and for all age groups. Life on the reservation had never looked so hopeful, so modern. There was money in Navajo hands, in paychecks, general assistance checks, and welfare checks. It seemed as if a new era had begun. In the words of Gloria Emerson, an activist during these years, "There was a great deal of energy, a great deal of confidence. . . . Suddenly it seemed as if it was possible to make a change, to make a difference."[1]

Richard Mike, for example, grew up in Kayenta, got his B.A. from Fort Lewis College in 1965, and went to work for the Chinle Head Start program. Raymond Nakai, Tribal Chairman, encouraged him to go into teaching rather than medicine, as he had originally planned, because, Nakai pointed out, he would be a visible role model for young Navajos. "Hundreds of Navajo kids will get to see you. If you go into the Indian Health Service, no one will see you."

Inspired by this encouragement and caught up in the excitement and the dynamic action of the times, when Richard started work on his M.A. he changed to education, and trained to become a teacher. In the early 1970s, his college degree in hand, he also became involved in Head Start administration. "For the first time, the federal government gave the Indians the opportunity to run programs, to become administrators, which had never happened before." It wasn't part of his plan, but it was challenging and exciting. Suddenly, he said, the reservation came alive.

I remember that we had to sleep on the floor in Window Rock because we were learning how to write proposals. Five of us, five for each agency, and Roger Wilson and Frankie Paul,[2] so the seven of us, and it was such an exciting time because before, white people would write proposals for us, and would put in the statistics and data. And here we were, learning to write, meeting federal criteria. . . . We more or less were—I won't say kicking the whites out, but we were taking their place. It was ONEO, the first program to start pushing the white administrators out. It was getting Navajos to start becoming administrators. [Richard Mike, interview with the author, January 2000]

Richard went to Chinle, where he worked for the Head Start program and contributed to a small radical Chinle newspaper, *Diné Bizaad*, writing articles and editorials. Later on he drew cartoons, inventing the comic figure "Super Navajo." All this he did under an alias to protect himself and his job from repercussions. The Chinle community had united in an action to try to replace Anglo school administrators with Navajos, assisted by the DNA lawyer in Chinle, Robert Hilgendorf and by his then wife, Lucy Hilgendorf, who was active in school education. The community caucus was successful.

We hired a Navajo superintendent. Here's a Navajo, the first thing he did, he got rid of his desk and drawers, his furniture, and he had a blanket on the floor. He had a Navajo hat, and he sat on the floor when he went into his office. . . . We were so idealistic—that was the Navajo way! . . . When you're young like that and you're idealistic you want your people to move and become part of society, become independent, sovereign, and part of America, I guess. Have their own homes, have plenty to eat, have their own money. [Richard Mike, interview with the author, January 2000]

Young Navajos spearheaded the move for change, for self-determination and independence; they felt it was up to them to help restore and recharge Navajo society. Gloria Emerson, who graduated in 1968 from Fort Lewis College, went to work for the Head Start program in Window Rock, one of the many bright young people who wanted to change Navajo life and bring about a shift in power and leadership. A few years later she went on to Harvard to earn an M.A. in education, beginning a long career as an educator and teacher.

A lot of things were happening on the Rez, as I recall. Part of it had to do with Johnson's War on Poverty. The funds that came to the Office of Navajo Economic Opportunity jump-started a lot of social action programs. . . . I remember many Navajo people going out to collect oral histories from one another, from families. I remember the beginning of the Rough Rock Demonstration school. The Navajo tribal college was in the making in that period. . . . We really were feeling, I guess, empowered. [Gloria Emerson, interview with the author, February 2000]

Lorene Bennett (now a Supreme Court Judge on the reservation) worked for ONEO and later for DNA. Ben Hanley, a counselor at the DNA Tuba City office, eventually became the first Navajo lawyer. Peterson Zah, of course, had been working for DNA since 1967, becoming assistant director of DNA in 1968 (and director in 1972). All of them were influenced by the Navajo scholarship program, and by the activism of the times, in which they became involved, and some were encouraged by their elders. DNA was part of that activism, and in Gloria Emerson's view played an important role.

> I think, what stands out in my mind, what was exciting to me, was the beginning of the legal aid program, the DNA. It was peopled by quite a number of young attorneys who had a strong sense of social conscience, and they were rubbing elbows with Navajo people who had a sense of destiny.
>
> I was a fervent supporter, because I knew we were ripe for it—that we needed to understand what our rights were, in consumer law, in other areas. [Gloria Emerson, interview with the author, February 2000]

DNA lawyers and staff were heavily involved in organizing and supporting Navajo activism, investigating, pressuring, and threatening lawsuits to everyone else. They were also influential in obtaining federal assistance for Navajos, suggesting in no uncertain terms that the Arizona Welfare Department bring its practices on the reservation into line with federal regulations. DNA lawyers in Crownpoint helped organize the Navajo Welfare Rights Organization, which first met in June 1969, in Crownpoint to discuss the food stamp program, the surplus food commodities program, and the problem of too few caseworkers and caseworkers who did not speak Navajo.

Notices of the first meeting of this organization were put out in the DNA newsletter, as well as by word of mouth, as were the outcomes of the meetings. One of the results was a petition stating that welfare was not a privilege but a legal right, and among its twenty-two demands, as with virtually every action in which the DNA were involved, it included one related to traders: that Navajos should be able to get food stamps somewhere other than at trading posts. This demand reflected the DNA's determination to move Navajos to a cash, rather than a credit, economy that would take the trader out of the center of economic activity.[3]

In 1970, when funding for the DNA program was looking more secure and Peter MacDonald—a strong DNA supporter—was running for Tribal Chairman, the DNA lawyers and tribal court advocates stepped up the pressure on traders. Traders had long been part of Navajo communities; DNA lawyers wanted to change that, to eliminate what they saw as the dominance of the trader and give that dominance to the Navajos. They searched for infractions of laws and regulations, wrote letters for every Navajo client with any complaint or grievance, and insistently characterized the extent of the traders' involvement in Navajo life as negative and ominous. The media gave them a little helpful coverage.

A trader, Maurice Tanner at Torreon Trading Post (63 miles east of the Crownpoint Agency), had been accused by the DNA in 1969 of assault and battery—waving a knife at a Navajo woman customer to force her to sign over her welfare check to pay her bill. Jack Anderson, a syndicated Washington columnist, wrote a sensational account, and the column, Washington Merry-Go-Round, appeared in major newspapers, including the *Albuquerque Journal*. Tanner was incensed, and had the customer sign a statement that her story was completely untrue; Ted Mitchell, equally up in arms, sent a DNA lawyer, Eric Treisman, out with an interpreter to get a counter-statement from the woman customer. Jack Anderson continued his story, beginning with a mock apology:

> This column owes an apology to the white Indian traders, white tribal lawyers, and federal agencies dealing with Indians. For good measure, we'll include the "Uncle Tomahawks" or "Uncle Tom-Toms" as those who do the white bidding are called. . . .

He described the battle of affidavits, and ended with a pitiful sketch of a Navajo customer:

> Women like Mrs. Ignacio are caught between their lifelong fear of the white traders' enormous power and the hope given them by younger Indian college graduates and the Poverty Corps lawyers.[4]

It was an irresponsible story, but it brought attention to the DNA and made good copy. Ike Merry, long-time trader and Secretary of the UITA, thought the article was reason for traders to become concerned. Merry, aware of the mounting anti-trader feeling, did not like the attitude or the goals of DNA lawyers. He disliked welfare, voicing the opinion of many traders that eventually it would rob Navajos of self-respect, self-reliance, and would turn the reservation into a ghetto. Traders firmly believed that they brought work to the Navajos in their communities, work that provided independence and the ability to purchase goods. But Merry's main reason for distrusting the DNA lawyers was the direction and philosophy of the program, as he wrote in a letter, "the thrust of DNA [is] to create an over-patronizing caretaker function of the Navajo far worse than that for which the BIA is criticized." He felt that Ted Mitchell and the DNA staff would "resort to any deceit, lie, and distortion to support the attacks they continually make against non-Indians and especially those in business."[5]

The irony of the situation was that welfare, in bringing money to the grass roots, brought customers to the trading post. Business on and around the reservation had never been better.

> Johnson's Great Society created a new breed of trader, who capitalized on everything that came along. . . . Traders never figured out that DNA was bringing cash money to the reservation. DNA changed the Navajos, but they really changed the trader. You had to have goods, a choice of brands. Like tires—at the trading post there was usually only one brand, or the trader went into towns and bought tires for the Navajos. Traders circumvented the process of choice for Navajos, and everyone wants choice. The traders didn't give it, or only some—Dinnebito when it enlarged and went self-service, it was fantastic. Navajos who had grown up with no selection, they wanted to try it all. [Bruce Burnham, interview with the author, November 1999]

The traders sought the Navajo dollar; DNA lawyers handling trader cases fought tooth and nail to keep it out of the trading posts. This was the period in which many traders reorganized their stores, brought in new items, and looked for ways to encourage their customers to shop in their store, rather than another. Competition existed, in their view, despite the fact of distance—the new pickup trucks had made sure of that.

> In the early 1960s, the desire of Navajos was to have a vehicle. And traders understood that, they helped that. But the vehicle was what allowed people to go to town, it was the means of travel. . . . By the 1970s, when everyone was in a pickup, traders realized the downside, the auto was the key to freedom. They had to compete—you didn't have to compete in the past. The tribe, the BIA, they guaranteed that the trader didn't have competition. [Bruce Burnham, interview with the author, November 1999]

In the small distant communities, traditional people, older people, were no more sure of what the general activism was all about than their Anglo counterparts were. But clearly, DNA worked hand in hand with a new generation of Navajos who wanted to drive change, to break with the gentler habits of their parents, to move from a position of subservience to one of strength. Gloria Emerson said of her own attitude from that period:

I felt that we were really oppressed as a people and as a society. I was very clear about the fact that we were living in a post-colonial environment, and I think that was how other young Navajo people felt, too.

It was her view that traders of this time period contributed to this attitude, that they had a strong sense of their superiority living among the poor. Older Navajos, she said, had different memories of earlier times.

My mother recalls how some of the traders intervened in their lives, helping them, making sure they got to the hospital in some really grave illness, helping with translation, interpretation. . . .

As I remember my mother's stories, it seemed like the traders who lived deep in the heart of the reservation were the ones whose barriers started to break down, who started to become more human. [Gloria Emerson, interview with the author, February 2000]

By the 1960s, however, the atmosphere was different, and so were many of the traders. The older people had always been convinced traders were cheating them "because you charge more for your goods than you paid for them." I've attributed this view of traders, who were for the most part the only and certainly the most consistent commercial business people that Navajos knew about, down to a Navajo ideal of sharing, an idea that you should not profit personally from exchange with neighbors. Profit, the means of sustaining business, was not evident in barter, but with cash, with Navajos working the cash registers and involved in ordering goods, it became visible, and the 1970s were times of very eager profit-making.

In addition, younger people were determined to fight against patronizing attitudes and the paternalism of centuries, evident in every store in every border town. Gloria Emerson said that during that time, for twelve years, she shopped in Albuquerque rather than Farmington to avoid the patronizing attitudes of storekeepers. Younger Navajos began to feel a resentment toward the administrators in the BIA bureaucracy, the schools, and to some extent, toward most white people who came onto the reservation. DNA lawyers were not exempt from this feeling.

I remember [Fred Johnson, a Navajo friend] saying, you're a good guy and everything, but the difference between you and me is that you can always leave this when you want. There's a little resentment in the phrase, as well as a positive thing. You know, saying thanks for coming, being here for two years, you've done some good things, but now you can leave and get on with your life and we can't. [Bruce Herr, interview with the author, October 1998]

In 1970, the Southwest Indian Development group (SID), put out their report on the results of their survey of the previous summer. It was a severe indictment against traders, as strident as anything that had been written by Navajos about non-Navajos, though it seems likely that DNA staff assisted in the writing. The authors castigated the institution of trading, portraying a trader as a figure who controlled every aspect of life in Navajo communities, and manipulated his "variety of roles . . . to his personal benefit." They, too, mentioned and quoted from Adams's book on Shonto. The traders' prices, the report said, were high and dishonest, they never had discount specials, they made gross "errors" that were clearly suspect, they were "mean" and even violent. To illustrate this, the Anderson column was reprinted at the end of the report.[6]

The authors suggested that it was illegal for traders to be Railroad Employment Agents. They pointed out that sanitation and safety were at a minimum inside the store:

> Older trading posts were generally unclean inside, with grimy floors, dusty and littered with trash, with sharp and dangerous merchandise hanging from the ceiling, which could result in serious injury. In one post a pick was hanging from the ceiling. Evidently the trader in that particular post had little regard for the safety of his customers.

The report concluded that

> It is revolting that a group of people should be kept dependent upon a small number of greedy individuals (and intruders) who, due to opportune circumstances, have the chance to relentlessly pursue their own ravenous material advancement at the others' expense.[7]

The authors acknowledged that traders had played "an essential part in the development of modern Indian society," but that this did not give them any right "to exploit and dominate to the fullest extent those very people who provided their livelihood." They attributed blame equally to the BIA, the Navajo Tribe, and the Trading Committee of the Advisory Council, and they called on the Secretary of the Interior to enforce trader regulations.[8]

This was a new note on the Navajo Reservation, echoing a radical tone that was being heard across the United States, not just among Navajos. Peterson Zah and Charley John wrote in a cover letter that the survey and its report constituted an independent action, not related to or carried out by the DNA. There is no question, however, that the report reflected Ted Mitchell's attitudes toward traders, as well as those of the SID Board members—Lorene Bennett, Bahe Billy, Gordon Denipah, Gloria Emerson, Ben Hanley, John Lewis, and Norman Ration. Traders living in Navajo communities had always represented Anglo-America, for better and, now that attitudes had changed and they represented "the intruder," for worse. The attack on traders had grown from specific complaints to outright hostilities, a battle for power.

Traders, at least those who paid attention to the thrust of this activity, began to turn to the UITA to help them with legal information and responses to DNA letters. The Association had continued to be an organization through which traders discussed items of interest, addressed problems and, once a year, met socially. Only half or perhaps two-thirds of all traders joined UITA: membership of an individual was derived from ownership of a trading post lease. Those traders who were committed to the association's role ran for UITA offices, which consisted of a president, vice president, treasurer, secretary, and nine directors. Each year, the Association held four Board of Directors' meetings, and one annual business meeting for all the members, followed by a dinner. The UITA dinner was an annual social event, a chance to see friends and colleagues. Members met to discuss such topics as livestock sales, suppliers, and BIA activities; but the most heated topic of all was the yearly discussion of whether the evening party should or should not serve liquor (forbidden to the many Mormon trading families). On the whole, however, most traders, though they might attend an annual meeting, carried on their business without much thought of the Association. Now, however, they felt the need for legal information and support, and membership began to rise.

The UITA directors had hired Charles M. Tansey as Association secretary and attorney, little realizing how essential legal advice would become. As anti-trader feeling and lawsuits mounted, traders had new concerns in addition to leases. Leading traders and those most aware of the situation began to write to congressional representatives and others in Washington, complaining about DNA. "Their political and social reform activities . . . have gone well beyond the terms of reference and have taken an abnormal amount of time of their staff away from the duties they were employed to perform" wrote Melvin Gibson, a businessman who had been a partner with Reuben Heflin in building a motel on the reservation, on the new highway that ran past Kayenta. Gibson wrote to Richard Cheney of OEO in Washington on April 2, 1970, hoping that

> DNA will provide legal counsel to individual Indians, but the representation should be within the prescribed terms of reference. . . . Many individuals who are working on the payroll of DNA are indulging in many facets of the life of the Navajo quite foreign to the work they are supposed to be performing under the arrangement between the DNA and the OEO.

And he wrote to Robert Robertson, of the National Council on Indian Opportunity, on the same date, agreeing with the need to "assist Navajos to improve conditions and change from old customs" but charging that DNA was "confusing" the Navajos, "to attempt to use them for purposes alien to the basic purposes of the DNA organizations."9

Traders were no more mellow in their opinion of DNA lawyers than the lawyers were of traders. More than anything else, traders deplored the social activism of the DNA lawyers. It was not merely that traders were conservative, but that they did not believe that what the DNA was doing would be helpful to Navajos. There could not have been more opposite philosophies than those of the DNA and the traders. Another round of letters soon went out, stating the opposition of the UITA's Board of Directors to DNA, as a federally financed legal aid organization:

> Under the pretext of assisting Navajo Indians with legal problems . . . DNA appears to be anti-business and anti-trader and is thus destroying the relationship [of traders to Navajos]. . . . The Indian traders have for years extended credit to Indians, the only businessmen who will extend unsecured credit. DNA destroys the Navajo ability to obtain credit by actually encouraging Navajos not to meet many of their obligations they have incurred with the trader.10

DNA lawyers continued to lodge complaints for fraud and negligence against individual traders. Although in almost every case traders could show that the pawn had long been sitting on the trader's shelf, usually with few or no payments made, it was becoming clear—to Tansey at least—that better accounting practices were in order. But traders were slow to change, especially in their system of record keeping, credit, and pawn. Despite the rumors of a coming storm, traders were far from its center, and, immersed in the daily round, refused to hear the warning rumbles.

Pawn had grown into an entrenched practice, one hundred years in the making, solidly set in Navajo community economics and social relations. Pawn had originally been a pledge against goods sold on credit, and credit a means of smoothing out the seasonal cycle of sheep and wool, the lean months of winter and summer, the fat months of spring and fall. By now, pawn had developed into a system of small loans, never intended to reflect the full value of an item, but to provide cash that would be paid back quickly. The BIA regulations required the pawn to be held for a year, and sometimes traders held it longer, recognizing the usefulness of the transaction, which brought in interest, especially since Navajos pawned pieces over and over again. But if a piece sat too long in the vault without any payments being made, the trader eventually sold it, usually to traders and pawn dealers in border towns (relatives or friends).

Border town traders were themselves dealing in pawn, as well as in new jewelry, and as the value of and interest in Navajo jewelry had increased rapidly during the 1970s, this made pawn ripe for sale. It became an explosive practice, a result of the value of heirloom jewelry, the different pawn laws in the different states, and the increased ability of Navajos to travel. In fact, the tendency of most on-reservation traders to deal leniently with their customers did not prepare Navajos for the dealings of border town pawnbrokers. Although many traders in Gallup, Farmington, and Flagstaff maintained relationships with Navajos they had known on the reservation, this was not always the case. Off-reservation stores were quicker to sell their goods, going by the state law—they were not bound by BIA regulations. Border-town traders were not the only ones taking pawn: automobile dealers, and, indeed, many other store owners accepted pawn quite readily even at some distance from the reservation, and followed idiosyncratic rules for informing and accounting and selling. The institution of pawn had ballooned into a widespread problem far beyond the confines of the reservation.

Tansey wrote responses to the letters from DNA lawyers on behalf of traders. He did his best to inform traders of the need for improved record keeping. This was an onerous task. Traders relied on ancient accounting habits and were reluctant to accept the advice. Many had operated for so long under simple accounting systems that they were not adept at record keeping. But a very large part of the problem was that they could not grasp the fact that the world was changing and that they needed to change with it. More than that, traders needed to be able to counter the charge of dishonesty, but in the absence of records, and in the face of evidence that some traders were indeed dishonest, they had no proof other than the word of their customers—word which, to the traders' shock and surprise, was not often forthcoming.

In the meantime, the DNA lawyers had found the legal leash to bring the traders to heel: the new Truth in Lending Act that had gone into effect on July 1, 1969. The new law had not gone unnoticed: Graham Holmes, director of the Navajo Agency of the BIA, had sent out a memo regarding Truth in Lending; but no one knew exactly what it meant or how they should meet its many, rather vaguely worded, requirements. Tansey asked for clarification, from the BIA, the Tribe, and the UITA, without much help, but he brought the new law up repeatedly at UITA annual meetings and board meetings.

Bud Tansey was a quiet, soft-spoken man who had studied law at the University of Kansas. A rural attorney, as he put it, "practicing in situations Abe Lincoln would have recognized and felt at home with," he began to practice in Carlsbad, then moved to Farmington. In 1950, he was hired by Norman Littell, general counsel for the Navajo Tribe, to work on matters relating to water and land; he had been involved in writing tribal legislation that imposed rent on trading posts. Tansey was an old-school western lawyer—gracious and polite—not at home with the cut and thrust of the young reformers and no match for their radical anger, and the fact that he knew something about the Navajo tribal government and Window Rock politics gave him no advantage. Tansey and DNA lawyers came from different generations and different perspectives, especially in their approach to traders.[11]

At the UITA board meeting in September 1970, Tansey pointed out that because of new laws for nonprofit organizations, the UITA officers could neither carry on any sort of political campaign, nor attempt to influence legislation. The officers gave some thought, at this meeting and the subsequent board meeting in November, to the idea of giving up the Association's nonprofit status in order to carry out lobbying efforts against the DNA anti-trader activities. They presented this possibility at the annual meeting, but the general membership voted against it, agreeing that politics was not, in the long run, their interest. The board and members discussed the pawn law, deciding that Tansey would write a memorandum on pawn, loans, and disclosure of interest rates to all members to clarify what they needed to know and do. Then the meeting continued with items of more interest to traders: livestock, brands, and a contribution of $500 they were making toward a scholarship fund at the new Navajo Community College.[12]

Throughout 1970 and 1971, Tansey approached the situation as such situations had traditionally been approached before the DNA arrived on the scene, with the idea that problems were resolved by reasoned discussion with interested parties. He wrote to officials of the BIA, the Tribe, and the DNA lawyer, to ask for meetings to discuss the new Truth in Lending law in order to arrive at solutions. His efforts were fruitless. The BIA was concerned with the Rockbridge mandamus suit, the thrust of which was to force them to act against traders (in September 1971 the U.S. Court of Appeals for the 9th Circuit reversed the dismissal of the case by a district court), and BIA staff discussions with the UITA would hardly be seen as an attempt at forceful regulation. The Tribal Council was busy, and with MacDonald as chairman, in full support of the DNA. The Navajo Council's trading committee was not yet ready to discuss traders, their problems, or their leases. DNA lawyers, of course, had no interest in aiding UITA or in a resolution of traders' problems with Truth in Lending. They perceived such assistance as counter to the interests of the Navajo—indeed, as unethical, since they were representing Navajo clients. Besides, the law itself was anything but clear, and it is quite likely that none of the lawyers, and certainly none of these institutions, could have clarified it.[13]

In late May of 1971, John Brown, chairman of the Economic Development Committee of the Navajo Tribal Council, wrote to Tansey to advise him that this Committee had taken over the responsibilities of the Tribal Council's old Trading Committee, and that he, Brown, would set a date for a meeting in approximately two weeks; would Tansey please propose items for the agenda. Tansey wrote asking for a later date, and listed the points for discussion: trading and problems relating to trading; leases due to expire, and the transfer of leases; problems regarding investment for improvements (traders were unable to obtain loans without collateral or leases); and the proposed new form of the lease. Tansey suggested that a representative of the Navajo General Counsel be present at the discussion of leases and regulations, and that undoubtedly the Committee would have other matters to add to the agenda; if Brown would let him know what these were he would raise them with traders. There was no response to his letter, as Tansey reported at a UITA board meeting that August, and he agreed to keep pushing for a meeting. In the meantime, he wrote a memo about compliance, attaching a drafted pawn ticket that he felt might meet the requirements, and sent it out to traders, urging them to use it and to change their record-keeping practices to comply with every detail outlined in his memo.[14]

DNA lawyers now focused their attention on the small loans provisions of the Truth in Lending Act, examining pawn tickets and the practice of pawn, on which loans were made. Early in January 1972, John Silko, DNA lawyer at the Chinle office, asked Clifford McGee, trader at Piñon Trading Post, for information on all of his assets, capital, and financial matters relating to the store, and summoned him to appear at a court hearing on January 24 in Phoenix. There were only a couple of plaintiffs, but the hearing was to determine if there were grounds for a class action. UITA board members met with McGee and his attorney, Edwin Powell, to discuss the action; Silko had, according to McGee, told him that if the court did not dismiss the case the DNA would proceed against other traders.[15]

The McGee case was a bad beginning—Tansey had repeatedly warned the traders at Piñon that their paperwork was inadequate and their pawn tickets likely to be questioned, but to no avail. In February, Ralph McGee at Leupp and Daryl Stock at Two Grey Hills received letters from DNA lawyers regarding pawn and pawn tickets; Tohatchi Trading Post was apparently already in court proceedings.

The UITA held a special meeting in March, attended by twice as many traders than usual. Questions flew. Could they even continue to give credit, under this new law? Could cash be loaned on pawn? In earlier days, pawn was only accepted as security for merchandise accounts, and traders had not paid cash on it, but the language of the BIA regulations had, everyone agreed, allowed cash loans also. What about due bills, credit slips—were all these forms in compliance? Every trading post handled their records differently, as they all acknowledged. Tansey could not possibly check every individual trader's set of forms, and it was agreed that the national forms were "too complicated to fit the operations at most trading posts."[16]

It also appeared that under the Truth in Lending law, the traders should have sent notices to all their customers, old and new, explaining precisely what their credit practices and charges were. No one had. Had it even been attempted, traders would have mailed the letter to customers (their address, of course, would have been in care of the trading post) who would need to have it translated and explained. This, of course, was what traders thought they were doing: explaining to Navajo customers the existing rules of pawn, and, indeed, of other aspects of non-Navajo life. And this was precisely the role that activists objected to.

However, the UITA officers announced that the Truth in Lending case against Tohatchi Trading Post had been settled reasonably, with only the named defendant receiving compensation. No class action would follow, but the case against Piñon was still pending, and there was no information on its progress. After the meeting, Tansey sent out a five-page memo, again summarizing the requirements of pawn, credit, and loans, and the questions raised at the March meeting. More meetings would be held, in June and September, to address concerns and respond to questions. The action was, however, too late—though perhaps once Ted Mitchell had made clear his stand against traders, shared by most of the DNA lawyers and Navajo activists, it would always have been too late. It seems unlikely that the traders could have taken any action to absolve themselves.

On Monday, August 7, 1972, in Los Angeles, Richard B. Lavine, regional director of the Federal Trade Commission, held a press conference at the Federal building. He announced that trading posts "were guilty of charging higher prices than off-reservation markets." An initial investigation "has uncovered evidence of deception, violation of Truth in Lending laws, usurious credit practices, unmarked prices, and manipulation" by the traders. The BIA and the FTC would, he said, carry out a series of public hearings on Navajo traders, on the Navajo Reservation, between August 28 and September 1. Complaints and testimony about trader practices would be aired. The sessions, open to all, would include Navajo customers, DNA lawyers, tribal officials, and traders. Half of his staff of twenty-five would be involved in these investigations. Ernest Stevens, director of Economic Development at the Bureau of Indian Affairs, also present at the press conference, said that the BIA, which had in the past been guilty of "flagrant mismanagement" of its trust responsibilities with regard to regulating trading posts, which it now wanted to rectify, was assisting the FTC in a joint investigation.[17]

The decision to hold hearings on trader practices was the culmination of discussions begun in the fall of 1971 between FTC and DNA staff and attorneys. DNA attorneys in the Chinle office, John Silko and Robert Hilgendorf, had invited FTC attorneys John F. Dugan and Robert H. Wyman to Chinle. There, they discussed what Hilgendorf and Silko felt were the three major transgressions of the traders that could be addressed legally: withholding welfare and other checks from customers in order to pay off and put credit on their trading post accounts; possible price fixing in which the UITA set prices for each item; and violations of the new Truth in Lending law, especially as it related to pawn. Following this meeting, FTC staff apparently carried out a "long and careful study" and concluded that "the situation cries out for action."[18]

The action the FTC proposed was a public hearing and a legal investigation of traders. Clearly, this would be a newsworthy event, an event that would make even the dry topic of business interesting, especially with such apparently obvious villains, such interesting victims. The FTC may also have been hoping for publicity that would bring them attention and credit, but this is pure speculation.

In April 1972, the assistant regional director of the FTC, George J. Zervas, and the two staff attorneys, Dugan and Wyman, requested formal approval of the project in a memorandum that explained the trading post situation on the Navajo Reservation and the charges being made. They noted that the BIA felt it had neither the personnel nor the expertise to investigate the claims, and that the FTC should take up the project, strike quickly, conclude a public and a private investigatory phase in as short a time as possible, write reports, and finish up whatever legal details might be necessary. They estimated this could all be accomplished quickly, because both BIA and FTC staff could work together, and the public hearings could alert the public "to whatever injustices the Navajos may have suffered" and thus create a demand for action. Closed hearings would be needed to develop evidence and proof of violation of BIA regulations so that BIA officials could enforce them "vigorously," as apparently they wished to do. At the end of the project FTC staff could set up a training program to help BIA employees regulate traders through procedures for record keeping and auditing. The FTC would also be able to instruct the BIA on how to build these procedures into new trading regulations. If the investigation was successful, the attorneys suggested that it could then "serve as a model for enforcement by other FTC offices" whose regions included Indian reservations.[19]

The assistant director of the FTC, Alfred W. Cortese, convinced by the memo that traders were involved in fraudulent practices, wrote in support of the proposal for action. The commissioner for Indian Affairs, Louis R. Bruce, wrote to confirm that BIA staff did not have the expertise to deal with this kind of problem. The FTC staff was trained and qualified to investigate "ghetto fraud," as the commissioners called it, and they recommended the investigatory project; at the end of May, the secretary of the FTC, Charles Tobin, and the Commission gave formal approval for legal action. Lavine announced the action to be taken as a result at the August 7 press conference, and the FTC staff in Los Angeles began to send out subpoenas.[20]

The public hearings were held at the very end of August, beginning at Window Rock, on Monday and Tuesday, August 28 and 29, moving to Shiprock and Kayenta (simultaneously) for one day each on August 30, then to Crownpoint and Tuba City on August 31, and finally at Chinle and Piñon on Friday, September 1. The hearings in Window Rock, held at the Navajo Civic Center, a convention hall capable of seating over one thousand people, set the tone. A panel, consisting of Richard B. Lavine and George J. Zervas, regional director and assistant director, respectively, of the FTC Los Angeles office; Alfred W. Cortese Jr., assistant executive director of the FTC in Washington; Louis R. Bruce, commissioner of Indian Affairs; and Ernest L. Stevens, director of Economic Development, BIA, presided over the hearings. Traders were called to appear, as were DNA lawyers, an anthropologist (Gary Witherspoon), an economist (Adlowe L. Larson), and Navajos. The panel opened the hearings with statements. They were followed by Peter MacDonald, chairman of the Navajo Nation, and Peterson Zah, assistant director of DNA, who each set forth the complaints against traders. Then traders were asked to give their markup, their gross receipts, and net profits. Ed Foutz, of Shiprock Trading Post, said his markup was 25 percent on groceries, 40 to 45 percent on hardware; his figures for 1971 were $450,000 in gross sales, of which he estimated the profit was between $20,000 and $30,000. J. L. McGee gave his 1971 gross sales as $360,000, his profit around $40,000. Saul Price was asked questions, also. Price was director of FedMart, a chain supermarket that had opened in Window Rock in the late 1960s with the express request from the Navajo Nation Council that its prices be identical to those at all its other stores. He testified to his shock at trader prices, his certainty that FedMart could prosper in Window Rock. He gave his gross sales figure—$7.5 million in 1971—but was not asked for his profit figures.[21]

G. Alfred McGinnis, District Manager of the National Federation of Independent Business, attended the hearings on behalf of the Federation, partly because of the publicity that the media had given the event. He was surprised that very few Navajos attended—he estimated no more than twenty present—and noted that the majority of the hundred or so people present were BIA employees, traders, and journalists. Only three Navajo witnesses testified on the first day, and McGinnis felt that the panel attempted to create an emotional atmosphere; he observed that "there is no doubt that on numerous occasions, prejudgements had been made."[22]

The hearings continued at Kayenta, Crownpoint, Shiprock, Tuba City, Chinle, and Piñon, and were smaller, though equally attended by the press. At the Kayenta hearings, Sandy McNabb, director of engineering at the BIA, commenting that some of the Navajo witnesses had failed to show up, pointedly asked one Navajo witness if she thought it possible that traders had threatened to cut off their credit if they appeared? To which the witness replied that it was probably so. McNabb continued to ask leading questions: could she read? No. How could she tell if the trader was writing down the right figure; was it possible he was cheating her? Yes, it was probably so. Positive testimony was also presented by witnesses who said that some traders were honest, treating customers with respect—Brad Blair of Kayenta Trading Post was mentioned—but the panel members were more interested in negative experiences, in deception, fraud, and threats.

George Vlassis, general counsel for the Navajo Tribe, asked to attend the final hearings in Piñon, to answer allegations that there was a conflict of interest between his office and a lawyer employed on his staff, Bruce Babbitt (the Babbitt family had early on set up a ranching and trading enterprise). Vlassis assured the hearings board that Babbitt held no stock in the trading post corporation, and after answering several questions, commented acidly that the hearings "in their zeal to root out evil had displayed a reckless disregard for the facts." The hearings board, he suggested, was more interested in character assassination than in improving trading regulations.[23]

The hearings began to make headlines, and the press had a field day. The traders were assumed to be guilty before they appeared at the hearings, and the complexities of the situation and the possibility of innocence were of little interest; besides, the situation made such good copy. A *Gallup Independent* article of August 31 began, "A type of slavery still exists on the Navajo Reservation. The slaveholders are traders who secure possession of a Navajo's welfare check and then refuses [sic] to convert it to cash." The *Navajo Times* and the *Gallup Independent* ran front-page stories, with photographs of those testifying, throughout the week; and papers in regional cities—Albuquerque, Denver, Las Vegas, Nevada—as well as Los Angeles and New York, carried the story.

The *Los Angeles Times* ran a front page article on September 4, 1972: "Navajos complain of Exploitation—Indians, White Traders: An Uneasy

Alliance." The journalist, Robert Jones, described the elderly Stokes Carson: "Now half crippled, an old man, he opened his first trading post in 1916. But the Navajos believe he has cheated them ever since, and Carson's era, a vestige of the American frontier, may soon end. Inside Carson's Inscription House Trading Post the Navajos say little as they buy food or pawn jewelry." The silence of the Navajos was an interesting detail. Jones could not be expected to know that Navajos were quiet, soft and unhurried in speech, and that they thought (then and now) that Anglos were loud and aggressive when they spoke. Navajo customers talked—to each other, to traders—though not necessarily when strangers were present. The story presented the perspective of the hearings that every trader was a thief and a cheat. Mildred Heflin, Carson's daughter, who, with her husband Reuben had been the trader at Shonto for many years, asked at the UITA annual meeting if a suit for libel could be brought against the journalist. But it was not encouraged, and in any case it would hardly have helped.[24]

There was nothing balanced about the hearings; from every account, it appeared as political theater, pure and simple, and was clearly intended to be. Jay Foutz, a long-time trader, was involved in the hearings, and remembered them well:

> Just like the circus up in a circus tent. . . . I mean, they had that testimony pre-empted and nobody could say a word. It was all pre-programmed, the whole outfit. . . . Even our lawyer, the Traders' Association lawyer [Austin Roberts], they wouldn't let him say one word. The only people that could say anything was the people that had been pre-programmed . . . no input of any kind. . . . Total farce, a disgrace to the human mind, really. [Jay Foutz, Beclahbito Trading Post, interview by Cline Library, August 1998]

Traders were assumed to be guilty of every accusation—dishonesty, fraud, graft, cruelty to customers, stale goods, high profits, low levels of safety, and the patronizing attitudes of "a bastard gentry," (the *Gallup Independent* quoted Michael Benson who worked for the Gallup Indian Community Center). The hearings were a media event (and welcomed, if not orchestrated, by the investigators) in which traders were blasted by everyone, Navajo and non-Navajo alike. Ernest Stevens closed the hearings by saying that new regulations would be coming out in two months, and that they would be translated into Navajo, available to everyone and posted on trading post bulletin boards.[25]

Traders were shocked and angered at facts and details that they felt had been twisted from reality. J. Lavoy McGee, of Red Mesa Trading Post, one of the directors of UITA, wrote a letter to the FTC and the *Farmington Daily Times* that voiced the traders' reaction. The hearings, he wrote, were "neither open nor fact finding;" they were a show put on by lawyers, in which testimony had been planned and witnesses coached, and did not represent a sampling of Navajo customers or their experiences. Nor did dishonest practices and isolated incidents, which he did not doubt occurred, represent a true sampling of trading practices.

> To those knowledgeable about the trading business and Navajo ways, these hearings were an affront to the trader, as well as the Navajo consumer, an outright miscarriage of justice. . . . Most traders have been in the business for some time and very close relationships have been formed with their customers. . . . Many times credit is extended, loans made, merely because there is a need, not because it would be good business.[26]

Lavoy McGee went on to say that traders could not compete with prices in large shopping centers whose higher buying power and volume allowed them to spread expenses more broadly and still make a profit.

But the traditions and continuity of trading were a problem: traders were too close to the ground, too bound up in the daily interactions, to see that changes *were* underway and to understand the need for them. The trading post was changing, and no longer played the role it had in the past, when the sheep was the center of Navajo, as well as trader, life and economy.

A few weeks after the close of the hearings, the FTC began the proceedings for closed hearings by sending summonses to six incorporated traders or trading businesses: Bruce Barnard of Shiprock Trading Post; Stokes Carson of Inscription House Trading Post; Roland Spicer at White Horse Lake and Lybrook Trading Posts; the Babbitt Brothers Trading Company (Warren, Cedar Ridge, Tuba City, Oraibi, Indian Wells, Red Lake Trading Posts); McGee Traders (at Piñon, Keams Canyon, and Polacca Trading Posts); and traders in partnership at Lower Sunrise, Sunrise Ganado, White Cone, and Lower Greasewood Trading Posts. The summonses informed traders that they were to bring documents: license and permits; ownership papers; financial records; names of creditors and of suppliers of goods sold; names and addresses of accounts receivable; names and addresses of all customers extended credit; lists of pawn sold and dead pawn held; pawn cancellation notices; names and addresses of all employees past and present, Indian or non-Indian; books and schedules for salaries, fees, and remittances paid to managers, stockholders, and employees; records of advertising costs and radio commercials; correspondence—including notes of phone calls the trader made to or received from the UITA, the BIA, the DNA, or any other trader—and any rate books, charts, tables, manuals, or documents used to determine finance charges.[27]

This second round of hearings, the legal investigation, took place in October. Traders were asked the same questions that had been fired at them during the public (one might say publicity) events, but more formally and with legal representation. The hearings were dry and straightforward, a fact-finding element of the investigation; though charges were not necessarily to be made, nonetheless it was inherently possible. To smaller traders, the hearings themselves, both public and private, constituted a charge of wrongdoing, a criticism of a way of life that had been misrepresented. Both Carson and Barnard took the private hearings hard.[28]

This was the end of the FTC investigatory activities. The FTC complaint cases resulting from the hearings did not begin until 1974. Legal action, however, continued, as DNA attorneys prepared to bring class action lawsuits against two traders, Raymond Blair and Clarence Wheeler, for infringements of the Truth in Lending law.

The issues, however, hidden behind the media events and the legal swordfights and never made clear, were what sort of economics should be in place on the Navajo Reservation? If traders were harried out of their niche, would anyone else go into the communities to provide goods and services, so much needed? If the system was changed to a carefully regulated, essentially nonprofit business, who would run such a business? Or could capitalism mix with Navajo economics?[29]

9

J·L

THE DUST SETTLES

Whatever reason they [DNA attorneys] may have had for the hearings, I think we all would agree that their intentions were to help the Navajos. However, good intentions don't always accomplish good results. Two fallacies they had going into the investigation were their preconceived ideas of the traders, and their own paternalistic attitude that said, "We [the DNA attorneys] know what's best for you, the Navajo, and we're going to fix it."

Claudia Blair, Letter to the author, 10/31/99

The FTC had, for the moment, finished with the traders; the DNA had not. The Piñon case, filed by John Silko of the Chinle DNA office in October 1971 as a class action suit, had been settled in the spring of 1972 by payment of $32,500 by the traders to the plaintiffs. Pawning at off-reservation trading posts was another problem, and DNA lawyer Paul Biderman began a lawsuit against a group of Gallup traders. That fall, following the FTC hearings, John Silko followed up his successful Piñon Trading Post case by filing two class action suits, one against Raymond Blair at Round Rock Trading Post (*Davis v. Blair*), and the other against Clarence Wheeler at Greasewood Trading Post (*Davis v. Wheeler*). The basis of the cases was the claim that neither Blair's nor Wheeler's operations abided by the requirements of the Truth in Lending Act.

Both traders were to be brought to court in Phoenix, and they retained a Phoenix lawyer, James K. LeValley of Streich, Lang, Weeks, Cardon, and French. LeValley felt that he had suitable defenses for Blair and Wheeler, but that defense was expensive and the ongoing congressional debate on changes to the Truth in Lending law unpredictable. Settlement seemed a more sensible approach. Silko, however, one of the DNA lawyers most active in pursuing traders, was hardheaded and determined, and opposed to settlement. However, in April 1973, he left the DNA and the Southwest, and his colleague at Chinle, Robert Hilgendorf, took over the handling of the cases. LeValley asked Hilgendorf what his objective in the cases was, and told Tansey that

> [Hilgendorf] said that he has almost no sympathy for the traders, insofar as Truth in Lending damages are concerned, because the Federal Trade Commission made it abundantly clear to them a year or so ago that they were subject to the Act and had a legal obligation to comply. He feels that they have ignored this warning and that they should suffer the consequences.
>
> He said he wants to use these suits to stop several practices commonly used by traders which are not perhaps illegal, but which violate BIA regulations and are unfair. The only specific that he gave me was the use of "due bills."

Due bills were negotiable slips for amounts owed by a trader to a customer. They were to be traded out in goods to the amount on the receipt. In a trade exchange of this kind, traders gave discounts, allowing more for goods than for straight cash. LeValley suggested to Hilgendorf that he come out to Chinle in May, visit trading posts with Hilgendorf and take depositions from both defendants and Navajo plaintiffs. Hilgendorf told LeValley that he would look at the cases, the proposed settlement, and his clients' wishes, and would respond in two weeks.[1]

As it turned out, the tide had begun to turn at DNA, and Hilgendorf agreed to settle. Both the Blair and Wheeler cases were settled out of court in October of that year, for small sums—$5,500 for Blair, $2,650 for Wheeler—to be distributed equally to all plaintiffs. But the path to settlement was thorny, and the exchange between the lawyers gives a picture of the thicket of politics, law, and economics in which traders were entangled.

First, the Truth in Lending law of July 1969 was not, of course, written specifically for trading posts. Many other institutions were in class action litigation as a result of its requirements, and in many of these cases, judges had decided against class action and, according to LeValley, had "expressed concern lately about the constitutionality of the damage provisions of the Act." Devastating liability could result (indeed, Raymond Blair and his wife, unprotected by any corporate entity, were worried about complete personal, as well as business financial ruin). As a result, revisions were being put before Congress, though the debate swung up and down from day to day.

The Navajo plaintiffs with whom Hilgendorf had met were expecting to get $100 for each pawn transaction they had made in 1971, and were not very interested in coming to an agreement with other plaintiffs, or in receiving less. Since a class action required that all the members of the class get the same amount, this made settlement difficult. Their expectation brought the figure in the Blair case to $427,700, far beyond the Blairs' ability to pay. Early in the case, Hilgendorf had been unwilling to settle because he felt that the UITA could pay, or contribute toward, these damages. LeValley told Hilgendorf that UITA could not do this, and that he certainly would not advise it. Hilgendorf countered with the suggestion that the DNA staff would not approve a settlement for less than 25 percent of the damage, still far too high a figure as far as LeValley (or the Blairs) were concerned. At this point, settlement seemed distant.

In June 1973, while these cases were being heard, the FTC staff published their findings on the trading post investigative hearings in a report titled "The Trading Post System on the Navajo Reservation." It was divided into seven sections, but the crux of the report was given in part IV, in a section titled "Abusive Trading Practices."

> The Navajos are a proud and dignified people. Territorial isolation and credit saturation obviate the necessity for ordinary business courtesy at many posts. Navajos complaining about abusive trading practices often assert that traders lack respect for them or for the Navajo people. When complaints are directed to traders, the Navajo is silenced by the perennial, curt reply: "If you don't like it, you can go to the store across the street." The nearest store is typically located twenty miles down a rutted dirt road.
>
> Many traders are well intentioned, earning moderate profits in an occupation that is exacting and tiring. Nevertheless, a significant minority of trading posts are riddled with abuses.[2]

The *Wall Street Journal* and the *Arizona Republic* reviewed the document, reporting the FTC's claim that traders were violating the Truth in Lending Act and exploiting Indians. Indeed, there was little doubt that traders were in violation of the July 1969 Truth in Lending law, having been too slow to change their accounting methods. Many traders were confused by the requirements, and certain that what was hedged with forms, agreements, and legal language would be as confusing to their customers. But they made the mistake of not paying attention to Tansey's urgings at UITA meetings. In June, LeValley wrote to Tansey, mentioned the articles, and, summing up the situation, said that traders could be driven out of business if they did not arrive at a truce with DNA, the BIA, and the Tribal Council.[3]

To some of the DNA staff, the end of trading posts might have seemed a useful outcome of the hearings. DNA attorneys had helped to set up a couple of Navajo trading cooperatives, at Piñon and Crownpoint (there was also Diné Cooperative at Chinle), to take the place of trading posts. The coops did not give loans or take pawn: sales were strictly cash. The markup was thirty percent, and the stores were making a good return, part of which went back to the community's coop members. There were, however, too few cooperatives—three—to make much of a difference, and they did not last long. Cooperatives require hard work and input from members, and they were no more prevalent on the reservation than they are in general off the reservation. Pawn—despite the efforts of the DNA—was an entrenched system, which Navajos did not give up, then or now. They were not alone; pawn has always been the banking system of those without real property but small personal valuables. Navajos approached pawn in very much the same way as they approached traders, with the idea that there was little difference between pawnbrokers' methods of pawning, and chose either whoever was closest or who was best known to them.

The legal efforts against traders on the reservation seemed aimed at annihilation rather than regulation. Truth in Lending violations were, in truth, not the real goal of the DNA: it was to minimize the role of the trading post. LeValley had asked Silko

> if he was concerned primarily with bringing traders into compliance as opposed to securing the maximum damages available for the members of the class. Silko assured me that it was the latter. He said he assumed that if he recovered a large judgment against each of these traders, compliance would automatically follow.

A large judgment in a class action suit would wipe out any trader. At this time, a large trading post in an area with many customers grossed from between half a million dollars to four million dollars; a smaller, more average post, between forty and a hundred thousand dollars. Net value—that is, profits after all costs, expenses, taxes, insurance, percentage to the tribe, and salaries—was around ten percent.[4]

However, the DNA changed its stand: by September of that year, five months after Silko had left, Hilgendorf indicated that there was less enthusiasm for class action suits at DNA, and he looked forward to settling the Blair and Wheeler cases. LeValley, who had preferred settlement all along, told Tansey that his interpretation of the change at DNA was that they recognized that class actions were taking up too much time and energy, and limited the ability of attorneys to attend to the problems that Navajo clients brought to them. He also wondered if the political opposition that DNA continued to face came from "overzealous use of the class action suit as a weapon of destruction."[5]

Settlement, LeValley noted, had its problems. Other Navajos could sue the traders, especially if it was learned that community members had benefited, and undoubtedly DNA would help them sue. On the other hand, holding out for legal resolution would be far more expensive in legal fees and, if they lost, in liability amounts. The Truth in Lending Act was before Congress for amendment of the civil liability clause; it had passed the Senate 90 to 0, and if it passed the House, it would limit any liability to 1 percent of net worth (approximately $2,000 to $3,000 each) and would prevent any others from suing for the same infringements in the same period as the original case. However, it seemed as likely that the House would not pass the amendment—would indeed change it to increase, rather than decrease, the liability amount. The amendment would alter the arguments LeValley used in court, and thus the uncertainty of the amendment's passage affected LeValley's defense. He asked Tansey to present these facts to the defendants and the Board, and let him know their decision.

Blair, Wheeler, and the Board decided on settlement. DNA staff also decided that settlement was preferable, although they warned that they would bring individual actions against traders if they heard of any mistreatment. By the end of December 1973, the two cases were closed, Blair agreeing to pay a settlement total of $5,500, Wheeler, $2,650. Tansey and the UITA Board announced the settlement at the annual meeting of January 1974. UITA, as the membership had agreed at a meeting in 1972, paid 80 percent of the attorney fees, both traders paying the balance, as well as the settlement charges. Everyone was relieved by the closure of these cases—and UITA meeting attendance fell somewhat as a result. Traders in general tried to go back to routines and practices that had been influenced by Navajos for decades, and which reflected an older way of life, one whose cycles reflected stock raising boom and bust. But it was not to be. They now had to make different disclosure statements for different kinds of loans, pawn, or credit, and new regulations had still not been approved by the BIA or the Tribe; no one had yet seen even a draft.

DNA objected to open-ended credit (the system now in common use by credit cards), trying to encourage a system of cash, not credit, for Navajos. This itself is a twist; traders had always been the ones to limit Navajo purchasing, learning to say *"doodah"* (no) in ways that saved face. The explosion of money in the 1970s had made them explore new ways of giving the customers what they wanted. New goods create new desires: consumer culture infiltrated the depths of the Navajo Reservation. Now it was the DNA who tried to limit and control spending. The basic anomaly for Navajos was that, while the DNA promoted modern (well-stocked) stores, they tried to keep a legal lid on Navajo spending habits. Throughout the following year, DNA staff continued to keep their eyes on trader credit and pawn, and to respond to every complaint against traders, usually concerning pieces that had been pawned a year or two earlier and on which no payments had been made. One by one, traders began to stop pawning, out of caution and self-defense. Their older customers had the same needs, the same request for pawn loans, and the same expectations of the old ways continuing. Even credit was cut by some traders, and everyone held it to a minimum.

Old-time Navajos did not understand why pawn and credit were stopped. Old-time traders did not understand why people from families to whom they had for a generation or more extended credit in the lean seasons, given generously at every ceremony, and felt that they had helped—with the phrase that what was good for Navajos was good for traders—had not stepped forward to support them at the hearings, had not said more to establish that there were relations of honesty, fairness, and friendship. Traders wondered why so few of their customers had put in a good word for them. Elijah Blair, then trading at Dinnebito, speculated that the reason might have been that Navajos thought that the same government that could take them to Hwéeldi, and take away their sheep, could make the traders do its bidding also: cancel debts, lower prices, change the way trading worked. Or perhaps it was due to the deeply seated feeling of Navajos, which the DNA lawyers obviously shared, that making a profit itself meant cheating customers. There were different cultural definitions for cheating. Elijah Blair said that "What makes the trader crooked in their eyes, and what makes the trader crooked in your eyes are two different things." Two words, in his view, explained this philosophy. One of them means "stingy" or "tight," *bithatso*, the other, *bina'adlo'*, means to be a cheater. "If you try to rise above the other members of the clan, then you become 'stingy'—*bithatso*—because it is a leveling philosophy." Traders, in Navajo terminology, were stingy-tight-cheaters, because they charged more for a can of beans than they paid for it. But this was proper in Anglo-American business. In the trader view, you were stingy and tight if you did not give to the community, if you withheld credit to a customer in dire need; you were a cheater if you gave the wrong change, cashed checks for the wrong amount, took advantage of the customer, or gave bad goods in an exchange. There were traders who fit this description, and it was accepted opinion among traders that the DNA lawsuits would not change them.[6]

Younger Navajos took up the radical ideas prevalent at the period, the opposition to business and commerce, and the negative view of traders, and incorporated it with their parents traditional ideas. Elijah Blair noticed this at Dinnebito Trading Post.

I had one guy come in, young guy, one time. This must have been many years after FTC and DNA. The guy says, well, Jaa'ii, you still here? You must be a millionaire now. He said, you stole it from all these Navajos. And you know, this was a young, educated Navajo. A lot of them felt that way, that we really cheated and stole—this started to develop in the sixties and the seventies. [Elijah Blair, interview with the author, May 1999]

The new regulations had been slow in coming, but in February of 1974, Clinton Jim, the Navajo Nation's head of the Commerce Department, had a draft ready that covered credit matters. Michael Jaenish, attorney for the Commerce Department of the Navajo Nation, asked Tansey, as secretary and representative of UITA, to get together information for a discussion related to new regulations. He wanted forms that met pawn and credit requirements, figures on the cost of producing these forms, an estimate of the number of pawn items that went dead each year, and an outline of necessary changes needed to current leases. Tansey, providing this in writing, said that leases needed to be simple, and they had to ensure the trader some ability to recoup his investment in building improvements. No trader had made improvements recently: not only were these expensive and required to meet building and sanitation codes, but without a lease such expenditures had no hope of return.

Tansey met with the Navajo Nation officials to discuss the draft of new regulations, which, he was told, had been written by Robert Hilgendorf on his own time. Tansey was critical of these drafted regulations: the seventy-three-page draft was, he told the UITA Board of Directors, all about consumer legislation. The drafted regulations would force traders to give credit, and provided neither protection nor dispute settlement for traders. There were changes in interest charges and paperwork required for pawn that Tansey thought were unrealistic, and the focus was on preventing open-ended credit. At the meeting, he urged the tribal officers to accept minimum charges—a set-up fee—for pawn and credit, similar to those set by the State of New Mexico. There continued to be disagreement between DNA lawyers and Tribal Council members and Committee heads. Jaenish and Clinton Jim were critical of Robert Hilgendorf and his draft, and Clinton Jim, in particular, was concerned that the regulations would not benefit Navajos. But in any case, there were to be no new leases, although many trading posts only had seven years left. In addition, there was heated discussion on the permissible percentage to charge on pawn.[7]

Pawn, as we've seen, began as a pledge against purchases on credit extended in lean times, before spring wool or fall lamb sales. Pawn for cash came later. It was always a small loan, with the same simple procedures: the customer was charged interest at a straight percentage rate that remained the same whether the piece was redeemed in one month or twelve; the retention period was a year.

> We had a twenty percent charge, twenty percent interest rate. Now, I'm not talking about annual percentage rate . . . but simple interest. If he pawned for ten dollars, you charged him twelve, ten dollar price plus two dollar interest. So you put that on this piece of pawn and you stored it. You kept this for a year, and it was twelve dollars; if he came back the next day and took it out, it was still twelve dollars, because there was no pro-rated charge or set-up fee. [Elijah Blair, Cline Library interview, February 1998]

Traders kept it simple: "everything was simple interest at that time." Nobody thought about annual percentage rates or set-up charges. The customer came irregularly to pay the interest, but as long as any sort of payment had been made within a year, traders kept the item. Traders tended to keep pawn because it was a disadvantage to sell it. Not only would the customers be upset, the trader also made money on the continued transactions on it over a period of time.

> There was no point to a one-time sale. You make more money over a period of time pawning and repawning and collecting interest, than a one-time sale, and you keep the customer happy. In off-reservation pawnshops they could do this, but we couldn't. Even if you kept pawn a long time and it went dead, even so customers were upset. Some traders' wives would wear it, and then people got really upset. [Elijah Blair, Cline Library interview, February 1998]

But pieces did go dead; traders did sell (usually to Gallup trader/dealers, rarely at the post). In addition, the fashion for Navajo jewelry had begun to grow in the late 1960s, and so did its value. The pawn vaults in trading posts were full of Navajo silver that was worth something, and arts and crafts dealers were begging for more. The closer traders were to the arts and crafts market, the more likely they were to sell dead pawn. Border town pawnbrokers, frequented by Navajos with vehicles, had entirely different rules, which Navajos may not have realized. They were not bound by BIA regulations but by state laws, and often they did not have the connection to the customer, and certainly not to any community, which reservation traders had.[8]

The regulations that were being proposed would limit the return on reservation pawn to an earned interest (24 percent per annum) or a two-dollar fee, whichever was more. They would ensure a twelve-month period for holding pawn, and limit pawn to cash, not permitting any pawn for merchandise—no barter system was to be maintained.

In August 1974, the Navajo Tribal Council passed a resolution stating that any Navajos who wished to buy the expiring lease of a trading post would be given first preference, that if a trader contemplated substantial renovations, the Tribe would negotiate a longer lease period (to allow reasonable profit), and if no improvements were contemplated, no lease would be considered until one year before it expired. A higher rent would be charged.

In July 1975, a year later, the Law Enforcement Services of the Bureau of Indian Affairs in Washington, D.C., held a meeting at which regulations for trading on the Navajo, Zuni, and Hopi lands could be discussed. Representatives of Hopi, Navajo, and Zuni governments and their attorneys were asked to the meeting, as well as Peterson Zah (director of DNA), eight BIA officials (from Phoenix, Albuquerque, the Navajo area, and Washington) and Hans Walker Jr., a solicitor from the Department of the Interior. UITA President Elijah Blair and Vice President Lavoy McGee were also invited to attend. Elijah Blair, his wife Claudia, and Lavoy McGee flew to Washington for the two-day meeting. It was hot and humid, but the Blairs had not been to the capitol before and toured around. Once in the conference room, Elijah thought that the daily problems of the Navajos could not seem real to the bureaucrats around the polished table.

> It was a board room with a long rectangular table; Hilgendorf and Peterson Zah were at one end of the table, talking about how we were exploiting the Navajo and our percentage rate. We were at the other end. FTC people maybe, or BIA, members of the hearing board were on either end. [Elijah Blair, interview with the author, May 1999]

Hilgendorf remembered that he had difficulties getting to Washington, missing a plane en route from Columbus, Ohio, and arriving at the meeting late and distracted by his travel problems. He had thought all along that the traders didn't really approach or tackle the problems, but in any case the meeting was being held merely to get all points of view (not just those from the Navajo Reservation) on the final draft and was evidently not an attempt to make any changes to it.

Pawn and credit were the first order of business, if not the main items. Lavoy McGee presented information on pawning, based on his own experience at Red Mesa. The average value of pawned items was $87.40; the average loan amount on pawn, $27.08. Average time of an item in pawn was four months, and approximately 32 percent of all pawned items were in pawn for longer and became dead. His own insurance costs were 65¢ per $100 of agreed value, and a deductible of $5,000, though he noted that other traders did not take a deductible and paid a much higher rate, $1.25 on $100. Traders paid the Navajo tribe 1.5 percent on the interest they received from pawn. He estimated that it cost him about $1.59 to make one such average pawn transaction, about $2.29 for pawn retained for six months, and about $4.34 for pawn kept for a year—figures that included the costs of notifying the pawner that the reclaim period was up. The total charge permitted in the newly proposed regulations was $2 or the finance charge of 24 percent, whichever was greater, but not both.[9]

Based on these figures, McGee asked that a minimum pawn administration fee be allowed, 20 percent or $5, whichever was less, on loans under $75, and 24 percent or $7.50 on larger loans. Hilgendorf said the $2 or earned finance charge was sufficient. Elijah Blair pointed out that this would basically eliminate small loans, but Steve Godoff, for the Navajo tribe, disagreed and said the $2 fee would give traders an incentive to make short-term loans.

Credit extension—so-called open credit—was to be stopped. Blair argued for the barter system in purchasing Navajo goods, pointing out that traders almost always gave more in goods than in cash. Godoff insisted that only cash or checks should be given in payment, "cash is healthy for the reservation economy and fosters competition." He was opposed to barter, especially merchandise pawn, not only because he felt a cash economy was healthier, but also because barter continued to tie a customer to a particular trading post.

There were also issues that differed between the two Pueblos and the Navajo. Zuni and Hopi required traders to give consent to be sued in tribal court. The Navajo tribe wanted no such provision, as it inferred that the tribe needed BIA action to obtain jurisdiction over non-Indians, a sovereignty issue. The conclusion of the meeting was a long discussion on sovereignty as it related to specific wording of the enforcement aspects of the regulations, and had little to do with the rules themselves. There was discussion over the request that Native traders not be bound by the same regulations: Blair said that UITA would prefer that all businesses compete equally. There was agreement on the new fee schedule to the tribe for traders, and on the exemption from disclosure requirements of any credit extended without a finance charge. Hilgendorf proposed a provision in which customer complaints could be initiated; these would have to be heard by the commissioner within a short period of time, and could be appealed if the decision did not meet with the customer's approval. Other details, among them such topics as food-handler training, specified meetings with the BIA or the Tribe, reviews of licenses, the date regulations would go into effect, and where or how prices should be shown, were also agreed to.[10]

Elijah Blair recalled a feeling of intense frustration. The die was cast, he said, and the regulations had little to do with the way things worked. It was not a meeting of minds, and Blair thought Hilgendorf just overpowered everyone. "There's a Navajo saying, *ó'pithlé*, in the dark, and that's what it was, they were all in the dark." No one had any idea how these rules would affect the Navajos. "I tried to say what would happen to Navajos if you stopped long-term credit and took pawn away. That was what was happening; we couldn't continue to pawn with these regulations in place." But the regulations went into place essentially unchanged; those requiring the use of standard credit and loan disclosure forms were to go into operation on January 1, 1976, and all other provisions would be effective thirty days after publication of the new regulations in the Federal Register.[11]

Peterson Zah said that the new trader regulations were needed. "The traders didn't like what we did, but I was there: we didn't have a choice. The complaints were just too overwhelming." Complaints were coming in to DNA staff about who was hired in the community for the Railroad, about checks being withheld, about pawn. Robert Hilgendorf was convinced that every trader was mishandling pawn, selling it too soon or sending it to Gallup traders to sell, misinforming customers on time and overcharging them on interest, that there was no way to distinguish good from bad traders—like his Navajo clients, he believed there was no essential difference.[12]

This was the crux of the situation: the trading post was treated as if the entire system was rotten. The claim traders made was not that trading was blameless, but that it was an institution that was different because it served customers of a different economy—the Navajos. Improvements, traders felt, should have been made that allowed the trading post to continue as a different kind of enterprise, allowed to survive as a viable economic operation that also served Navajos. Instead, they were vilified and shamed.

The attention to bad traders needs to be looked at: What constituted bad trading? Dishonesty, of course, was an abhorrent element in trading as in any business. A trader, taking advantage of lack of literacy might add to and pad accounts, or cash a check for less, say, $1170 for $170. A comment illustrates one trader's thinking:

> They're very naive on any kind of business. I can get a Navajo to sign anything. Doesn't matter what it is, I can get him to sign anything and they'll never question me.[13]

Attitude was a problem, and trader attitudes could be extraordinarily patronizing. Even worse were traders who revealed a negative view of Navajo life, in which they portrayed themselves as saving their customers from bad habits or ignorance.

> He's a Navajo and doesn't know what to do. I was down there [at a Navajo customer's house] yesterday. . . . A lot of things down there that I would just do; he's got the fence all tore up, the gate all tore up, he's got the pump all busted, he's got a bunch of goats, and geese, and chickens, and every-thing else down there, there's animal manure all over where the little kids are playing. His wife is uneducated, and she's not very intelligent; why he ever married her I never could figure out.[14]

Nor did such traders seem to recognize the evident disrespect and a lack of appreciation or even knowledge of Navajo culture and ways of life. Remarks and behavior made these attitudes and inaccurate ideas evident.

> Like friendship—they have no way at all of being a good friend, like the white people do or the Spanish people do. The biggest part of them, it's very difficult to get any kind of show of appreciation out of any of them. . . . They have no way at all of showing gratitude. They think you're supposed to do it [help]; the softer you are on them the more they try to work you.[15]

These are comments of traders who clearly do not have an interest in or respect for Navajos.

Violence was a minor note in trader relations, but almost every trader, man and woman, has had some kind of challenge, a test of sorts, occasionally from people who had had too much to drink. How traders dealt with or handed out threats can be considered part of what distin-guished "good" from "bad" traders. A few traders had relied on the com-fort of visible firearms, and had guns hanging on the wall of a trading post's office, well into the 1960s. A trader and his wife commented on a predecessor.

> When we first came to the post, there were all these knives and sticks under the counter, and guns hanging up behind it. We changed that. We took them all down. We never needed it, not once.[16]

Dealing with drunks was occasionally necessary, but it takes a mean trader to enjoy it:

The first fight I got into was about nine-thirty at night, and I was in the trading post all by myself, there was no one there but me. This bunch of Navajos was banging on the door. I didn't have any electricity, all I had was the Coleman light that I used . . . turned around and started to go back into the house and [one of the Navajos] just came on through that door like it wasn't even there. Now, he said, I'm going to get me some stuff. No, I said, now you're going to get shocked. I had a gun in my hand then, I'd reached down under the counter—I had a .32 automatic—I said you go on and get back in that car, and get the hell out of here, and come back when you're sober. . . . And he just came right on through, and I said, uh-oh—I didn't want to shoot the son-of-a-gun in the trading post, because if somebody dies in a trading post, it's chindi and then you got to build a new store. . . . I knocked him down and got the door back opened up and then when he started to get up I got him by the back of the neck and the seat of the britches and I just high-boyed him out right in front of the car. I dumped him right in front of the headlights, and I put my foot down right on his neck, and I said . . . you just lay there, because if you try to get up, I said, I'm going to kick you right in the face and I'm going to kick every one of your teeth out.[17]

The difference between a "good" trader and a "bad" trader is not always easy to detect, and it is a distinction that few Navajos make. Bruce Burnham thought that it was not entirely true that they did not have a choice of traders. "In spite of all the stuff you hear about economic servitude and all that thing, competition was keen."

The fact was that Navajos did not think there was much difference between posts. "Most trading posts operated the same way, and dealt with people the same way." "All traders are alike." Constancy, however, meant something to the Navajo community. It was not so important to like the trader as to know who they were, to be able to predict behavior rather than to like it. Peterson Zah described the two trading posts near Keams Canyon, near where his parents lived.

They were different in the sense that with Cliff McGee, he knew the people very, very well, it seems—the people who went into the store, that did business with him, the Navajo ladies that took Navajo rugs to him. . . . And so there was more trading activities that was going on at the McGee trading post, and it seems like all of the other people who were working at the trading post were the offspring of Cliff McGee.

But with the Lee Trading Post, a mile up the road, was run by some-body else . . . he always had different people there working, depending on what time of the year it was. And so it seems the people didn't know the new people that were commanding the trading post there. They weren't there all year round. [Peterson Zah, Cline Library and author's interview, March 1999]

As Paul Begay put it, "The only thing as far as a good trader and a bad trader is, I think, just that I don't know one trader personally, and I know the other one."[18]

Navajos did notice the differences in prices, especially in wool. Walter Scribner said that in his day (from about 1935 to 1970) Navajos were pretty clever about working one trader against another.

They'd say, what are you paying for wool; well, I'm paying so much. The guy down the road there, he's paying two cents a pound more than you. Stuff like that. Traders help each other, but at the same time they were competitors.[19]

It was rare that Navajo opinions about anyone—whether Anglo or Navajo—interfered with any interaction they might have with that per-son. In their own community, it was essential to be able to work or get on with everyone. At the same time, Navajos had different ways of assessing people, different reasons for liking people.

You have to make an Indian person very comfortable in order to win his trust . . . so the trader had to break through this . . . they first have to learn the language. . . . Teasing is a big thing among the Navajo people each day. . . . It's a way to interact.

When you say "in-law" to a white man, you're basically saying, "Oh, he's good enough, so I wish he could *be* my in-law." This is what they're actually saying. It's not going to become, but it's just a way of teasing among the Navajo people. And so when they say "my in-law" they're grabbing at his clothes, and he's doing the same thing to the Navajo. Maybe he's grabbing the Navajo's clothing because he owns a lot of jew-elry and has got a big concho belt. "Huge! Looks like a wealthy Navajo. I want *him* as my in-law." And so this is a way to build good rapport, a good relationship between the trader and the Navajo. [Paul Begay, Cline Library interview, February 1998]

Certain traders were especially well liked for specific reasons. Paul Begay talked about Elijah Blair.

> He's the only man that I know that speaks fluent Navajo in a Kentuckian accent. And so it is possible to learn how to talk Navajo . . . and so this was the way to win the hearts of the Navajo—learn their language, learn their lifestyle, learn their way of teasing. [Paul Begay, Cline Library interview, February 1998]

The institution itself was considered to be pretty much the same all over the reservation. "There was always a little anger set toward the trader. But then it's also understood we cannot live without the trader, also." But if Navajos like a person, they might even go after them to see them, to visit with them.[20]

Traders had an inside view, and a set of values by which they judged themselves and other traders. Many had a very specific sense of who made a "good" trader and who did not, and a highly critical attitude toward their fellow traders. Asked to define a good trader, the response was usually, if they get on well with the community. Asked to define a bad trader, the answer was if they cheated, took advantage of Navajos, padded bills. Bruce Burnham said that traders would have weeded them out eventually, but the trouble was the DNA treated all traders as if they were bad traders.

> It was the guillotine: "swoosh." Your head was gone. It [change] was already happening. There was no reason for them to do that. . . . Had it not been a class action, then they were absolutely justified in ferreting out the bad apples. But they took a whole group of businesses out. . . . If they had dealt with them individually, and left it in place, they wouldn't have hurt the Navajo people so bad. [Bruce Burnham, interview with the author, July 1998]

In October 1975, before the new paperwork requirements went into effect, UITA carried out a survey of the approximately 125 traders (that is, trading posts), by postcard, to find out what their current practices were, and what traders were planning to do about pawn and credit. Fifty-four cards were returned: twenty traders no longer took pawn at that date, twenty-five were planning to stop pawn at the end of the year, and three were planning to continue it. Six would resume pawn if the minimum charges were increased, and twenty-seven would resume it only if the entire regulations were changed. Thirty-three said they gave merchandise credit, twenty-eight (three of whom were undecided) would probably continue limited credit, fourteen would probably stop credit, one would stop credit on all who failed to pay, and five would give credit on a thirty-day basis only. Many of the respondents noted that they only gave credit and pawn to people in their community.[21]

Traders were outraged at what they considered to be an unfair and unbusinesslike situation created by the new regulations. Once these were in place, pawn slowly came to an end. Regulations did not allow a set-up fee. They required additional paperwork—a contract, monthly notices, notices of dead pawn—more thorough documentation (probably necessary) and specified time frames for it. They also made selling pawn even more inevitable, as traders now could not keep pieces but had to sell them and return to the original owner the difference between the pawn loan (minus charges) and the sale price. Using newly drawn-up pawn forms did not seem to guarantee that DNA lawyers would not continue to hound them. Every trader was convinced that any error they made in pawn procedures would be proof of guilt and the basis for a crippling lawsuit. Pawn ceased at trading posts.

DNA attorneys still do not quite accept the traders' response, despite the fact that the Truth in Lending law was, as Hilgendorf acknowledged, a complicated statute.

> My reaction to their all uniformly dropping reservation pawn was that now that they had to follow the laws that everyone else was following, the disclosures and the interest rate, and the sale of pawn, the big issue wasn't the interest rate and the disclosures, the big issue was that you had to give back to the Navajo the difference between what you lent him and what you sell, after your cost of sale; all their profit is gone. [Robert Hilgendorf, interview with the author, October 1999]

For the solid community trading post it made little sense to sell pawn pieces unless the pawn was long dead. A customer would pawn a piece over and over again, and that was what made the difference. But there were too many stores on the reservation, too many reasons to sell, and too many dealers and buyers ready to purchase. Eventually, traders realized that state pawn laws provided a better deal for pawnbrokers. Since Navajos had vehicles and used them, and pawn was still being taken by a wide variety of enterprises, many traders set up off-reservation businesses, with their old customers. Pawn, which now consisted of car titles, rifles, small appliances, radios, as well as jewelry, Pendleton blankets, peyote paraphernalia, or saddles, was an aspect of Navajo business that did not so much change as move. So, after the regulations, pawn went off the reservation, where state laws predominated, which included the required disclosures of the law *and* allowed a reasonable return. The state of New Mexico in 1978, for example, permitted a $7.50, or 10 percent, set-up fee.

Raymond Blair continued to try to work pawn and to be harassed by DNA lawyers, and grew bitter. In 1976, he wrote to his brother Elijah, "I got sorry for an old girl and accepted partial payments after the pawn was dead, and then sold it after she quit paying on it." Frustrated, he wrote to James LeValley about the situation, asking for advice. LeValley clarified the legal situation, advised him not to accept more payments or enter into oral agreements, and added:

> I can sympathize with your feelings of almost hopeless frustration which result from so much hassle by government bureaucrats and lawyers. . . . The situation for the small businessman, generally, is almost intolerable, and someone like you who extends consumer credit on a relatively small-scale basis is really in a quandary. The regulations affecting the businessman multiply like rabbits but with less reason. Your problems are compounded by the fact that you must deal with an additional, sovereign government . . . as well as . . . the BIA, the FTC, and DNA. Inasmuch as these groups seem to have made a policy decision to the effect that the best interests of the Navajos are served by driving the white trader off the reservation, the cards are really stacked against you.[22]

Raymond Blair sold his post to Clarence Wheeler, and retired. Slowly, traders began to leave: older traders retired, a few traders found they could not make a living, and a couple of trading posts—Wide Ruins, Pine Springs—burned down and the traders decided it was not worth rebuilding. The effect of trading post closings for Navajos in the community was the disruption of an old economic system on which they had relied and grown used to over many decades. The heady days of OEO and ONEO programs and money were already virtually over, and stock market crashes and the collapsing economy that occurred around 1977 meant that there was no funding for many of those fighting the war on poverty, who folded up their tents and melted away. Cash economy came to some Navajos, but by no means all. Tribal, state, and BIA bureaucracies began to take on some of the responsibilities traditionally carried by trading posts. The trading posts also felt the pinch of the tighter economy. For Navajos, too, this was the end of an era.

> Some of the people were told that the trading post was going to be closed, and I remember some of the people were upset and sad because they knew they had to travel farther now and had to get more supplies to last at least a month. Everyone went to Gallup, to the Little Bear Trading Post and the Navajo Trading Post. Everything was the same, expense-wise, but the travel was farther. Sometimes people used to camp out between here and Gallup. [Cecilia Yazzie, interview with Arlene Tracy, June 1999]

The FTC's report of 1973, "The Trading Post System on the Navajo Reservation," is an interesting government document, well footnoted and quoting from many different sources including a transcript of the hearings. It described "abusive trading practices," off-reservation problems at automobile dealers, and the situation with pawn. It sketched the responsibilities of the BIA, and the way in which the Navajo Tribal Council could play a role. Many of its recommendations were sensible, others reveal the fact that, underlying the report was the older issue of assimilation, the need to adjust and change to modern-day America. It was not just traders who were expected to modernize, but Navajos.[23]

This is a critical implication. DNA lawyers and Navajo activists fought, with exceptional energy, for equal treatment for Navajos, equal rights before the law. Their action against traders was intended to bring low prices, goods and services identical to those in stores in the rest of America (by implication more types of goods, regular prices, and fewer unrelated services), and relief from paternalistic, patronizing attitudes. Attorneys had argued that few of their clients could read (either English or Navajo), or speak English, and that they were being taken advantage of because of their different culture. The documentation and written information which, under the Truth in Lending law, traders were required to send, thus seemed to be a tool of change and assimilation. These requirements were obviously intended to provide for informed, open dealings that could be legally regulated; perhaps lawyers hoped to make Navajos more aware of the transaction formalities and their own responsibilities.

Traders had adapted to the Navajo ways, but it left them open to appearances of dishonesty since it provided no trail of proof. DNA, in essence, encouraged change in Navajo society by urging the adoption of procedures in order to ensure evidence of above-board dealings, and introducing litigation. Traders argued that they themselves had been less forceful agents of change. "We accepted them as they were. We didn't have to become Navajo; we didn't ask them to change."[24]

In fact, the DNA brought about changes that were beneficial to the traders. Traders had to cease doing both pawn and credit as the Navajos knew it, but long-term credit had been a problem for traders: like most businesses, they had many accounts that went unpaid. When the new regulations came out, only thirty-day credit accounts were permitted, and the trader could legitimately refuse further extension and cite the regulations. Pawn was a different matter. Though many traders found it a relief to cease taking pawn, almost all of them thought that pawn was a way of life on the reservation and would continue. Stiff regulations—and traders thought the new regulations were unreasonably stiff—did not take into account the fact that the reservation was not a world apart: Navajos traveled, shopped, and pawned in border towns. This move to border towns by Navajos who could afford it affected the patterns of community economics, and, in particular, the economics of the elderly and those who rarely left the reservation.

New stores came. In the mid-1970s, Thriftway convenience stores, a local chain built up by Jerry Clayton, appeared all over the reservation. The company promised to train Navajo managers and, after a prescribed number of years, pass the lease on to them. Thriftway stores carried the usual range of items for travelers and basic goods like milk and bread at exceptionally high prices. More recently, the company bought up a few trading posts and converted them. Another convenience store chain, Circle K, built a few stores in "high traffic" communities. Trading posts continued in the distant communities. Travel to larger, better stores was expensive, but they were new, modern, and had a vast array of goods. Though they provided no livestock dealing, no loans, no credit, less information, Navajos were treated like any other customer, impersonally and as cash-only customers.

The first supermarket on the reservation, FedMart in Window Rock, closed, but by 1983 another chain supermarket, Bashas', opened its first reservation store in Tuba City. Other Basha stores were built, also in the larger communities—Window Rock, Chinle, Kayenta. Bashas' was considered an "anchor tenant" for shopping centers, a tenant that would pull in customers for essential groceries so that other stores could rely on a flow of people, and was usually given benefits and breaks. As such an anchor tenant, Bashas' was provided with new buildings at very low rent. High-priced convenience stores along highways filled in the gaps between supermarkets; fast-food restaurants followed.

Navajos themselves had demands and ways of operating that did not always match the outside world's customs. This, too, changed, as Peterson Zah pointed out.

Navajos were going out. More and more Navajos were going out to Flagstaff, Winslow, Cortez, and Farmington to shop. And they were beginning to see the difference between the trading post, what it has to offer, and the shopping centers out there. They were beginning to compare prices, they were beginning to compare the quality of the merchandise they were buying. And to me, it was just inevitable that this thing came about in the manner in which it did. It was one of those things that just had to come at that time, in the history of the Navajo people. [Peterson Zah, Cline Library and author's interview, March 1999]

It was always only a matter of time before supermarkets came out to the reservation. During the period in which traders were beginning to leave the reservation, the Navajo Nation gave large concerns strong incentives to open branch stores. On the other hand, very little was done to develop Navajo businesses or train Navajo people in the formal business practices.

Traders had always believed that Navajo culture, with its strong emphasis on sharing with relatives, was not the environment out of which commercially successful people grew. However, with time, new attitudes began to grow up. Yet, setting up a business, or taking over an old one, on the reservation was and remains difficult, time-consuming (it can take years to obtain lease and loan approval), as hard for Navajos as for outsiders. The Tribe sought industry; funding was given to larger businesses and enterprises—Peabody Coal, the Navajo sawmill—to start up on the reservation, but less help was extended to individual Navajos who wanted to set up businesses. Betty, Louisa and John Wetherill's Navajo foster daughter, grew up and married Buck Rodgers, an Anglo-American rancher from Texas. Encouraged to start a trading post by John Wetherill, Betty and Buck Rodgers ran various stores and businesses on and around the reservation throughout the 1960s.

The Navajos really didn't know my husband, and me, being a full-blood Navajo myself, why, they just didn't know about it. They just didn't know whether they wanted that white man in there or not. Well, I guess they didn't. They gave us heck all the time we were there. . . .

You had to get a lease, so many years, and when that expired, you had to . . . renew it. . . . But me being a Navajo, I could stay there forever. But they didn't have that much sense to know. They really gave me a hard time. [Betty Rodgers, Cline Library interview, July 1999][25]

And Richard Mike, a Navajo businessman in Kayenta, noted:

No reservation institutions nor any school systems taught Indians that small business was a viable vocational career. There were no Indian role models and the notion of an Indian business owner simply did not exist. [Richard Mike, interview by the author, January 2000]

Loans, training, and encouragement for individuals still seemed hard to obtain in Window Rock. The question was how culture might change and still retain its identity; whether new economic forces could be harnessed by a society without destroying its values and practices.

10

⌐·⌐

TRADING AT THE END OF THE TWENTIETH CENTURY

It saddens me that several years ago the Wide Ruins post was completely destroyed by fire. Jimmy Toddy phoned me from Chambers to tell me the news. I understand the site has been bulldozed. But it still exists in my memory and I often reconstruct it in my dreams.

Sallie Wagner, 1997: Wide Ruins,
Memories from a Navajo Trading Post, *146*

Trading posts, despite the changes, continued with a certain vitality through the 1980s. As before, trading was sustained on the two different principles that have already been described as "traditional" and "progressive." Traditional traders continued to run their store along old-fashioned lines, stocking basic goods that exactly matched the desires and needs, as the traders had learned them through years of living, of their traditional customers. These traders grossed enough to pay the bills and a salary, living in quarters behind the store, usually investing in a small property off the reservation, to which they might later retire. Some never owned a trading post at all, but worked for an owner, sustaining a long relationship with Navajo customers just as the owner-trader did, and retiring with memories. They sold a traditional inventory: canned goods, fabric, bacon, cold cuts, hats, flour, coffee, salami, and cheese, all the basics, all the goods the customers liked, in the color and the brands they preferred.

"Progressive" traders, usually younger, ran their store as a modern business enterprise, providing a wide range of goods and eager to find out what new items their customers wanted. These traders changed their posts into self-service style stores in the 1970s, and they tried to provide a variety of other services, not only the traditional ones of buying wool and lambs and crafts, but novel ones: auto mechanic service, hardware, a café, and, later on, video rental and laundromats. Many trading posts active throughout the 1980s fitted this description, though each had its own approach to new times, new ideas.

Ed Foutz, trading at Shiprock Trading Post, remarked on the faster pace of change in the 1970s and 1980s, and the way traders adapted to it.

> The roads, of course, came along, the area of transportation changed. And with that the demands of the people changed. I think the really big change came about with the advent of communication: radio and the Navajo Hours that were aimed almost straight at the Navajo people in the way of advertising and things. And it used to be at the old trading post that fashion lagged maybe two or three or fours years behind the fashion, let's say, in the country. . . . With the advent of radio, and especially with TV, the young people, as well as everyone else, were brought into the world today. So if chocolate Cocoa Pops were popular as a cereal, that's what you'd better stock in your store, because that's what the kids would be coming in and telling their parents they wanted to buy. . . . You couldn't carry just the good old standard things that we used to in the early days. . . . We started carrying a greater selection of meat, instead of just mutton and lamb, we carried chicken and luncheon meats and things like this. [Ed Foutz, interview with author, September 1998]

Progressive traders found out what the community wanted and supplied it; they changed with changing times; some had pension plans for their employees, or a profit-sharing plan. As Bruce Burnham put it, "We're dealing with people . . . not just an 'ethnic group.' They are a people. We're in Rome and they are Romans."

> As we try to honor and respect tribal culture and tribal identity, the government's sole purpose, it seems, is to bring these people into the mainstream. The trader's been the buffer between those two cultures. . . . We don't try to change the Navajo. We deal with the Navajo on the Navajo

standard on one hand, and we deal with the white world on the other hand. [Bruce Burnham, interview with the author, July 1998]

A few new trading posts opened in the latter years of trading, but not for long. A store called Baby Rocks was built around 1978 just below the cliffs known as Tse Awe (Baby Rocks), a few miles east of Kayenta, on Highway 64. The store was handsome, built of local stone in the shape of a double hogan, the inside light and airy, the exterior blending into its surroundings. Recognizing change, it catered primarily to the tourist trade that was beginning to grow at the end of the 1970s, and carried a small amount of groceries. Kayenta was already a hub of activity at this period: there were two motels, two trading posts, garages, a laundromat, a café, and a tour operation taking visitors around Monument Valley. The competition was fierce, the costs high; by 1987 Baby Rocks Trading Post had closed. The handsome building still stands, forlorn and abandoned, under the red cliffs. This period saw many closings, stores like Warren's Trading Post in Kayenta, Navajo Mountain, Wide Ruins, and Pine Springs. New regulations came out in 1975, but by 1985, trading days were numbered. Time was inevitably more potent than the regulations.

Lavoy McGee, who had been vice president of UITA in 1975, had grown up at Red Rock Trading Post. In 1965, he went into partnership at Red Mesa Trading Post with his father, Jewel McGee, and his uncle, Roscoe McGee, who had moved the store to the new paved Highway 160 just a few years earlier, and ran it until 1984. Red Mesa was a good area for livestock, especially for mohair goats, and Jewel, Roscoe, and Lavoy McGee traded for wool, mohair, and cattle.

> Out in this country, people sheared once a year, so when they did their shearing, it was a good long staple. Lots of other areas, like Texas and so on, they'd shear twice a year, so it wasn't the nice staple that our mohair was. And they had good quality goats, did a good business in mohair. . . .
>
> We'd have buyers who would contact us and bid on our mohair. We had several people that were interested so people would contact us, or we'd know of buyers and check for the best price. . . .

In 1984, Lavoy McGee gave up trading and left Red Mesa.

> By that time my family was pretty big, and the wife was living in town and the kids were growing up. We just felt it was time for our family to make

the move. And trading wasn't the same as it used to be. Things were changing drastically out there. People weren't as loyal to you, and things were just changing so fast. . . . With the highways and cars and more of a cash economy, and the superstores in town, maybe our need [the need for traders] was just fading away a little bit. [Lavoy McGee, Cline Library interview, March 1998]

He and his family moved to Farmington, and he opened a pet supply store.

As I look back, I don't see how we made any money out there on the Reservation. We did so many things that probably weren't sound business-wise. Now we're in a store, and it's a cash business. If we haven't sold it, it's on the shelf; if we have sold it, the money's in the drawer, and it's just a lot simpler. The trading post business was a complicated business, with all the things that we did. [Lavoy McGee, Cline Library interview, March 1998]

As the flow of money to the reservations came to an end in the 1980s, trading post businesses grew more cautious and pulled in credit. By 1990, traders began to stop cashing paychecks; the drive to a distant bank for large sums of money was time-consuming, took away trading post staff, and was a drain on cash flow. Only a few bought lambs or wool. The live-stock and wool trade had changed, and the Tribe discontinued the wool buying program it had instituted in the 1970s.

Navajos living in small communities still straddling old ways and new were the ones who suffered from the changes, and were the ones who most missed the trading posts. The system of cooperation could no longer prevent a widening gap between better-off and less well-off families. At Shonto, only half an hour from Bashas' supermarket and other stores in Kayenta, the trading post changed from one carrying an extensive stock, including a variety of dry goods, hardware, and groceries, to one with a smaller inventory of basics. Grace Brown said people disliked the change.

There's a lot of them complain at the Chapter meeting, they say the store isn't like it used to be. And then, I guess they say, we're not going to sign the lease again. . . . And then some say, well, what are we going to do after that? If it closed down—there'd be nothing. [Grace Brown, interview by the author, June 1999]

Individuals in communities without trading posts got together to pool rides, and paid each other for gas and rides to town, though there were no phones to coordinate trips. Changes in families, work, and the way people spent their time made changes in the system of cooperation and shared work. The shift to cash, desired by many both in and outside the Navajo tribal government, took place—is still taking place—very slowly and unevenly. Pawn continued—and continues—to be part of the way Navajos manage their economic resources.

Some traders recognized that some of the changes were helpful to traders; a few even held the view that the FTC hearings had been necessary. And, it was certainly the case that the federal presence on the reservation and its attempt to regulate trade was not a new thing and had always been resented by traders. Jim Babbitt was a third generation Babbitt from one of the largest trading concerns, the Babbitt Brothers. Five brothers, David, William, Charles, George, and Edward came to Flagstaff from Cincinnati in 1886, and began a ranching and trading business, owning at the peak of the company's business as many as twenty trading posts in the western sector of the reservation. The company was the leaseholder, but after the first Babbitt generation, usually hired traders to manage the posts.

> My grandfather [C. J. Babbitt, one of the five Babbitt brothers] . . . expanded fairly rapidly, and with his partner, Sam Preston, got the old Tuba Trading Post right at the turn of the century, and then they built this new building about 1902. Well, along at the same time, they got a third trading post over at Willow Springs, which is up under the Echo Cliffs, beyond Moenave. So by 1901 or 1902, they had three trading posts. But even in those days, trade was regulated by the U.S. Indian Service. And whoever was sitting back at the traders' licensing desk in Washington saw the third trading application come through for Babbitts, and he said, "Nope, can't have this," because to him, back there, he thought they were trying to develop a monopoly. And he thought if they could get a monopoly on the Indian trade, they would raise prices and cheat the Indians. [Jim Babbitt, Cline Library interview, July 1999]

Throughout the decades, the BIA had attempted to prevent monopoly, dishonesty, and too high prices by limiting the total number of stores in the 1950s, trying at the same time to ensure traders a thriving enterprise and thus avoid a situation in which they would charge even higher prices to be certain that they could make a living.

By the last decade of the twentieth century, the traditional and entre-preneurial activities of trading, taking pawn, acting as a broker between cultures, making a living for all concerned, indeed, trading itself—the ex-change of one kind of goods for another—had ended. Though many traders carried on, trading posts became very different. A number of trad-ing posts on the reservation, located in the same old buildings, now rely on arts and crafts, on tourists and visitors, to supplement the "trade" of a community. Their owners, or managers, may retain the title "trader," but it is a nod to tradition, to a vaguely romanticized past. As Ed Foutz, of Shiprock Trading Post, put it "if you were to say 'Indian trader', I don't even know if that fits; you could say, 'I'm a businessman on the Navajo Reservation.'"[1]

Those trading posts on the paved road, or near an attraction or a nat-ural stopping place, use the strength of their historic buildings, and, to outsiders, exotic environment, to pull in visitors. A few old posts have been bought by Thriftway, which has turned some, like Nazlini, into con-venience stores, and maintained others, like The Gap, in a closer resem-blance of the trading post they once were. Many traders continue to work in arts and crafts, acting as middleman between a sophisticated market and skilled, usually well-informed, artisans. Almost none deal in livestock or raw wool, but may sell specially spun and dyed skeins of wool for their weavers, as well as items of special interest to Indian consumers, such as items for Native American Church services or buckskin and baskets for Navajo ceremonies. The world of the Navajo Reservation and that of the dominant society now mix and mingle; there are guidebooks to trading posts, giving short histories, or information on location, hours, what arts and crafts they sell (and whether they are a member of the Indian Arts and Crafts Association), what kind of credit cards they accept, whether they have handicapped access and provide services for shipping purchases.[2]

There are about two dozen trading posts that continue to provide old-time services, as well as goods, even though the regulations do not allow them to "trade" and they do not take pawn. Many of them are off the beaten track: Borrego Pass, Red Rock, Old Red Lake, Naschitti, Inscription House, Tsaya, Piñon. Some are now on a paved highway, such as Beclahbito, Teec Nos Pos, Big Rock, Fruitland, Blanco, or in larger reservation communities, such as Kayenta and Shiprock Trading Posts. The stores in distant commu-nities do yeoman service for their customers, bringing in groceries and goods, providing a post office, sometimes check cashing and other kinds of services, and in rare—very rare—cases, continuing to buy sheep and wool. Though current-day traders recognize the old-fashioned, ultimately vanishing, nature of their operation, much vitality remains. Some younger people from trading families continued, or came into the business, looking for a change or a shift in career, and usually a return to roots.

The Ashcroft trading family, for example, has one such modern-day trader. Andrea Ashcroft had been a social worker in Portland for many years when her father, Jim Ashcroft, mentioned that Rough Rock Trading Post was empty, boarded up, had been a pretty good store once, and suggested she take a look at it. "I got very homesick for the desert, the Southwest," Andrea Ashcroft said; "it gets in your blood, there's no way to get it out . . . and my dad has always tried to get me back." So she went to look at Rough Rock.

> It was all boarded up. There were windows broken out. It was a mess. I squeezed through a place on the door, looked around, and thought, it's awfully nice back here. [Andrea Ashcroft, interview with the author, June 1999]

She moved out to Rough Rock and began working on repairs, fixing plumbing and plaster herself, getting help with the electric wiring. Jim Ashcroft, a trader himself, managed to obtain a lease for Andrea through the Chapter, and she opened in 1996.

Rough Rock is a small community tucked under the eastern edge of Black Mesa, north of Many Farms, southeast of Kayenta. The community is known for its school, which in the mid-1960s became an experiment in Navajo self-determination: Rough Rock School was a model, run with a Navajo school board, managing its own programs, in which the teaching of Navajo language, and the development of Navajo language materials, was paramount.

> The first day, I opened this place with an initial inventory order of $4,000, opened the first day and did $500 in business, and I was just happy . . . and it has grown from there—it's in a viable location.
>
> I told myself when I opened that I really did want to run it like an old trading post and so, you know, I carry a lot of credit, I really do.

She operates strictly on cash herself. "I pay for everything as it comes through the door." But she loans money.

> Sometimes it's big. I have a couple right now that have pawned the title

to their automobile. I don't know what interest those places charge, but these folks were paying $300 a month and their balance kept getting bigger and bigger. And they were about to lose their vehicle. I gave them a lecture about . . . "know what you're borrowing, and how much you're going to have to pay for it" and loaned them the money, like $1,500 to get their truck out of hock so they wouldn't lose it. [Andrea Ashcroft, interview with the author, June 1999]

Loans are risky. Though in this particular case she is being paid back, there are times when she is put at the bottom of the list of bills to be paid "simply because I am community."

The stock in the store is a mixture of standards goods—Unida biscuits, cans of sardines, Spam, tomatoes, corn. Fresh produce is difficult, but she carries a little. Milk is expensive ($4.65) to get out to the store, but she has it, but WIC (Women and Infant Children) checks from the tribe cover milk for families with children. Soda pop is still an important item, and the store also has a video rental section. Like many trading posts, she does not sell gasoline. Ten years ago, the Environmental Protection Agency ordered trading posts to replace old gasoline tanks.

It would cost me a minimum, with no contamination, a minimum of $60,000 to put in gasoline. I just chuckle. If there's contamination in the ground, which there probably is because those tanks have been there for years and years, it could be a million dollars plus. [Andrea Ashcroft, interview with the author, June 1999]

The EPA has been good in working with her, looking into declaring them abandoned tanks; the cost of cleaning up contamination would wipe her out. "I would," she says, "pack up my bags and leave."

Andrea wanted to run a trading post because she wanted to get back to the desert, and because she felt trading was a link with her family's past.

I really pride myself on my family—my grandfather, my father, myself, on our honesty and straightforwardness and our fairness with the people that we work with. That's very important to me. . . . When my grandfather opened, he would sell flour—it was a business decision—but he sold flour at cost. So he had flour, the cheapest flour in town because he wasn't making a penny out of it. And then my father always sold flour at cost, and I sell flour at what I paid for it—I don't make a penny on flour. And it's just

little things like that that I take a lot of pride in. It's sort of a family tradition selling low price. . . .

I think it's a community institution. It is more than—almost more than
a business. Yes, it's me they come to when someone in the family dies, and
they need money to bury them, or someone was ill and they need to pay a
medicine man for a ceremony, which is kind of nice. I'm more than a shop-
keeper. [Andrea Ashcroft, interview with the author, June 1999]

But trading posts, though they continue, are a special niche, an
anachronism. In some communities they are necessary, if small, businesses
catering almost exclusively to the community. Each trader meets special
challenges and changes, retains some of the trader traditions, bends some
of the others, though most of them usually work with and focus on the
crafts. Andrea remarked of the Foutz trading family, related to her own,
"It's the girls who are carrying on the store, the daughters, and the sons are
really backing out of it." In many, if not most, communities, traders also
cater to tourists—Cameron, on the route to the Grand Canyon, is one example. The Hubbell Trading Post is another, rather special, example.
Owned by the National Park Service, Hubbell's stands as a historical
monument to trading on the Navajo Reservation, preserving the architecture and furnishings of a period that changed little between 1900 and
1940. But Hubbell's also continues as a working trading post, selling groceries, buying rugs and baskets, jewelry and pottery, while tourists wander
round the buildings and examine, and buy, the crafts.

Other traders continue to run stores in outback communities, like Red
Rock (Jed Foutz), Borrego Pass (run by the Moores), or in the border com-
munities of Sanders (Bruce and Virginia Burnham), or Waterflow (the
Manning family). Community needs and trading traditions still go hand
in hand. Hank and Victoria Blair run Totso Trading Post, in Lukachukai.
Hank Blair's parents, Brad and Carolyn Blair, had come to the Southwest
from the east, their last store the successful operation at Kayenta Trading
Post. Hank grew up on the reservation, left as a young man to serve in
Vietnam and to try various other types of work. Then he came back to
Kayenta to run the trading post for his father, Brad Blair, from about 1976
until 1984, the year after his father died.

In about 1982, Hank and Vicky submitted a proposal for managing
Totso Trading Post, with prepared financial statements and a plan of operations, to the Tribe. The lease went to two other traders who had written a sketchy—even unbusinesslike—proposal on a sheet of paper. They

went bankrupt in fairly short order, as had the previous three or four traders, and in 1984 the Blairs got the lease and began to put the store back on its feet, doing everything themselves.

Totso, like all trading posts before it, is one of the centers in a small community that is not well-off and has little in the way of services. Hank returned to trading because he liked it, because it was never dull, because "I got four kids that are Navajos, and I enjoyed growing up here." The trials of running a trading post are constant and varied. The Blairs manage and fix everything. They live behind the store, and are almost never "off duty." Vicky Blair is from Kayenta, and does the bookkeeping, and much community work. She stays out of buying and selling crafts.

> When [Hank] does business, if he buys a rug, if he buys anything, they are doing that business with a white man. When you do it Navajo to Navajo, because of the clan system, because of the helping system . . . they want you to buy it higher, they want you to sell it to them for less. [Vicky Blair, interview with the author, June 1999]

She says, "Hank is from a trading family, this is what he has done all his life." Elderly women come to the store, "they come in and they say 'shiyaaz', which means my little one . . . and it's because they want something!" Hank goes to their aid. Vicky is more pragmatic: the customers, she says, know this about wives. "They always call the women 'ashkeegi,' 'the ones that get after you'." Totso Trading Post is a source of gifts and contributions for a variety of events. Vicky and Hank put together what she calls a Squaw Dance package: flour, salt, baking powder, sugar, coffee, and potatoes or pop, for the summer sings.

> We donate for graduations, for weddings, for funerals, for Sings and dances, for kids going on trips. If the kids get As on their report cards, [Hank] gives them a dollar. I stand behind him and say, shima—your mother—wants you out here, your grandmother wants you out here [in the store].

Through Vicky the store is tied into all the community's vital needs.

> It's such a small community, and if you learn to work together, it's so much easier. If the bread man forgets to come, if she [the cook for the kitchen at the school] is closed at five and if the bread man comes at five, he'll leave the bread for the boarding school here. . . . If the Arizona food bank comes

and the Chapter house is closed, I let them do the food bank here in front of the store. The need is so great, and when there is not a place for that to happen, they do it at the store. . . . The community health worker, he wants to know who the new babies are, who the girls [the new mothers] are. . . . I tell him, he goes around and visits them. [Vicky Blair, interview with the author, June 1999]

Trading is hard work, but it makes a living. As a younger man, Hank worked in California.

Not very long, but I worked in a machine shop, Douglas Aircraft, worked construction. I think I consider myself to be a people person, and to do this [run a trading post] you kind of sit here and you get to talk to anybody who comes in the door. . . . There are a lot of different responsibilities . . . you don't know whether the water line is going to freeze up or the meat case is going to blow—you've got to love it. [Hank Blair, interview with the author, November 1998]

There is new blood also: the ancient, tiny store at Oljato is run by Evelyn Jenson, born on Black Mesa a few miles south of Kayenta, who had been manager of the bank in Kayenta for several years. Oljato Trading Post, one of the older trading posts in an area that was once one of the more traditional and out of the way reaches of the reservation, is a tiny store. It is a classic trading post, like Hubbell's but different, and in its prime traded with a very traditional and staunchly Navajo community, unique and different, as each community across the Navajo Reservation is different. Evelyn Jensen, though she does not come from Oljato, is from the Bit'ahnii clan, which is strong in the area and gave her an entrée. Her own family raised livestock, and her mother wove.

Maybe it had something to do with my upbringing and going to a trading post. And how romantic I thought it was to have a trading post in some remote area, with a potbelly stove and a blue coffee pot, and just having people come in and visiting and having a cup of coffee. So back in 1991, November of '91, Winona, who is the daughter of Virginia and Ed Smith [traders for decades at Oljato] contacted me and asked me if I would be interested in operating Oljato Trading Post. And before I really thought about it I said "sure!" [Evelyn Jensen, Cline Library interview, February 1998]

The community did not want the trading post to close down. So Evelyn Jensen started with a booming business, giving credit to all who requested it, and serving a local community whose members had called Oljato home for many generations.

> And maybe two years, three years down the line, people would start drifting off and not come back and pay their credit, so in the end, it hurt me. . . . That was a lot of learning on my part there. . . . I still offer credit, but to very few . . . and I have to set a limit; it has to be on a monthly basis.

After eight years, she is still waiting for her lease.

> The lease is just a piece of paper that says you have so many years. . . . You have to have insurance, you have to have a sanitation permit, and all this good stuff. But that's one part of the lease process, you know, that I really don't understand, even though I didn't build this trading post. If I was a new tenant, and if I were to build a trading post, when I leave at the end of my lease, I leave the building and I walk out. [Evelyn Jensen, Cline Library interview, February 1998]

This has always been the case, of course: the land belongs to the Navajo Nation, not to any one person, and new buildings (by U.S. law, anywhere in the U.S.) always belong to the landowner. It has been the reason that many traders were reluctant to rebuild or improve the store, except in cases where they could be certain of a good return on sales, or perhaps after a fire, with insurance money.

Evelyn sells groceries, buys rugs and everything that is locally made— pottery and baskets—and sells the crafts to tourists, of which there are a steady flow. She succeeds in keeping up some of the old trading patterns, donating to local ceremonies.

> That's from the Navajo part, too—they had a lot to do with it because they just kind of expect you to donate, just because you're here as a trader. I know that has happened to me before, too, especially as a Navajo, I think. From here, there's a lot of the To'ahani people, who are like my aunts and cousins, and anytime that there is a ceremony, they expect me to donate.

But Evelyn combines old trader practices with new ones. Oljato is close enough to Kayenta and Monument Valley to be something of an attraction, and Evelyn has put signs up on the highway to promote tourist trade. Although the store is something of a communication center for the Oljato community, Evelyn feels that the role of the old trader is long gone.

> When I came along, I wanted to be everyone's best friend, and try to help everyone—loaning money or loaning this and that. And after a while, you get to know some that you shouldn't trust very much. You have to be a little bit mean, and you have to say no to certain things, because once you loan a person some money, the word will go around.

She feels a change in Navajo culture, too. She loves to ride, and sees older men and women riding around, herding sheep or just going about, a sight that is getting rare anywhere else on the reservation.

> This is the last of them—the grandmothers and grandfathers, the grassroots people. This is why I consider myself lucky to be amongst them, because once they're gone, that's it. And it's so sad, maybe to see a grandmother out there that maybe their grandkids are not being very nice to them, or being rude to them. It makes you want to cry. Sometimes you have older men—in their seventies, their late seventies—they come into the trading post and they exchange jokes. You know how they grab each other. You don't see that anymore. . . . It's an era that is fast going, and I'm just glad to be a part of it, I guess, a very small part of it. [Evelyn Jensen, Cline Library interview, February 1998]

Many traders, taking one strand of the trader bundle of activities, chose to deal specifically in arts and crafts. They work with weavers and silversmiths, basket makers and potters, selling the products of the artisans in a competitive market. Bruce and Virginia Burnham took this direction. Bruce, after years of working at trading posts, now has two stores near Sanders, just off the reservation. One store, Painted Hills, is "100 percent trading post" and the other, R. B. Burnham's, is a gallery selling arts and crafts. "Somewhere back down the line I kind of lost focus on the profit motive and just started relaxing." He began to leave the concerns of the store behind and do what was most interesting and rewarding—"not financially rewarding necessarily but just gratifying"—working with weavers.

> Those that I deal with, I have a very long-term relationship with. I told

my wife one time, it's almost like a romance. I said, I court these gals, and I'm interested in their lives and their families, and everything. [Bruce Burnham, interview with the author, July 1998]

Virginia Burnham, who had for years worked in a trading post managing the cash register and keeping the books at Dinnebito where she met Bruce and then at their own stores, began to make jewelry, first in silver then in gold. She and Bruce opened a jewelry store near Querino Canyon, west of Gallup, and worked with silversmiths—at the height of their operation, forty-five silversmiths worked for them full time. But Bruce felt uncomfortable outside a trading post, and in 1974 he built R. B. Burnham's, a mile off I-40, selling goods and buying and selling crafts. Virginia bought jewelry and baskets from the northern part of the reservation, around Navajo Mountain and Tuba City, and later on also from San Carlos Apache Reservation, while Bruce bought rugs. They began to go on buying and selling trips, and attended shows, at the Gallup Ceremonial, the old Flagstaff powwow, and in Tucson. The shows, the heart of working with arts and crafts, a place to meet people interested in high-quality workmanship and new styles, were important. The Burnhams' children were always "in the business."

From the time we started having kids, I always had a kid under my arm, doing the show. We have pictures of our kids, they're sleeping under a table or on a pile of rugs at a show. . . . We taught them how to count change at a really early age so they can take money for merchandise, make the right change. [Virginia Burnham, interview with the author, January 1999]

Bruce sold carded wool, known as roving, which was being used by weavers everywhere on the reservation since the late 1970s. Weavers would spin this wool into a very even yarn, and rugs woven from it were uniform and fine. In 1984, however, Bruce became a supplier of this wool, obtained from Brown Sheep Wool Company in Nebraska, to other traders, as well as his own weavers. As he pointed out, "Not every household has access to wool anymore, because there's just not enough land to support that many sheep."[3]

After a few years, Bruce found another mill in Germantown, Pennsylvania, that was producing carpet yarn. He worked with them to develop a wool he liked better, reproducing the old, true three-ply

Germantown yarn, good yarn for Navajo weavers. He had it dyed in special colors—the brighter colors of traditional Germantown rugs from the nineteenth century. Burnham's carries other colors, too; Bruce found that some weavers were better spinners, asked them for advice on carding, spinning, and colors, and had some of them spinning the carded wool he bought. By 1998, Bruce had encouraged weavers in a new style of rug, the Burntwater rug. He supplies the wool, to save weavers time, and works closely with a small group of weavers.

> Not a whole lot of them. But the things that I do with the weavers that weave for me almost exclusively is we influence a lot of other weavers. We end up, I think, having a major impact on rugs all over the reservation. . . . We've pretty much made the Burntwater into the rug it is today. We started a revival of the transitional period rug weaving—the chief's blankets and the late classic period. . . . We've made the Newlands outline rug what it is today, the latest rug to be recognized as an area style weaving. [Bruce Burnham, Cline Library interview, July 1998]

Virginia runs the Painted Hills Trading Post a mile away while Bruce runs R. B. Burnham's. She manages the groceries and accounts, and does some pawn. Much of what she does involves credit, trying to help older people with details of social security and managing their money, as well as trying to explain financial dealings to younger people, the way stores and banks work.

> There's still quite a bit [of pawn]. . . . We send a first notice, we call it a first notice, saying that next month your pawn item number such and such, in the amount of [such and such], will be on display, or whatever. Anyway, we give them a notice, and a second or final notice. This is always big and yellow, so you can really see it . . . so that they will know that that pawn is going to be dead. We send that notice to everybody that pawns, so they can come and take it out. This woman came in and she was so outraged about how much interest we were charging her, that we were crooks, you know, everything about bad traders. . . . She hadn't paid anything on it for about seven months that we'd had it here. There are some—most of these young people—they don't understand the interest. I always tell them, well, go to the bank and borrow some money. . . . With merchandise that they get, groceries and things like that, we don't charge them interest on anything that they buy on account. We put it on

account for thirty days. [Virginia Burnham, interview with the author, January 1999]

Virginia clearly has a good business head, managing big city arts and crafts dealers, to whom she and Bruce have in the past sold some of their products. In fact, Virginia's mother, a Navajo, was a trader who together with her sister and her sister's husband built and ran a small trading post, right next to their mother's house. Lorenzo Hubbell helped them start out, and they paid him in installments. Later on, when Virginia and her brother and sisters were small, Virginia's mother sold goods out of her own house. She carried basic staples, coffee, sugar, cans, flour. Every now and then, she would get a ride down to Ganado, and buy goods from Lorenzo Hubbell, bringing them back home to trade. Virginia likes the life.

> We've really enjoyed, I have, I know Bruce has, trading post life. We got to talking about that one day, Bruce saying he was fourth generation Indian trader, and I said I was the first trader in my family. And then it just hit, you know, that my mother had been trading, even today she still does: baskets, wedding baskets from people who've made baskets, for meat. [Virginia Burnham, interview with the author, January 1999]

Many other traders were involved in the craft enterprise. Rug designs have long been known by the names of trading post communities, but the ownership and innovation of designs combined with the weavers' creativity and choice make rug styles extraordinarily fluid and the range of traditional motifs has always been broad. Silver and baskets, too, reflect various influences and cater to special markets, and Navajo pottery has seen a recent flowering. Traders continue to play a role in the art market, though the choice of whom to deal with is now much greater for Navajo artisans, and not restricted to traders. Indeed, traders, as Ed Foutz pointed out a few pages ago, is a loose term, and may mean "dealer" more than anything else.

The picture of trading blurs into the large businesses of dealing arts and crafts. This is not new—the UITA was created for the express purpose of hallmarking authentic Indian handwork, particularly in the case of look-alike jewelry. Dealing in arts and crafts was a different kind of business to trading, requiring something of an eye for workmanship, a nose for the aesthetics of the time, and a head for business. In this field, Herman Schweitzer is a legendary figure, buyer in the 1920s and 1930s for the Fred

Harvey Company, itself a legendary name in travel, in opening up the west to tourism. There were other wholesalers. John W. Kennedy, for example, was the son of a trader who went under in the depression and later moved into the oil business and established Kennedy Oil. John W. grew up in trading posts, worked for C. G. Wallace at Zuni from 1943 to 1947, and had a wholesale house in Gallup—Gallup Indian Trading Company—from 1952 until 1979, buying rugs from virtually every trader on the reservation. He employed a sales force of ten, who concentrated on the west, including Chicago, New York City, and, to a much smaller extent, the east. The wholesale dealers pushed the traders who in turn influenced the weaver or the silversmith.[4]

> You try to improve the product and come up with innovations that will help the producer better his [sic] situation. That was the main play, because you can always buy rugs, but how many good rugs can you buy? [John W. Kennedy, John D. Kennedy, Cline Library interview, December 1998]

Traders did not, on the whole, seek out or enjoy working with tourists. According to John W. Kennedy, most traders ran "maw and paw operations" taking in pawn, working with sheep and wool, selling rugs or silver or pawn only if the rare visitor came in a moment of calm. Carolyn Blair, trading with Brad Blair first at Red Mesa and then at Kayenta Trading Post, said if there was a tourist, they were lost. This was no longer quite the case after 1966 when the road across the reservation was paved and Kayenta, near Monument Valley, saw more visitors than most Navajo communities. But the "country traders" (as the bigger concerns referred to them) attended to Navajos. The wholesalers focused on buying and selling crafts. They carried big inventories, went to big wholesale shows in Los Angeles, Dallas, and Denver, and sold large quantities. Kennedy bought from traders, but they also sought out Indian craftspeople, by word of mouth and by radio, and traded with them, giving them a trade slip for merchandise in the store until the new regulations forbade it at which point he paid cash. He hired silversmiths to work in the building as well: Zuni inlay cutters, Navajo silversmiths, and people whose work was to polish the silver. He advanced silver and turquoise to smiths who worked on their own, taking the finished piece for a small payment. At the height of the firm's business, he employed about forty people all told, as salespeople or artisans.[5]

Wholesalers catered to the demand for Native American crafts, especially to collectors. As the demand exploded in the 1970s, so did the number of Gallup wholesalers, from around twelve to as many as four hundred. M. L. Woodard had been director of UITA during the 1930s when its main goal was to ensure quality and authenticity of Indian crafts. Tom Woodard, his son, learning about the quality of Navajo crafts from boy-hood, worked as a dealer in Tucson, Gallup, and, subsequently, Santa Fe between 1960 to 1986.

> Vogue magazine came out, and there was a gal wearing a squash blossom necklace . . . and I bet there hadn't been two squash blossom necklaces sold in New York in the preceding ten years. But they ordered ten of them. . . . Pretty soon it just went wild. It was way over what we in the business could control. [Tom Woodard, Cline Library interview, December 1998]

At the same time the copycat jewelry business exploded as well, (and to a smaller extent, weavings) and in recent years an influx of foreign copies—frequently sold as authentic—brought the business down. Kennedy remarked that some Gallup wholesalers that were doing $6 million a year are now doing $1.5 million, and no one knows if they are buying the real thing or not.

Authentication of Indian crafts had been the primary reason for the cre-ation of the UITA in 1931, as a nonprofit organization that battled compe-tition from machine-produced jewelry copying Indian designs. The UITA's concern was the arts and crafts market and the livelihood of Navajos—and other Indian craftspeople—and traders. During World War II, at a time when precious metals were not available, it obtained a commitment from the government to obtain a certain amount of silver for Navajo smiths, in recognition (after the Meriam Report of 1928) of their need for income.

However, after the war, UITA found that it was handling quantities of precious metal, in a business that was now inappropriate for a nonprofit organization. It changed its focus from arts and crafts, and became an or-ganization assisting the reservation traders with information, as well as providing a social event at the annual meeting. When the traders came under attack by the DNA, UITA was a focal point for disseminating information, legal assistance, and action. With that crisis past, UITA tried to reshape itself to focus on modern business, and in 1979 it took the name Indian Country Business Association. But the focus was less clear, the need less pressing. Membership slowly decreased, from 90 in 1975 to 38 in 1981. Although the twenty-five-year leases came to an end around 1980, the Tribe provided no resolution for new leases. Although George Vlassis, Tribal Counsel, from time to time gave the Association updates, these amounted to nothing more than acknowledging that the situation was under review. The Association made little headway, and shied away from the possible publicity it thought would attend any attempt to raise the issues. By 1985, as trading posts continued to close, and the end of trading—as most traders had known it—was evident, the board of directors began to talk about dissolution of UITA. At the end of 1997, the Association dispensed funds in a series of gifts for projects and scholarships—to Northern Arizona University Foundation, to the Farmington Museum, and to other universities and museums—and it seems likely that when these projects are done the organization may be dissolved.

A few Navajo artisans are beginning to set up for themselves. Raymond C. Yazzie, a creator of silver and lapidarian jewelry, and his wife Colina, a young Navajo entrepreneur and businesswoman, own and manage Yazzie's Indian Art in Gallup.

> I was brought in, asked to work with Joe Tanner. . . . Joe Tanner, I guess, always worked with my family. . . . Those years that I spent with him, I think I've probably made some of my best pieces in those days. [Raymond Yazzie, Cline Library interview, January 2000]

Colina Yazzie started their business—Raymond says "my wife is the one that really put the store together the way it needs to be"—a store that sells jewelry of several artists, as well as Raymond. When they began, they called the store Yazzie Trading Company.

> I don't really have an opinion on how the traders dealt because I really didn't deal with them, but I do know that the Navajos have . . . hard feelings toward traders and that was the reason why we changed our name. [Colina Yazzie, Cline Library interview, January 2000]

Raymond grew up dealing with traders, and had slightly different thoughts.

> I guess when you've dealt with trading, that kind of sticks with you, just because of the personality that they had, or the kindness that they had. . . . To me there was a lot of goodness in them, the way I think about them, because it fed a lot of families, no matter what they were doing. [Raymond C. Yazzie, Cline Library interview, January 2000]

Perhaps this is an illustration, in one modern family, of the complexities of Navajo-trader relations.

Reservation traders are shifting toward dealing. In some areas, they continue to make changes in craft production. For example, Jed Foutz is trying to persuade Shonto weavers to make different kinds of rugs, more finely woven and with more variety of design, rather than the soft, striped saddle blankets that for so long have been made in the area. The trader approach is that it is up to the trader to increase the value of weavings, to raise the standards—as well as the standard of living—up to those derived from the current appreciation of Indian crafts linked with museums and collectors. This approach encourages Navajo weavers to produce more rugs that cater to this taste—that will sell for more and ultimately make more money for the weaver and her family. Weavers accept this challenge. The saddle blanket has been, in fact, one of the "traditional" weavings of the Shonto/Inscription House area, but few dealers appreciate them. Navajo saddle blankets, often quickly woven, thick and soft (the word *diyog* means shaggy or fluffy, and *diyogi* is a Navajo blanket) and inexpensive, were once sought after by cowboys and others who rode for precisely that purpose—to put under the saddle (they often doubled as a sleeping blanket). They do not meet the current interest in finer Navajo weaving, and their day is perhaps over.

Trading days are also over. In 1990, after twenty-five years of trading there, Elijah Blair walked out of Dinnebito Trading Post—it was in the Hopi-Navajo disputed area, and consequently had even more problems than most stores—and closed the door. The name "trader" will persist for reasons of history, charm, the appeal of earlier (often little understood) times, but the word has true resonance only for Navajos, who know the meaning and the history of the trading post, and traders. Now, with traders more often functioning as art dealers, the trading post era is over. Bruce Burnham summed it up:

> Someone referred to me as a mustang the other day, and I said, "Well, what do you mean?" And he said, "Well, you're a dying breed." We truly are. And we're just one of many, many businesses in the United Sates that have made the crossover into the computer age and not survived it. It was more pronounced for us because we went from seeing our customers riding in a wagon to data processing in forty years. That's a tremendous change. [Bruce Burnham, Cline Library interview, July 17, 1998]

11

⅃·L

A FEW FINAL WORDS

We can no longer think of societies as isolated and self-maintaining systems. Nor can we imagine cultures as integrated totalities in which each part contributes to the maintenance of an organized, autonomous, and enduring whole. There are only cultural sets of practices and ideas, put into play by determinate human actors under determinate circumstances.
Eric Wolf, 1982: Europe and the People without History, *390–91*

Change is a fact of life, often creeping up on us unexpectedly and with unpredictable results. It almost always causes us to regret the past. So it was with the Navajo trading posts and the traders. Despite the fact that a few trading posts still thrive, the trading post era is over. It's history. The many stores that call themselves trading posts—located in urban environments, utterly unlike their historic predecessors, or on paved highways on the reservation that bring a completely different clientele through the doors—are not true trading posts. The label continues, evidence of the place of trading posts in the imagination, as well as their connection to traditions of Navajo (and Hopi, Pueblo, Ute, and Apache) life and crafts.

I've tried to present the description of trading posts through the words and memories of people from two trading generations, drawing on interviews done by oral historians from Northern Arizona University. I draw, too, on my own interviews of traders, done over twenty-one years: I've been present at the very end of an interesting American institution. I'm also telling a story: how trading was radically changed in 1972—a radical time in America—what happened and why, and the role the UITA played in the drama. This story includes lawyers who came out to the reservation in the activist sixties, and Navajos who were trying to make changes in their own society during this time, and I've been able to interview them, too.

I see the story a little differently than any of those I interviewed. My view isn't the same as that of DNA attorneys and Navajo activists, whose convictions and ideals I admire and respect, nor does it quite match the traders' own ideas of their business. I've seen trading from the inside, though I think I have a special view—a view from trader informants who, I suspect, are not typical of their profession. Their insights are too thoughtful, too philosophical, and in all cases they speak more Navajo than their peers. Traders weren't all alike (neither were DNA lawyers, as one of my DNA informants assured me). The trader who most impressed me early on, Madeline Cameron, who traded at Navajo Mountain Trading Post until the early 1980s, would not talk to me about trading at all, though she refused most delicately and indirectly. Her silence on the topic was instructive. Madeline merely took me into her house; she gave me a cup of coffee and showed me some small, ancient pieces of pottery found near the store, let me sit around, and told me about the cottonwood trees (Zane Grey, she said, wrote about them) while a Navajo child played on the floor of her living room, watched by his mother who was eating her lunch. Obviously, these were the traders I thought about while I wrote this book.

There are other kinds of traders, less interested in Navajo life. I have described the kind of challenge that traders frequently had to deal with, a challenge of wit but also (especially but not solely to male traders) of physical and personal confrontation. I don't think this is in itself unusual in any situation in which one is a cultural outsider, but I am sure that some traders enjoyed—perhaps initiated—the threat of violence, and responded in kind.

I have described the trading post exchanges, the way credit and pawn played a role and money didn't. I've described dealings with checks, as if they were commodities, and the attempt of traders to insist that Navajos use them to pay bills. Traders were old-fashioned businesspeople from their own world, who believed in entrepreneurship, in the benefits of profit, and in hard work, and (usually but not always) in making money. They insisted on the payment of their bills, not so much at the expense of Navajos, but because, in their view, Navajos liked and wanted the goods traders brought and did not completely understand the capitalist exchange system, and needed to be guided in what they bought and how they paid for it.

The basic rule of exchange is that you exchange one thing of value for another of similar value. In trade across cultures, a far more frequent aspect of the world economy for far longer than you might realize, the difficulty lies in trying to figure out what the exchange value is, because very different rules of worth apply in each group. The rules for barter also differ: is it set fast by rules? Is it surrounded with etiquette and ceremony, by religious systems that control both behavior and objects? Is it a game of wit and cunning, in which haggling over the exchange is permitted, even encouraged, or is this sort of behavior not only frowned on but forbidden? In addition, there are constantly shifting alliances, large and small corporate entities, predominant economies and the informal economies of small markets, peddling, exchanges of unassailable things. People have to learn not only a new language, the tones of voice and the kinds of taboos that exist, but the nature of the exchange, and new meanings—not only *of* the goods, but of the relationships that surround them, the way people treat each other, and the way work—labor—fits into, or changes, the picture. They need also to recognize their own cultural trading practices. Behind all these concrete details lie politics: who rules, and what is the nature of their laws and their enforcement of them?

As the traders I know tell it, they thought the Navajo economic system was different from their own, and they did their best to integrate the two systems. Trading, of course, changed through time, also: at the beginning it was not the same as it was at the end. And in the century and a half of trading there were traders who were dishonest, or greedy, who used cross-cultural misunderstanding to increase their own profits—and did not care about their customers at all. Traders reflected both their own culture and their own individual personality. Navajos, too, were individuals of all varieties, sharing aspects of Navajo culture but acting out their own particular understanding of its integration with another culture.

The trader-weaver interaction went to the heart of this particular economic relationship. Traders changed Navajo weaving. From early times, they provided (or even insisted on) notions of design and of selling that came from a specific Anglo-American cultural context: aesthetic ideas, economic ideas, ideas about Navajos and other Indian people, as well as the practical aspects of business, of museums and collecting, of moving goods by trains and trucks, of value in dollars and cents. Not only did traders—however little they might really know about either weaving or business—influence aesthetics and weaving standards, they also altered Navajo means of subsistence, altered the relationship of weavers and rugs, subtly as well as in obvious ways. Navajos had always been known for their weaving from earliest times—Anglo-Americans were not the first traders for Navajo blankets. They were, however, harbingers of a different economic system and new ways of making a living, bringing in new goods, encouraging the labor of weavers and silversmiths, of basket makers and potters, intensifying specialization and the Navajo craft complex.

However strongly traders influenced Navajo economics, they seem never to have entirely restructured it, shifting but not completely changing the Navajo context of kin and clan and local connections. Those traders who thought about economics in the abstract thought they had, for a century or more, brought capitalism to the reservation. They thought of themselves, as Lije Blair, Bruce Burnham, and Hank Blair do, as middlemen between two economic systems, their own entrepreneurial, capitalist system, of which they were proud, and the Navajo system as they recognized it, of obligations, cultural networks, and kinship ties, which they respected. For example, traders did not challenge the role of medicine men, and systematically incorporated ceremonial needs and economies into the trading exchange despite BIA rules. In certain areas, trading posts stocked (and continue to stock) peyote ritual items for the Native American Church ceremonies; in other areas, they keep the right kind of buckskin, and Navajo baskets, for sings. When the ceremonies are over, they will readily buy back the items: a skin, a basket, may change hands over and over.

Where once Navajo people had made items—silver, rugs—as part of their annual cycle, traders encouraged a full-time craft occupation. By the end of the twentieth century, this occupation provided a cash income (and, for certain weavers, a very good income). It was an enterprise for the weaver that involved timesaving innovations, the imposition of tax, costs, and expenses, and other aspects of the dominant economy. Yet, it was not a factory line; it was not outside the community; and it was both wholly Navajo and entirely cross-cultural.

Over and under the Navajo-Anglo exchange lay the institutions that determined the rules of the trade. The arm of the federal government that most affected trading was, of course, the Bureau of Indian Affairs, itself a changing organization, staffed by changing people, who reflected not only the times they lived in, but the role and position of the U.S. government, the final arbiter. The Navajo tribal government was another integral part of trading, but with a vital difference: it could not set the rules. Trading between these two cultures was ultimately regulated in law only by the federal government. The Navajo Nation, however, was at this time a government growing in strength and vision. It, too, reflected movements in the larger American society, of which it was—despite its important differences, its distinct sovereign existence—a part. The actions of the Johnson administration created a new office, the Office of Economic Affairs (OEO), and stimulated an economic change of major proportions. On the Navajo Reservation OEO funneled funds through the Office of Navajo Economic Affairs (ONEO), for programs and ultimately for paychecks in the pockets of Navajos. It was OEO that enabled the creation by Ted Mitchell of the Dine Beiina Na Agaditahe, the DNA organization (although unique to the Navajo Reservation, there were many other poverty law programs created across the country at this time, all funded by OEO). The attorneys staffing DNA were the individuals putting into action radical ideas that swept the larger nation. Lastly, the FTC was another arm of the federal government, though it played a small role here, wheeled on by the DNA and the BIA to provide the machinery and staff for an investigation (which had really already been done) and the institutional script for a political drama, held in full media spotlight on the Navajo Reservation.

The law is a tool, and though justice is often depicted as blind, legal argument is not. The arguments in law always reflect a set of ideas specific to the time, place, and culture, and (like all the organizations and their staffs mentioned above) change with changing times. In the interviews of ex-DNA attorneys, I have been impressed with their probity, and most of all with their insistence on treating Navajos, whose society most of them came to know, as if culture made no difference. I was puzzled by their lack of insight into trading. But this is naive of me: in fighting cases, it is necessary to hold a particular, often sharply black-and-white, view that accords with the goal of a cause and the case in question. If a broader view creeps in, how, in honesty, can a lawyer argue with conviction and win?

As an anthropologist, I feel my role is to understand all sides and to unpack the way in which they interact; but I'm not unbiased here. I've taken the traders' side, to a very large extent—I've tried to present their point of view through their own words—the side opposite the lawyers. I have been unfair to the lawyers, perhaps, after their willingness to be interviewed and the clarity of their details, but I, too, have a specific argument.

Someone else will have to tell their side of the story. The efforts of legal, federal, and governmental action to change the trading post "system" did not do away with corruption, nor turn bad traders into good (though it may have blocked some bad practices). It did not turn trading posts into supermarkets (though many were bought by chain convenience stores—with even higher prices), but that was not the intention of the various bodies that tackled traders.

The way the changes were brought to trading posts was, however, outlined by lawyers, not economists or businesspeople from another field (or members of any other profession) and it might be fair to point out that the DNA lawyers knew as little about business as traders knew about law. They seemed to have a predisposition to dislike trade and business in general, but perhaps it was in the hope of improving the economics of the system in which they lived. Their actions against traders, however, seem to me to hint at a kind of class distinction—Ivy League takes on the Wild West. I don't think they thought this; it seems a shadow that lies behind their actions. Traders were conservative, blunt—they were rather like the saddle blankets I described in the last chapter, rugged, practical, and indigenous. Perhaps the lawyers could be compared to Teec Nos Pos rugs, which echo extraordinarily fine and complex patterns derived from Oriental rugs.

The crisis seemed to lie in what, exactly, these bodies thought trading posts *ought* to be doing and how, ideas that had a great deal to do with what outsiders might understand about Indian, specifically Navajo, life, and what they knew or thought about economics. To further add to the confusion, trading posts had also changed. They began as an institution introducing new goods and a new economy; moved into a phase in which they solidly backed a traditional Navajo lifestyle and even managed Navajos' purchasing behavior in order to make sure that they did *not* buy more than they could afford; and finally became (in some cases were driven into) a competitive entrepreneurial operation that sold Navajo customers whatever they wanted and tried to minimize the risk in doing this. Capitalism, in other words, was changing, too, from smaller to larger operations. At every stage, traders were regulated, as were other businesses. In the case of trading posts, the constant theme was to ensure that, in a cross-cultural situation, fair financial exchanges (as defined by the dominant culture) were maintained.

But what was fair? By Navajo standards, individuals should share all goods—including cash—until there were none left. In trader economics,

an entrepreneurial social system should fit into the Navajo communal social system, and should seek creative ways to bring Navajos enough wealth
that they could afford trader goods. In activist ideals, Navajos should have
an ensured income (through social security and other federal programs)
that would allow them to remain on the reservation, continuing traditional life if they wished (but an inactive one), at the same time engaging
in modern practices of cash economics and the bureaucratic formalities of
welfare and credit, and using loans as a last resort.

Both traders and activists were encouraging assimilation to Anglo-
American life, but on different terms. Young Navajos tried out their own
ideas, helped by ONEO funding for a while. The current direction of
Navajo economics seems to lie in extracting tribute at the tribal government level from money-making concerns, and in a sort of shadow economy of peddlers and individuals selling a variety of small items (food,
clothes) at the community level; Navajo-owned, entrepreneurial businesses still struggle to exist on the reservation.

Trading began and evolved as a cross-cultural exchange. Traders, both
newcomers and old-timers, were united by the economics and traditions
of Navajo families and by the economics and traditions of trading.
Though they acted as rugged individualists, they did, in fact, comprise a
"system"—though not precisely that described by critics—rooted in the
barter of different goods that had grown up over a century. They were
bound by two different kinds of rules, those of the Navajo community in
which they worked, and those of their own society. The weakest of these
rules were the BIA regulations. Traders believed in free enterprise, and an
individual, often libertarian, freedom, and disliked all constraints. The
strongest rules they submitted to were the values and principles of trade—
of not giving something for nothing—and the idea that making a profit
was fair. They worked in a particular social situation that was half Navajo
and half Anglo-American. Traders were as caught up in credit and debit
as their customers, but it was a system they believed in and lived by.

Their customers had an entirely different set of economic beliefs and
practices, one that depended on a culturally enforced sharing of labor and
resources (including cash money). Navajo individuals could not get out of
this network of obligations and cooperation, any more than traders could
escape the financial rules of their society. Navajo communities did their
best to engulf the traders in as much of their own network as they could.
It did not really make a difference what the trader was like (as we've seen,
Navajos defined a good trader as one they knew, and did not bother to

define a bad trader). Navajos wanted them all to practice specific acts of giving, Navajo-style, while also carrying out their Anglo roles of bringing in services, jobs, wages, post offices, taking care of problems (of health, or with rules from outside), and of introducing and explaining new things. Traders, of course, needed to carry out their business according to Anglo-American culture, and they, in turn, tried to inculcate Navajos in its economic methods. The result was a wobbly amalgamation of practices from each society, and it will not be surprising that the dominant society's practices predominated.

Most traders, whether they recognized the Navajo construction of trading post practices or not, knew their community well, and acknowledged and, to different extents, bowed to its pressures. There were those who did not, who broke the tacit Navajo rules by which trading was done (and there were also wholesalers and other related businesses off the reservation, which were entirely different concerns run by entirely separate pressures, however tied into trading they might have been). A bad trader—bad, that is, measured by how little he or she carried out the Navajo expectations of trading—could rarely be influenced or changed by the community, and no other trader could (or would try to) interfere. Violence and unpleasant exchanges, though these have always occurred in trading, appear to cluster around traders who do not keep to the cross-cultural norms that had been worked out over a century. Force made little difference to this sort of trader, but sometimes, subtle means had an affect. Bad traders had a hard time keeping their trading post assistants; the community, for whom paying bills was a form of loyalty, had more outstanding debts; there might be more theft in the store, more drunks, and more weapons around the counter or the trader's office. But the community needed the store too much to abandon it altogether.

All this, of course, marked the trading post exchange up until the end of the 1960s. By the 1970s, hard cash coming to the reservation made a sea change in trading. As Evelyn Jensen put it, "It seemed to me that there was a different set of traders, they had different values; it was more like they were after making money." The picture is more complex: Navajos were also more interested in money, bowing to outside pressures to change their way of life, and everyone was more interested in Navajo arts. Most important of all, Navajos began to own vehicles. Bruce Burnham said, "You wouldn't think a set of car keys would make that much difference." For the first time, traders had real competition with stores in border towns, for goods, services, and pawn. Customers could not be taken for granted, and a trading post could no longer count on being the sole, most convenient, supplier. Nor could they count on their bills being paid. Traders, caught up in their own commercial values, had to woo the Navajo consumer.

The Navajo consumer, however, was beginning to become like all other consumers anywhere in the country. There was a greater mix of customer preferences, from those who kept traditional lifestyles and values to younger Navajos whose shopping habits were similar to those of a shopper in, say, Phoenix or Albuquerque. "Progressive" traders went self-service, stocked a greater variety, put in refrigerators for meat and pop, gave more credit, pawned more items, cashed checks, and even, in one or two cases, went into partnership with auto dealers to help Navajos get vehicles. Much later they put in soda-dispensing machines and video games, and rented videos. Navajos demanded to be treated just the same as everyone else—being Navajo should make no difference either to the goods they were sold or to the respect due to a customer—and they were backed by the DNA. Yet the resistance of Navajos to some of the ideas of the larger economy continued. This resistance was illustrated by the words used by older Navajos, *bithatso*, to be stingy and selfish, and *bina'adlo'*, to cheat. Making a profit made traders both *bithatso* and *bina'adlo'* in Navajo eyes: it was un-Navajo and traders, living in Navajo communities, seemed to be submitting themselves to Navajo rules. Younger Navajos, fighting for civil rights in the company of many of their non-Navajo peers, took up current ideas about monopoly capitalism and rights to social assistance, some of which matched the Navajo ideals of shared resources and communal cooperation.

Traders, like all American businesses, used profit to pay for services and salaries, including their own, to buy new equipment (like cash registers, refrigerated cases, freezers), and make renovations or put up new buildings. On the reservation such improvements were cautiously done. The trader, having no rights to the land or the buildings, could only recoup large investments by selling the lease, and the contents of the store—but, of course, not the store itself nor the land—to another trader. A trader, like a doctor buying a medical practice, bought (in theory) the goodwill of the customers. Usually outgoing traders stayed to assist, for several months, until friendship and loyalty to the new trader was built up, as Navajos often considered bills as personal responsibilities to a specific individual, which could be abandoned if a newcomer was behind the counter.

The two economic systems, Anglo and Navajo, often clashed. Complaints about traders—and some praises of them—were voiced at the

Tribal Council continually. The BIA agents, changing from decade to decade in both personnel and policies, were in principle, as a regulatory body of Indian trade, supervisors of traders. They, too, as part of the entirely different federal government system (itself forbidden profit in commercial terms), were often wary of private enterprise on a reservation. Agents often recognized a community's needs and the way traders contributed to and worked in the community, despite periodic tension that was always increased by the greater influence of a trader in a community. By the 1950s, the BIA generally was a low-key supervisor of traders, and the Navajo tribe had created its own Trading Committee. But this Committee was unable to play a strong-arm role. We've seen that its one attempt to control traders, in 1953, was put down by the Commissioner for Indian Affairs. As I've mentioned, the U.S. Constitution rules that Congress alone may regulate Indian trade, a responsibility it delegates to the BIA. Like traders, most BIA personnel were unprepared for the reservation politics of the 1960s, and, challenged in court by DNA to regulate traders, unversed in business or accounting practices, they were caught in a crossfire.

DNA lawyers were newcomers, breaking up everybody's patterns of relationships and connecting directly with young Navajos who wanted a new world. DNA staff, Anglos and Navajos alike, following Ted Mitchell, had a deeply negative attitude toward traders, seeing them as dominant and essentially exploitative figures. They believed that traders did not even pay lip service to Navajo culture. They felt strongly that traders were making too much money, sucking Navajos dry and taking their heirloom jewelry, which, many DNA lawyers believed, traders took extreme advantage of in their pawn practices, selling it early and reaping the highest prices in a market now eager for Indian jewelry.

Pawn was a long-entrenched system on the reservation, taken up with swift acceptance by Navajos who had objects valued in both cultures. But the changes of the 1970s made pawn volatile. The ways in which it had always operated—by words, not paper; by need, not value; by trust, not law—were Navajo ways, developed within the Navajo community context, of which the trader was part. Off the reservation, however, places that took pawn (and there were many of them, from respectable trading concerns to hastily created "trading posts" to car dealerships and garages) were not bound, as community traders were, by pressures and actions a community could bring to bear on a trader. DNA attorneys, drawing on their belief that traders were an all-too-powerful system in Navajo society, imposed Anglo lending rules on reservation trading posts—with one exception, that of Paul Biderman's case against Gallup traders.[1]

The DNA lawyers, recognizing that pawn practices were almost always specific to the relations of trader and customer (and not to regulations), used a new Truth in Lending law to control trading by threatening lawsuits for any trader they felt was overstepping the boundaries, whether these related to pawn or not. Navajos responded to the anti-trader fervor. Many acted in good faith or political belief, a few in the hope that goods would be cheaper or bills would be forgotten, others worked off grudges, and many responded to years of patronizing trader attitudes. Both Navajos and DNA attorneys used traders, in part, as political straw figures, symbolic of the larger society that had dominated Indian societies. The 1970s were, in many ways, a turning point in Native American economic and political life.[2]

The DNA lawyers went to work with their own values and principles, their own philosophy of legal assistance for those whose rights appeared to be trampled on. Being well-trained, they used manipulation, media events, and impressions to bring change. They succeeded, though many of them claim that it was Peter MacDonald and, later, the arrival of chain supermarkets onto the reservation that really made the difference. If so, the irony was that in the end it was a bigger business that appears to have accomplished what the regulations and the law did not. By this logic, traders should have been allowed to become larger concerns rather than restricted to small ones. Change, created by the pressures, demands, and subsequent lawsuits, filtered unevenly from one corner of society to another, like water in an old irrigation system, blocked by weeds in one area, flushing out underbrush in another, constantly flooding over or running dry.

The cessation of pawn that resulted from the new DNA-drafted regulations and threats of lawsuits was not precisely what DNA lawyers had in mind, nor was it the most beneficial result, at least to many traditional Navajos. The resource gap, now measured in cash income between families, grew wider. Traders were not altruists, nor saints, nor anthropologists, nor social workers; indeed, they prided themselves on not being "do-gooders." They were entrepreneurs: they took a challenging situation, and tried to turn it to good (economic) advantage (and often succeeded), not only for themselves but for all their customers. There were, as traders say, "bad apples" and they believed, but without any empirical evidence, that these would have been weeded out eventually.[3]

Trading posts began to disappear. The kind of central role the trader and the post played, for better or for worse, was exceptional, and the kind of services they brought were not provided anywhere else. Their role began to be taken up by a range of Navajo institutions—the local Chapter, various departments at Window Rock, community schools and school programs—and many non-Navajo organizations, including state social services and missions. A chain supermarket, Bashas', responding to Navajo Nation incentives, came out in the 1980s to agency towns on the reservation. This created more shopping centers somewhat closer to a few communities, but in distant communities shopping could be—and still is—a major undertaking, involving ownership of a vehicle, or claims to someone who has one, money for gas and challenges of the weather and the unpaved roads.

Despite the fact that trading, at least in the view of many traders, had no future and would under any circumstances have slid into its current small niche, the events of 1972 did affect it. Treated as greedy monopolists by the FTC, as minor potentates by the DNA, and as patronizing outsiders by the younger generation of Navajos, traders were everybody's villains. Many felt hurt, and a few were bitter. Some retired, some moved off the reservation; others stayed where they were and continued trading, especially those in the most distant reaches of the reservation.

Attitudes have also changed, on the reservation and around it. Gloria Emerson, radical activist, involved in education on the reservation, observed that life at the beginning of the twenty-first century was different.

> Nowadays, there's so many Navajos who stand up for their rights and are so articulate; they know what their rights are. It seems to me that the racism that I lived with in this country all my life has taken a different turn because of the colleges. . . . San Juan Community College has brought so many of the Navajo and White people together so now there's a whole new different relationship. [Gloria Emerson, interview with the author, February, 2000]

There are many different topics in this story, and I'm going to end with a small, but important, point. Trading post history is Navajo history. A trading post in Pine Springs, an hour from Gallup, burned down around 1975, and the trader, Norman Ashcroft, retired. Much of the old stone building still stood intact, though the rafters of all but the main room had caved in, and wind and snow had wrought havoc with the plaster. Many years later some of the community members thought about restoring it, but a Navajo family had set up their trailer on the grounds shortly after the fire and had lived there ever since. The ruined building, however, was considered part of the community's past. Cecilia Yazzie told her daughter,

> After the last trader left, which was Norman Ashcroft, the trading post was never opened again. Now the building is just sitting there and some people do not know how precious that building is because our great grandfathers and our fathers and uncles built that building with their own bare hands. It is a historic building. It is a shame to see people doing damage to it instead of trying to preserve it by keeping an eye on it and protecting it. [Cecilia Yazzie, interview with Arlene Tracy, June 1999]

Traders have come and gone. The trading interaction grew and changed shape and altered everyone in the course of 130 years. It did not stand still, and neither did the Navajos nor the larger society, nor the economic systems of either. Navajo society is broad and complex. Colina Yazzie, managing her store in Gallup, said the only time she tries to explain Navajo culture is in very specific situations "where [Anglo-Americans] have questions about what the person was trying to do or say, or the way they were treated."

> Growing up at the time that I did, I'm able to understand the more modern ways of life. And then at the same time, I also remember the traditional ways of life. So there are two. A person may—I've known of friends and relatives who have taken more traditional ways of life, therefore their ways are different, in approaching who they talk to, who they deal with. And there are some that are very modern ways of life, and they also have their ways of dealing with the public and people that they meet. So that's kind of a two-party thing, where it's one or the other or both. It's hard to describe. [Colina Yazzie, Cline Library interview, January 2000]

I'm going to let the traders have the last word. Jack Lee, who had traded with both Hopis and Navajos at L and A Trading Post in Keams Canyon for thirty years, said, "It's over, and I'm glad. I'm glad that it is. It was hard to leave—some of those old families that we traded with, all the while we were there"—"They're all dead, too," his wife Evelyn reminded him—"They're all dead, too, but when we pulled out of that canyon, they stood there and just cried like babies." And Evelyn added "You know, there's a cycle for everything, and the day of the trading post is over." (Jack and Evelyn [Sammie] Lee, Cline Library interview, August 1998.)

◢·◣

NOTES

Chapter 1

1. Frank McNitt, 1962: *The Indian Traders*, vii.

2. Joseph Schmedding, 1951: *Cowboy and Indian Trader*. Frances Gillmor and Louisa Wade Wetherill, 1952: *Traders to the Navajos: The Wetherills of Kayenta*. Elizabeth Compton Hegemann, 1963: *Navaho Trading Days*. Franc Johnson Newcomb, 1966: *Navaho Neighbors*.

3. William Y. Adams, 1963: *Shonto: A Study of the Role of the Trader in a Modern Navaho Community*. Navajo, the current spelling, was also spelled Navaho by many authors of earlier decades.

4. There are other more recent accounts of trading post history, usually about specific traders, among them *Thomas Varker Keam: Indian Trader*, by Laura Graves (Oklahoma 1998), an excellent book that describes a remarkable trader, his role, and the general history of that period of trading.

5. In the succeeding pages, long quotes will be followed by the name of the person talking, who did the interview, and the interview date. For a complete list of all the trader interviews, by Cline Library staff and by the author, see pages 264–66.

6. Mormon settlement of Tuba City area: Frank McNitt, *The Indian Traders*, 95n.

7. This was traditional turn-of-the-century dress for men, and can be seen in many photographs, for example, by Ben Wittick, from the 1890s.

Chapter 2

1. There are many excellent books on Navajo life and history, and the following are only a few: Garrick and Roberta Bailey (1986): *A History of the Navajos: The Reservation Years*; Peter Iverson (1981): *The Navajo Nation*; Clyde Kluckhohn and Dorothy Leighton (1974, Rev. ed.): *The Navaho*; Frank McNitt (1972): *Navajo*

249

Wars: Military Campaigns, Slave Raids, and Reprisals; Ruth Underhill (1956): *The Navajos*; Robert W. Young (1978): *A Political History of the Navajo Tribe*.

2. Amsden, 1934: *Navajo Weaving: Its Technic and History*, 126–27. He notes that the early references indicate that Navajo, Navahu, or Nabaho is a region; Bailey and Bailey, 1986:12–14.

3. Bailey and Bailey, in *A History of the Navajos*, 17, suggest that the rise in herding occurred after the Navajos moved out of the Dinétah, which was too rugged for livestock. They argue that the shift from an economy based on farming, hunting and gathering to herding with some agriculture and hunting may have been a result of raids on Navajos, herds being less susceptible than fields to depredation.

4. Charles Amsden, 1934: *Navaho Weaving*, 166.

5. Underhill, *The Navajos*, Chapter 11.

6. Underhill, *The Navajos*, 133–36, 144–63; Bailey and Bailey, *A History of the Navajos*, 28–29.

7. The details that follow come from: Kluckhohn and Leighton, 1946: *The Navaho*, David Aberle, 1966: *The Peyote Religion Among the Navaho*, Young, 1978: *A Political History of the Navajo Tribe*, and Underhill, *The Navajos*.

8. There are male weavers also, and many women silversmiths.

9. Bailey and Bailey, *A History of the Navajos*, 41–47, 77–88.

10. Bailey and Bailey, *A History of the Navajos*, 94–95, 104, 203. They give figures for 1890 of 70 to 95 sheep per person; for 1900, 19 sheep per person.

11. Bailey and Bailey, *A History of the Navajos*, 96–101.

12. Schmeckebier, 1927: *Office of Indian Affairs*, 251.

13. Dorothea Leighton, Clyde Kluckhohn, 1947: *Children of the People*, 73.

14. Interview, from Leighton and Kluckhohn, 1947: *Children of the People*.

15. Bailey and Bailey, *A History of the Navajos*, 169.

16. Kelley and Whiteley, 1989: *Navajoland*, 214–15; Coffey, 1918: *Productive Sheep Husbandry*.

17. Brugge, 1980: *A History of the Chaco Navajo*, 154; Roberts, 1987: *Stokes Carson*, 58–59.

18. Stock reduction, arguably poorly thought out and implemented, was originally supposed to take few or no sheep and other livestock from small herders in poorer family units, and more from Navajos with over a thousand head of sheep, as well as larger numbers of horses and cattle. For fuller history, see Parman, 1976: *The Navajos and the New Deal*, and Boyce, 1974: *When Navajos Had Too Many Sheep*.

19. Bailey and Bailey, *A History of the Navajos*, 184–93; Kelley and Whiteley, *Navajoland*, 101–17; Nash, 1984: "Twentieth-Century United States Government Agencies," 265–68. Bailey and Bailey note that the details of how the Stock Reduction Program was carried out in its later stages are not clear. Kelley and Whiteley suggest that small stock owners suffered more under the reduction program than large stock owners.

20. Bailey and Bailey, *A History of the Navajos*, 244–47. Kelley and Whiteley, *Navajoland*, 212, give the following figures: in 1911 the wool sold was 3,668,463

lbs.; in 1940, 2,446,668 lbs. Average weight of a fleece was 3.1 lbs. in 1891, 5.9 lbs. in 1940, and 7.4 lbs. in 1956 (no figures given for 1911, 1935, 1940).

21. Robert Young, 1961: *Navajo Yearbook 1951–1961*, 539. He notes that some names given to Navajos were unprintable. The use of census numbers for Indian people was introduced in 1928–29 because of naming problems.

22. Edith Kennedy, Cline Library interview, March 1998.

Chapter 3

1. McNitt, *The Indian Traders*, 45–46.

2. Bailey and Bailey, *A History of the Navajos*, 61, note that there was only one licensed on-reservation trader in 1877, Romulo Martinez, and he was still the only on-reservation trader in 1880 thought there were half a dozen off-reservation traders. By 1889, they say there were seven on-reservation posts.

3. Bailey and Bailey, *A History of the Navajos*, 60; they give a complete set of figures for early trade and early trading posts.

4. McNitt, *The Indian Traders*, 200–201.

5. Roberts, *Stokes Carson*, 17. The Fort Defiance posts were run by Reeder, Donovan, and Clark and Aldrich (McNitt, *The Indian Traders*, 66).

6. The source for these names, and for most of the Navajo words used throughout this book, is Robert W. Young and William Morgan, 1980, *The Navajo Language: A Grammar and Colloquial Dictionary*. When I transliterate words heard from Navajo speakers, I have tried to match it to this dictionary and have followed their spelling. There are a few words that I cannot place in this manner; I've given the speaker's translation and spelled it as best I can.

7. Klara B. Kelley, 1983, "Ethnoarchaeology of Navajo Trading Posts."

8. McNitt, *The Indian Traders*, 73–74.

9. For violence against traders, see McNitt, *The Indian Traders*, 324–27; Roberts, *Stokes Carson*, 30–32. Kelley and Whiteley, *Navajoland*, 67, quote from the U.S. Senate *Survey of Conditions of the Indians in the United States* (1937:17967) details of an incident in which a Navajo hogan was burned by a settler who first ordered its Navajo occupants outside. Day's letter to Bursum of September 30, 1924: Day Family Papers, Series III, Box 2.

10. Navajos trading rugs with other Indians: Bailey and Bailey, *A History of the Navajos*, 60; figures of rug sales: Amsden, *Navaho Weaving*, 182.

11. Goods: McNitt, *The Indian Traders*, 75; sheep shears, wood carding equipment: Amsden, *Navaho Weaving*, 32–36.

12. For a discussion of original breeds of sheep, see Roberts, *Stokes Carson*, 52; Ruth Underhill, *The Navajos*, 155–56; Amsden (*Navaho Weaving*, 198–99) was told by Robert Prewitt "a merchant" that he had heard the Treaty sheep were Kentucky Cotswolds; he was also told that the opinion of "a government livestock expert" was that "the sheep were a very mixed lot bought up cheap by the Government, undoubtedly English strains American bred."

13. McNitt, *The Indian Traders*, 75.

14. Leupp, 1910: *The Indian and His Problem*, 188.

15. Caskey, 1994: *Fringe Banking*, 13. He notes that references to loans on personal property are mentioned in biblical times in the Near East. Pawnshops, he suggests, may have been first set up in early times in China; they are currently important throughout Asia.

16. Pawn: Caskey, *Fringe Banking*, 16–17. Navajo pawning: Adair, 1944, *The Navajo and Pueblo Silversmiths*, 109 fn., notes that Lieutenant Bourke's journal of April 25, 1881, comments that Navajos do not like to sell their jewelry, but "when pressed for cash, they will pawn them at the trader's, but the pledge is always redeemed promptly." Problems in Navajo pawn in 1887: McNitt, *The Indian Traders*, 56. Santa Fe pawning: J. S. Candelario Papers, History Library, Museum of New Mexico, Santa Fe.

17. Leupp, *The Indian and His Problem*, 188.

18. Leupp: *The Indian and His Problem*, 188.

19. McNitt, *The Indian Traders*, 250, 283; Day Family Papers, Series IV, Box 2.

20. McNitt, *The Navajo Traders*, 221. Day Family Papers, Series IV, Box 2; McNitt, 252.

21. Day Family Papers, Series III, Box 2, Folder 58. The letters, written between October 1923 and September 1924 when Herman Schweitzer met him in Albuquerque to "conclude the matter," are not clear on whether Sam was doing the drawings himself or having a Navajo Singer make them. Geary sends colored inks and white paint to mix with them, and the inference is that Sam Day is doing the paintings.

22. Day Family Papers, Series I, Box 2. Nils R. A. Hogner at Cross Canyon, August 18, 1920; J. J. Kirk at Kirk Brothers, Gallup, N.Mex., October 17, 1923.

23. Day Family Papers, Series I, Box 2, Folder 18. There is no indication in the papers as to how the situation was resolved.

24. McNitt, *The Indian Traders*, 158–59. Day Family Papers, Series I, Box 2.

25. Numbers of trading posts: Bailey and Bailey, *A History of the Navajos*, 148–49.

26. Bailey and Bailey, *A History of the Navajos*, 162; automobiles: Day Family Papers, Series III, Box 2, Fd. 58.

27. It was not until the late 1950s—in part due to complaints of Navajos that precious grazing was eaten up by traveling herds—that trucks came to the posts and sheep were loaded into them—a time-consuming and labor intensive operation—for delivery to the point of sale.

Chapter 4

1. Grey Mustache said this to John Adair in 1938. Adair, *The Navajo and Pueblo Silversmiths*, 8. Sand-cast silver is made in molds carved in sandstone; for a description, with illustrations, see Adair's book.

2. Jonathan Batkin, 1998: "Tourism is Overrated," 291–92, suggests that the curio dealers' catalogue business played far more of a role than tourism in creating a market of, and for, Indian objects, especially Southwest Pueblo pottery.

3. Neil Harris, 1978: *Museums, Merchandising, and Popular Taste: The Struggle for Influence*, 143–45. Harris discusses the role of museums and expositions in bringing a wide range of information to the public, in particular relating to Native

American culture. The Chicago display was directed by Frederick W. Putnam of the Peabody Museum, and also showed other activities of different Native American groups. The San Diego exposition of 1915 had several exhibits, directed by Edgar L. Hewett, which included Pueblo pottery and Edward Curtis's photographs. See also Rushing, 1955:7–8.

4. W. Jackson Rushing, 1995: *Native American Art and the New York Avant-Garde*, 7–8, gives an interesting description of these displays, and the thinking behind them.

5. See for example Marta Weigle and Barbara A. Babcock, Editors, 1996: *The Great Southwest of the Fred Harvey Company and the Santa Fe Railway*.

6. Trading with Utes: Adair, *The Navajo and Pueblos Silversmiths*, 6–7. Navajo trading dates: W. W. Hill, 1948: "Navajo Trading and Trading Ritual: A Study of Cultural Dynamics."

7. Traders supplying curio dealers: Jonathan Batkin, "Tourism is Overrated."

8. McNitt, *The Indian Traders*, 200–222.

9. McNitt, *The Indian Traders*, for Hubbell and Cotton, 222; for Hubbell discouraging Germantown yarn, 209.

10. McNitt, *The Indian Traders*, 218.

11. McNitt, *The Indian Traders*, 252–57; quote from Moore's catalogue, 225.

12. Bloomfield and Davies: McNitt, *The Indian Traders*, 259–61; Shiprock fair: Amsden, *Navaho Weaving*, 196.

13. Navajos used "teasels" or dried heads of stiff plants to card with; James, 1914: *Indian Blankets and their Makers*, 109; see also illustration in Amsden, *Navaho Weaving*, 32. Amsden notes that Navajos spin with their fingers, 9. Arny, the agent at Fort Defiance in 1875, ordered hand looms and spinning wheels for use by Navajos, but they were ignored (McNitt, *The Indian Traders*, 154).

14. Photographs of the turn-of-the-century frequently show Navajos, especially men, wearing Navajo-woven blankets (women of the period seem to have begun already to wear Pendleton blankets). By 1920, Navajos in snapshots, except for Singers and elders, can be seen in purchased coats or Pendleton shawls. McNitt notes that C. N. Cotton was the exclusive wholesaler of Pendleton robes in the Southwest, as well as of Arbuckle's coffee—the two most basic items of trade, brand names that Navajos recognized and insisted on. Other traders bought these goods from Cotton, at a marked-up price. McNitt, *The Indian Traders*, 222.

15. James, *Indian Blankets and Their Makers*, 20–24. He cites Josiah Gregg, *Commerce of the Prairies* (1844); Lieut. J. H. Simpson, *Report on the Navajo Country* (1852); John Russell Bartlett, *Personal Narrative of Explorations and Incidents in Texas and New Mexico* (1854); and a Smithsonian Report of 1855 by Dr. Letherman.

16. James, *Indian Blankets and Their Makers*, 202–5.

17. Date and development of silversmithing: Adair, *The Navajo and Pueblo Silversmiths*, 3–7, 25–28. Fort Wingate soldiers commission pieces: 25. See especially photographs by Ben Wittick, and others of the late nineteenth century. Smiths do not copy: 72. Tools: Adair lists the tools of a 1938 smith, noting that, at the current prices charged by traders, they were expensive—several hundred dollars, 62–63.

18. Adair, *The Navajo and Pueblo Silversmiths*, 29.

19. Adair, *The Navajo and Pueblo Silversmiths*, 25–26. Between 1898 and 1902, Thoreau, according to McNitt, was a terminal for the Hyde company's wagons in

and out of Chaco Canyon. The trader there was Al Wetherill, Richard Wetherill's brother, with a Hyde employee, W. S. Horabin. Later it was taken over by A. B. McGaffey in partnership with Horabin (McNitt, *The Indian Traders*, 234). Kirk Brothers: the full heading of their notepaper reads: "Wholesalers of Navaho blankets, furs, wool, skins, hides, general merchandise, silverware made to order." (Day Family Papers, Box 2, Fd. 31.)

20. Adair, *The Navajo and Pueblo Silversmiths*, 114.

21. For details of silverwork, see Adair, *The Navajo and Pueblo Silversmiths*, 114; for details of competition and its effects, see Schrader, 1983: *The Indian Arts & Crafts Board*, 248.

22. Byron Harvey III, 1996: "The Fred Harvey Company Collects Indian Art: Selected Remarks," 74, refers to Huckel, Schweitzer, and Colter as a team of "significant tastemakers." Hubbell's sale to Harvey Company: McNitt, *The Indian Traders*, 211.

23. For an excellent and detailed account of the situation surrounding Indian arts and crafts, and the activities of the Indian Arts and Crafts Board, see Robert Schrader, 1983: *The Indian Arts & Crafts Board*, from which this account is drawn, esp. 46–51.

24. For DuPuy's activities, and for traders' discussions and activities to try to get arts and crafts protected: Schrader, *The Indian Arts & Crafts Board*, 24–27. For traders' meeting in Gallup: Amsden, *Navajo Weaving*, 203.

25. United Indian Traders Association, Certificate of Incorporation. UITA Papers, Box 1, Fd. 2.

26. See Schrader, *The Indian Arts & Crafts Board*, 89.

27. Amsden, *Navaho Weaving*, 203. UITA Papers.

28. Schrader, *The Indian Arts & Crafts Board*, 52–57. Schrader notes that "the phrase 'press cut and domed blanks' used by Maisel was an inadequate indication to the public that a machine press was used."

29. Adair, *The Navajo and Pueblo Silversmiths*, 209.

30. W. Jackson Rushing, 1992: "Marketing the Affinity of the Primitive and the Modern," and 1995, *Native American Art and the New York Avant-Garde*, has written extensively about Rene d'Harnoncourt's role in Indian arts and crafts, and the flow of influences between Indian art and modern art. My account draws on his work. On d'Harnoncourt: "Marketing the Affinity of the Primitive and the Modern," 197–98. Adair's survey for the Indian Arts and Crafts Board: Adair, *The Navajo and Pueblo Silversmiths*: Appendix IV, 201–9; on traders and jewelry: Adair, 14.

31. Margery Bedinger, 1973: *Indian Silver: Navajo and Pueblos Jewelers*, 120; Adair *The Navajo and Pueblo Silversmiths*, 201.

32. Rushing, "Marketing the Affinity of the Primitive and the Modern," 191–236; D'Harnoncourt's exhibits in San Francisco and at the Museum of Modern Art: 191, 223.

33. Bedinger, *Indian Silver: Navajo and Pueblo Jewelers*, 120.

Chapter 5

1. Quote from Robert Young, *A Political History of the Navajo Tribe*, 71.

2. Vogt, 1951, *Navajo Veterans*, 1951:158. Evon Z. Vogt Jr., an anthropologists who was himself a young veteran of World War II, interviewed Navajos to see how they

were managing to return to their lives; his monograph describes their experiences before, during, and after service, in their own words. He suggests that for those who already spoke English and knew more about the dominant culture often saw more military action and had a harder time adjusting to regular life in their communities.

3. Vogt, *Navajo Veterans*, 65, 164.

4. Iverson, *The Navajo Nation*, 56–57. See also Robert W. Young, 1968: *The Role of the Navajo in the Southwestern Drama*, 70–74, for mention of: Elizabeth P. Clark, September 10, 1946, Report on the Navajo; A. L. Wathen's economic report of 1947; Navajo Agency's The Navajo Welfare Situation, 1947; and Max Drefkoff's Industrial Program for the Navajo Reservation, 1947. See also: U.S. Bureau of Indian Affairs, 1949: *Report to the Commissioner of Indian Affairs on Navajo Trading*, prepared by Moris S. Burge; U.S. Department of the Interior, 1948: Report of the Navajo—A Long-Range Program of Navajo Rehabilitation (which incorporated Drefkoff's Industrial Program) prepared by J. A. Krug, Secretary of the Interior.

5. Young, *The Role of the Navajo*, 75; Iverson, *The Navajo Nation*, 52–53. Littell was Tribal Attorney for twenty years.

6. According to Elijah Blair, Navajos bred sheep, often, for their color: *dibélichí'í* is a reddish-tan colored sheep; *dibé dootł'izh'i*, a blue sheep; *dibé binishba'i*, a gray sheep. Elijah Blair, personal communication, July 1999.

7. Gallegos Trading Post, in the checkerboard region southwest of Farmington, was built by Richard Simpson, an Englishman, whose first two wives were Navajo. His first wife was a weaver of Yei rugs (see Amsden, *Navaho Weaving*, 106; Roberts, *Stokes Carson*, 25). In the 1940s, Progressive Mercantile, in which Russell's father and uncle were partners, bought Simpson's Gallegos store.

8. Adair, Deuschle, and Barnett, 1988: *The People's Health*. Between 1955 and 1960, Cornell University ran an experimental medical clinic at Many Farms, jointly funded by the university, the Navajo tribe, and the Public Health Service. The project involved Navajo health workers and medicine men, interpreters, and a thoughtful inclusion of Navajo language to try to elicit the right information for diagnosis and for explanations of cures.

9. Education: Aberle, *Peyote Religion Among the Navaho*, 103–4; he notes that at Mexican Springs, near Gallup, 44 percent of parents put all their children in school in contrast to the 4 percent at Aneth. The total number of children enrolled in schools in 1952–53 was 9,659; in 1960–61, it was 15,759 (Iverson, 1981:64). Family approach to work: Louise Lamphere, 1977, *To Run After Them*, 23–25.

10. Individual income: Bailey and Bailey, *A History of the Navajos*, 263; see 244–64 for income details. Young, *The Navajo Year Book 1951–1961*, estimates average *family* income in 1960 as $3,225, including various free goods and services. In 1956, the Tribe received $34.5 million in oil royalties from the Aneth oilfield alone (Iverson, *The Navajo Nation*, 68). For detailed information on the activities of the Navajo Tribe, and development on the reservation of this and later periods, see Iverson, Chapter 3.

11. Bruce Burnham, interview with the author, July 1998.

12. Adams, 1963: *Shonto: A Study of the Role of the Trader in a Modern Navaho Community*, 167–68.

13. Joe Tanner, Cline Library interview, March 1999; J. B. Tanner, Cline Library interview, August 1998. The Navajo Shopping Center was a financial disaster, partly due to J. B. Tanner's drinking (by his own admission), and they folded into bankruptcy barely two years later.

14. William Y. Adams, 1963: *Shonto: A Study of the Role of the Trader in a Modern Navaho Community.*

15. Adams's criticism of traders: *Shonto*, 273; profit and loss of Shonto Trading Post, 184.

16. Changing role of traders: Adams, *Shonto*, 229; anachronistic traders, and quote: 290; criticism of Navajo herding: Adams, 1971, "Navajo Ecology and Economy;" Adams, *Shonto*, 79; Quote on making a living, 73.

17. Scott Preston: Peterson Zah, Cline Library interview, March 1999, Peter Iverson, *The Navajo Nation*, 71–72. For details of the 1950s see Iverson, Chapter 3. Legal reform: Iverson, 76; Major Crimes Act (of 1885) Baca, 1988, "The Legal Status of American Indians," 236–37; the 1950s as a golden age, Young, *A Political History of the Navajo Tribe*, 162, and Iverson, 82, where he states that "The 1950s had indeed witnessed the birth of the Navajo Nation."

18. Southwest Indian Development Inc., 1969: *Traders on the Navajo Reservation: The Economic Bondage of the Navajo.* Window Rock, Ariz.

Chapter 6

1. Kluckhohn and Leighton, *The Navaho*, 51–53, give the Navajo population density at 2.1 per square mile, contrasting with 1.8 in rural areas (Coconino County, Arizona) and 16 in township areas (McKinley County, New Mexico).

2. Population: *Navajo Nation Fax 88: A Statistical Abstract* (1988, 2). Young, *The Navajo Yearbook 1951–1961* gives the figures of 80,364 or 83,116 (322–23). These are the BIA Agency estimates, but population figures were always difficult to obtain, and, of course, many Navajos lived off-reservation. Navajo population was estimated at 8,354 in 1864 (Young, *Navajo Yearbook 1951–1961*, 315). Quote: Myrtle Begay, in Broderick H. Johnson, Ed., 1977: *Stories of Traditional Navajo Life and Culture*, 66–67.

3. For this and the following paragraph, see: Kluckhohn and Leighton, *The Navaho*, 53–64 (generalized for 1940–1958); Adams, *Shonto*, 194–227 (in-depth for one community, circa 1955); and Louise Lamphere, *To Run After Them*, Chapters 6, 7, and 8 (in-depth for a different community, circa 1965).

4. Adams, *Shonto*, 167–68; quotation, 168.

5. Philip Reno, 1981: *Navajo Resources and Economic Development*; coal: 106–8; uranium: 133–36. Uranium mining brought problems of radioactive pollution and cancer. Many miners died or contracted lung disease, though their families received compensation after lawsuits.

6. U.S. Bureau of Indian Affairs, 1949: *Report to the Commissioner of Indian Affairs on Navajo Trading*, prepared by Moris S. Burge; 1–3. Up to that time, traders had operated under three-year permits from the Commissioner of Indian Affairs (3).

7. *Report to the Commissioner of Indian Affairs on Navajo Trading*, 1949, 2–3; staff: 5.

8. Burge considered this figure of 24.5 percent gross profit to be reasonable. *Report to the Commissioner of Indian Affairs on Navajo Trading*, 1949, 10.

9. *Report to the Commissioner of Indian Affairs on Navajo Trading*, 1949, 10. Figures from Youngblood's survey of 1935 are interesting in this regard. They show the profit markups on items, and the fluctuations of these markups from season to season within a year. For example, in the first half of 1933, markups on men's work socks was 110 percent, on flour 43 percent; in the second half of 1933, 94 percent on socks, 21 percent on flour; in the first half of 1934, it was 87 percent and 19 percent, respectively (U.S. Department of Agriculture, 1935, *Navajo Trading: A Report*, prepared by Bonney Youngblood, 68).

10. *Report to the Commissioner of Indian Affairs on Navajo Trading*, 1949, 8.

11. *Report to the Commissioner of Indian Affairs on Navajo Trading*, 1949, 17–18.

12. *Report to the Commissioner of Indian Affairs on Navajo Trading*, 1949, 14–15.

13. *Report to the Commissioner of Indian Affairs on Navajo Trading*, 1949, 16–17.

14. "Proceedings of the Meeting of the Navajo Tribal Council, Window Rock, Arizona, January 5–23, 1953;" 260, 263, 264; quote from Council Member Frank Bradley, 269.

15. Seco, or tin money, common around 1920 when there was virtually no cash, consisted of counters made in various denominations by a trading post, usually bearing the name of the post. Customers received these counters instead of money, and usually could only spend them at the specified trading post. "Proceedings of the Meeting of the Navajo Tribal Council," 268–70; interest, 274.

16. Code of Federal Regulations, Title 25-Indians, 1940, 469–74.

17. Code of Federal Regulations, Title 25-Indians, 1940, 469–74.

18. "Proceedings": Howard Gorman quote, 274; George Hubbard quote, 281; Jimmy Largo quote, 273.

19. The Tribal scholarship fund was added to, in 1959, bringing it to $10,000,000. The number of grants rose steadily, from four in 1953 to 361 in 1960–61. By 1961, 120 Navajos had earned degrees on these scholarships, and others had used the funds to become accountants, nurses, mechanics, and clerks. Young, *Navajo Yearbook 1951–1961*, 353–54.

20. Bruce Burnham, interview with the author, July 1998.

21. This was the period during which the Ralph Lauren company and other manufacturers (echoing a similar development from the 1920s) developed the "Santa Fe style" with its influences from traditional Navajo skirts, Navajo silver jewelry, and western design elements.

22. Jay Springer, Cline Library interview, December 1998.

Chapter 7

1. For a full account of this period, see Iverson, 1981: *The Navajo Nation*, Chapter 4. Industrial development during the Nakai administration: Iverson, 100–114. See also Philip Reno, *Navajo Resources and Economic Development*, and Kent Gilbreath, 1973, *Red Capitalism*. There was criticism, also, for the considerable economic assistance given to companies to locate on the reservation. Many of these industries did not stay long.

2. See Iverson, *The Navajo Nation*, Chapter 4.

3. Iverson, *The Navajo Nation*, 89–91. He cites funding from federal grants for ONEO of $20 million for four years, 1965–1968, and a staff of 2,720 (only forty-six non-Indians).

4. Iverson, *The Navajo Nation*, 92 and fn.

5. Taylor McKenzie: Iverson, *The Navajo Nation*, 155, 159. Mitchell's agenda: every DNA lawyer interviewed seemed to feel that Mitchell had an agenda. Mitchell's focus on breaking the power of traders: Eric Triesman, interview with the author, November 9, 1999; and a CBS Documentary by Mitchell, described in The *Navajo Times*, May 23, 1968. OEO was directed by R. Sargent Shriver, whose hope was that the poverty law program would not only help the poor in specific problems, but would "get them out of poverty once and for all." See Michael Gross, 1973, "Reckoning for Legal Services," 78.

6. People who described Ted Mitchell used the phrases: "brilliant and charismatic," and "flawed." Support and respect for Mitchell, opposition from Wauneka: Bruce Herr, interview with the author, Oct. 1998; Michael Gross, interview with the author, Oct. 1999; Eric Treisman, interview with the author, Nov. 1999.

7. DNA caseload: DNA newsletter, *DNA in Action* vol. II(4) December 30, 1969, 1; the newsletter states that 19,600 cases were opened, 15,418 cases closed, the balance pending, and gives a breakdown by DNA agency offices. OEO poverty law programs: for a broader history of OEO's legal services, see Earl Johnson Jr., 1974, *Justice and Reform: The Formative Years of the OEO Legal Services Program*. DNA was by no means the only program with a social agenda and a focus on law reform.

8. Peterson Zah, interview with the author, March 1999.

9. Bruce Herr, interview with the author, October 1998; Paul Biderman, interview with the author, December 1998.

10. There were exceptions. Eric Triesman took several courses, one from Clifford Barnett, and later learned to speak Navajo well enough to tell a joke; interview with the author, November 1999. Martha Blue and Roy Ward were at the University of Arizona, and knew the Southwest well (see, for example, Martha Blue's book, *The Witch Purge of 1878*); there may have been one or two others with this kind of experience and background.

11. DNA staff: Iverson, *The Navajo Nation*, 94. In addition, there were fifteen interpreters, three education and community relations specialists, and thirty-two staff members. See also Jack August, 1994: "The Navajo and the Great Society," fn. 10. Wauneka and Nakai: Annie Wauneka was a member of the Old Guard, which did not support Raymond Nakai; Iverson, 84–85.

12. DNA was, in fact, funded by OEO money, through ONEO, not by grants per se. It *was* Mitchell's vision and plan, and as director he would have been responsible for annual reports and funding requests.

13. Gross came to the Law Reform Unit at DNA in 1968, and left in 1970, having fallen out with Ted Mitchell, disillusioned with the basic system of DNA. He felt that unless a client paid for legal services—however minimally—the client could not determine the focus or the activities of such services. The providers of the service would—and in the case of DNA, he felt, did—choose legal actions that furthered the goal of the organization. See Gross, "Reckoning for Legal Services."

14. Iverson, *The Navajo Nation*, 95.

15. Gross suggests that the disruption of the Tribal Council meeting resulted from Wauneka's actions, not Mitchell's. For a full description of the incident, see the *Gallup Independent*, August 9, 1968. Wauneka is quoted there regarding Mitchell's "silly, dirty laugh." Congressional complaints about Mitchell: Jack August, 1993: "The Navajos and the Great Society," 22.

16. Navajos liked traders for precisely the same sort of reasons.

17. Eric Treisman, interview with the author, October 1999; Iverson, *The Navajo Nation*, 98.

18. Types of cases handled by DNA: Iverson, *The Navajo Nation*, includes a table of DNA cases from April 1967 to August 1968, 94. Of 7,909 cases, 1,230 related to consumer and employment problems; 535 to administrative (welfare, social security) types of problems; 1,949 to family situations; 31 to housing; and 4,164 to "miscellaneous," which included juvenile school cases, misdemeanors, criminal procedures, and "other" cases that included trader cases. In a detailed list for 1970 (Iverson, 99), out of a total of 11,950 cases, 2,929 cases were listed for "Other (land disputes, pawn, grazing rights)." Welfare Rights meeting: Dine Baa Hani, October 1, 1969.

19. The *Navajo Times*, April 15, 1968.

20. The McClanahan case was a test case that established that Navajos working on the reservation did not have to pay state, but only federal, taxes.

21. Mitchell's agenda: Robert Hilgendorf, Mike Gross, Eric Treisman, Interviews with the author. Mitchell's TV documentary: The *Navajo Times*, May 23, 1968.

22. Herman Becenti, *Proceedings of the Navajo Tribal Council Meeting 1953*, 275.

23. Hoskie Cronemeyer, *Proceedings*, 1953: 277–78.

24. *Proceedings*, 1953: 268–69. The quote on what traders say comes from council member Frank Bradley.

25. The *Navajo Times*, May 23, 1968.

26. J. Shirley to R. Blair, March 13, 1969. UITA Papers, Box 8, Fd. 135.

27. R. Blair to J. Shirley, March 17, 1969. UITA Papers, Box 8, Fd. 135.

28. R. Blair to J. Shirley, March 20, 1969. UITA Papers, Box 8, Fd. 135.

29. *Gallup Independent*, June 12, 1969. Regarding traders charging state taxes: no on-reservation trader appears to have done this, or to know of such taxes being charged by any other trader. The off-reservation traders did charge state taxes, as all stores did, then and now, no matter who shopped there.

30. I. Merry to G. Holmes, July 23, 1969: 9–145. UITA Papers.

31. Navajos in Vietnam: On April 17, 1969, for example, The *Navajo Times* listed twenty-two Navajo warriors killed in action. Alcatraz and radical activism: T. Johnson, 1996, *The Occupation of Alcatraz Island*, 31. AIM originated as a Bay area group focused on local Indian civil rights, and moved to broader, nationwide activism in 1970–71 (Johnson, 39).

32. no. 25437, In the United States Court of Appeals for the Ninth Circuit; 3, 38.

33. I. Merry, letter to all directors, UITA, June 26, 1969. UITA Papers, Box 9, Fd. 145.

34. C. M. Tansey to E. Blair, January 28, 1969. UITA Papers, Box 9, Fd. 145.

35. Ike Merry to C. M. Tansey, July 23, 1969. UITA Papers, Box 9, Fd. 145.

Chapter 8

1. Gloria Emerson, interview with the author, February 2000.

2. Roger Wilson, Frankie Paul, were Navajo administrators; Frankie Paul became superintendent of the Tuba City Agency Superintendent, and in 1978 was vice-chairman in Peter MacDonald's third term of office. Iverson, *The Navajo Nation*, 216. Richard Mike went on to become a successful Navajo entrepreneur, and co-owns several Burger King franchises and a Hampton Inn on the reservation. He feels the DNA destroyed the old barter system, fundamentally changing, for the worse, the way traditional people lived.

3. Copy of petition, UITA Collection, 9–148, Cline Library, NAU. Other demands included: receiving general assistance when no employment was available within commuting distance from the reservation; obtaining surplus foods that Navajos like to eat—"ask what we want;" a review of the way livestock were considered as a factor in evaluating a family's need for welfare so that the cultural reasons for keeping sheep were recognized; and having Navajo caseworkers deal with Navajo caseloads: "fire the deadwood Anglos if there are not enough funds for Navajos."

4. *The Albuquerque Journal*, February 1, 1970. Eric Treisman, retold the story: "I took my interpreter-investigator . . . he was an extremely cranky guy. . . . So we went out and browbeat that lady into giving us an affidavit. . . . She said that the reason that she gave an affidavit to the traders was that they took her up in an airplane and 'made her heart to stop.' . . . And so then Jack Anderson wrote another story and used that affidavit, and we decided she was a lady who would sign anything for anybody. So I don't know what the truth was, but that was our part in it." Treisman, interview with the author, November 1999.

5. I. Merry, March 17, 1970, to M. Gibson. UITA Papers, Box 9, Fd. 148.

6. The Southwest Indian Development Report was sent out to various agencies with an accompanying letter (undated) from SID President Charley John explaining how the investigation was carried out and the report written—there were apparently claims that DNA attorneys had written it, which he refuted. Copies can be found in the Law Library at the University of New Mexico, and at Cline Library Special Collections, Northern Arizona University, among other places.

7. Railroad Agents: SID Report, 8. A DNA lawyer worked up a memo about traders as railroad agents, and the possibility that this was illegal, but nothing came of this attempt; UITA Papers, Box 4, General Correspondence. Sanitation and safety: SID Report, 21–22; conclusions: SID Report, 26.

8. SID Report, 26–27.

9. M. Gibson to R. Cheney, April 2, 1970; Melvin Gibson to Robert Robertson, April 2, 1970. UITA Papers, Box 9, Fd. 148.

10. Letter from UITA Board of Directors, to U.S. Senators and Representatives for Arizona, Colorado, New Mexico, and Utah, May 28, 1970. UITA Papers, Box 9, Fd. 145.

11. Charles Tansey, Cline Library interview, March 1998.

12. Minutes of UITA meeting of November 21, 1970, UITA Papers, Box 2, Fd. 31.

13. The Rockbridge case (see DNA Newsletter Law in Action IV(1) September 24, 1971) eventually influenced the Commissioner for Indian Affairs to turn to the FTC for expert assistance in regulating the accounting practices of traders: memo

of April 19, 1972, Zervas to Commission, Federal Trade Commission archives. DNA lawyer Robert Hilgendorf noted that "the whole Truth in Lending statute . . . was a complicated statute that had specific disclosures. The banking industry and everyone had to hire attorneys and figure out what the best way to do it was." Not only was the law complicated, each lawyer interpreted its requirements differently. Robert Hilgendorf, interview with the author, October 1999.

14. J. Brown to C. Tansey, May 20, 1971; UITA Papers, Box 9, Fd. 150.

15. Minutes of UITA Meetings of September 16, 1970; November 21, 1970; January 22, 1972. UITA Papers, Box 2, Fds. 25, 26.

16. Minutes of UITA Meeting of March 16, 1972. UITA Papers, Box 2, Fd. 26.

17. The *Los Angeles Times*, August 8, 1972.

18. Memorandum, Federal Trade Commission, to Commission, from Attorney-Advisers, Los Angeles Regional Office, April 19, 1972; Federal Trade Commission Archives. Meeting with DNA attorneys at Chinle, 2 of memorandum; planning and goals of project, 6.

19. FTC Memorandum of April 19, 1972 (see above); planning and goals of project, 6–7; recommendations, 7–8 (last page is unnumbered).

20. Memoranda of April 26, 1972; May 1, 1972; May 15, 1972, FTC archives; subpoenas were dated August 24. *Los Angeles Times*, August 8, 1972.

21. FedMart left in the early 1980s.

22. McGinnis, memo to George J. Burger Jr., Assistant to the President of the National Federation of Independent Business; UITA Papers, Box 9, Fd. 141. McGinnis was by no means an unbiased observer, though he noted that he was "bearing no brief for either the traders or the Navajo Nation." He certainly held strong opinions about the nature of business, opposing Commissioner Bruce's idea of "a [reservation] economy in which Indians will only do business with Indians," which, he noted—apparently in all seriousness—"is rank communism." His comments about Louis Bruce, Ernest Stevens, and the DNA are negative in the extreme, though he was impressed by MacDonald.

23. Vlassis: *Gallup Independent*, September 2, 1972.

24. *Los Angeles Times*, September 4, 1972, front page.

25. Stevens: The *Gallup Independent*, September 2, 1972. Navajo language: Father Berard Haile, at St. Michael's Mission, had written a dictionary, and Gladys Reichard had taught Navajo literacy in hogan schools in 1935 (part of the Collier program). Navajo was primarily a spoken language at this period, but during the mid-1970s, two Navajo-run schools, at Ramah and Rough Rock, published Navajo language materials for schools. Robert Young and William Morgan's dictionary, *The Navajo Language*, was published in 1980.

26. Undated clipping from the *Farmington Daily Times* in UITA records.

27. Subpoena to Roland Spicer, White Horse Lake Trading Post, to appear at Gallup October 26, 1972. UITA Papers, 8–63.

28. Jo Drolet, Mildred Heflin, Interviews with the author, 1979, Chaco Archives, University of New Mexico; Bruce Barnard, personal communication, 1979.

29. The Indian Agency had, two centuries earlier, proved the singular failure of government-run trading houses. The Navajo Nation made some attempts to help to develop Navajo-run businesses, but the focus in economic development seemed to

be on bringing outside businesses in. Many observations were made of the problems Navajos had in trying to run businesses, from the need to pay bribes to the problem of developing an entrepreneurial culture, seemingly in conflict with Navajo traditions and responsibilities to family; see, for example, Kent Gilbreath, *Red Capitalism*.

Chapter 9

1. J. LeValley to C. M. Tansey, April 26, 1973, UITA Papers, Box 8, Fd. 131. For a while, Robert Hilgendorf also suspected traders of conspiring, through the UITA, to set prices.

2. The Trading Post System on the Navajo Reservation, Staff Report to the Federal Trade Commission, 1973, 29. The "perennial reply" is a quote of a trader from William Y. Adams, *Shonto*, 210–11. Adams did not use the phrase "perennial reply" nor the adjective "curt." He does not list it under "Joking" (287–88) where it might be considered to go; but cross-ethnic joking is, in any case, fraught with implications. The FTC report may not have been sent to the UITA president; Charles Tansey apparently had not seen it in June 1973 when an article on the report appeared in the *Wall Street Journal*.

3. J. K. LeValley to C. M. Tansey, June 18, 1973; UITA Papers, Box 8, Fd. 129; *Wall Street Journal*, June 15, 1973; The *Arizona Republic*, June 16, 1973.

4. J. K. LeValley to C. M. Tansey, June 18, 1973. UITA Papers, Box 8, Fd. 129.

5. J. K. LeValley to C. M. Tansey, UITA Papers, Box 8, Fd. 129.

6. Elijah Blair, interview with the author, July 1998.

7. C. M. Tansey to M. Jaenish, Tansey to UITA directors February 5, 1974. UITA Papers, Box 6, Fds. 96–97.

8. In 1972, Paul Biderman took a case against Gallup traders to make much-needed changes in the way they handled pawn, also based on the Truth in Lending Act. Paul Biderman, interview with the author, December 1998.

9. E. F. Suarez, Division of Law Enforcement Services, BIA, Washington Office, to Elijah Blair, July 21, 1973, enclosing formal notes of the July 8th meeting. UITA Papers, Box 6, Fd. 87.

10. E. F. Suarez, Division of Law Enforcement Services, BIA, Washington Office, to Elijah Blair, July 21, 1973, enclosing formal notes of the July 8th meeting. UITA Papers, Box 6, Fd. 87.

11. Elijah Blair, personal communication, May 24, 1999.

12. Peterson Zah, Cline Library and author's interview, March 1999; Robert Hilgendorf, interview with the author, October 1999.

13. Willow Roberts, The Trader Project interviews, 1979, Chaco Archives, University of New Mexico.

14. Willow Roberts, The Trader Project interviews, 1979, Chaco Archives, University of New Mexico.

15. Willow Roberts, The Trader Project interviews, 1979, Chaco Archives, University of New Mexico.

16. Willow Roberts, The Trader Project interviews, 1979, Chaco Archives, University of New Mexico.

17. Willow Roberts, The Trader Project interviews, 1979, Chaco Archives, University of New Mexico.

18. Paul Begay, Cline Library interview, February 1998.

19. Willow Roberts, The Trader Project interviews, 1979, Chaco Archives, University of New Mexico.

20. Paul Begay, Cline Library interview, February 1998.

21. Survey of traders, cards returned. UITA Papers, Box 11, Fd. 178.

22. R. Blair, letter to E. Blair, n.d. (received March 10, 1976); James K. LeValley to R. Blair, March 2, 1976; UITA Papers, Box 11, Fd. 177.

23. U.S. Federal Trade Commission, 1973, The Trading Post System on the Navajo Reservation. Staff Report to the Federal Trade Commission.

24. Claudia Blair, interview with the author, May 1999.

25. See Gilbreath, *Red Capitalism*; Francisconi, 1998, *Kinship, Capitalism, Change*.

Chapter 10

1. Ed Foutz, Cline Library interview, March 1998.

2. For example, Eddington and Makov, 1995, *Trading Post Guidebook*, 2nd edition.

3. Bruce Burnham, Cline Library interview, July 1998.

4. John W. Kennedy, John D. Kennedy, Cline Library interview, December 1998.

5. Caroline Blair, Cline Library interview, February 1998. John W. Kennedy, Cline Library interview, December 1998.

Chapter 11

1. Border town businesses and wholesalers are a topic only peripherally touched on in this account. During the period when traders on the reservation pawned, many people also pawned at a variety of places off the reservation. The situation was one in which Navajos expected similar treatment to that of their home trading post, while pawntakers—who often did not know the pawner at all—were going by laws of the different states, and were indifferent to the customer. Paul Biderman's class action case against Gallup pawnbrokers struck at this problem, and won the support of traders as well. See Paul Biderman, 1979, "The Impact of the Revised New Mexico Class Action Rules upon Consumers."

2. Partly as a result of public attention to Native American issues (Alcatraz gained sympathetic publicity), the Nixon administration canceled the Termination Policy. A change in government policy and attitude toward Indian tribes began in 1970, and continued in legislation for tribal self-determination and land reparation bills; see T. Johnson, *The Occupation of Alcatraz Island*.

3. Traders' scorn for do-gooders: Robert Parks, one of the University of Chicago's great sociologists of the 1930s, and an activist, opposed the idea of "do-gooders" in sociology. Different perspectives, but there are ideas here that are worth examining. Weeding out bad apples: this seems unlikely. The UITA had no institutional aim, and nothing in their by-laws, to stamp out dishonest or unfair practices. Certainly no individual traders ever did anything in regard to such practices, when they knew or suspected them.

J·L

LIST OF INTERVIEWS

The Oral History of Trading interviews were carried out by Bradford Cole, Manuscripts Curator, Special Collections and Archives Department, Karen J. Underhill, Head, Special Collections and Archives Department, both of Cline Library, Northern Arizona University, and Audio-visual technicians, Lew Steiger and Gail Steiger, of Steiger Brothers.

Interviews by the author were carried out specifically for this book.

All interviews are part of the United Indian Traders Association Collection, Cline Library, Northern Arizona University. (Earlier interviews by the author referred to in footnotes can be found in the Chaco Archives, Zimmerman Library, University of New Mexico, Albuquerque.)

Andrea Ashcroft, interview with the author, June 19, 1999.
Jim Babbitt, Cline Library interview, July 21, 1999.
Mary May Bailey, Cline Library interview, July 13, 1999.
Paul Begay, Cline Library interview, February 10, 1998.
Paul Biderman, interview with the author, December 30, 1998.
Carolyn Blair, Cline Library interview, February 12, 1998.
Claudia Blair, interview with the author, July 21, 1998.
Claudia Blair, Cline Library interview, February 9, 1998.
Elijah Blair, interview with the author, July 21, 1998.
Elijah Blair, Cline Library interview, February 9, 1998.
Elijah and Claudia Blair, interview with the author, May 16–17, 1999.
Hank Blair, Cline Library interview, August 13, 1998.

Hank Blair, interview with the author, November 16, 1998.

Marilene Blair, Cline Library interview, February 12, 1998.

Victoria Blair, interview with the author, June 17, 1999.

Martha Blue, interview with the author, November 16, 1999.

Grace Brown, interview with the author, June 19, 1999.

Bruce Burnham, interview with the author, July 9, 1998.

Bruce Burnham, Cline Library interview, July 17, 1998.

Virginia Burnham, interview with the author, January 19, 1999.

Bob Bolton, Cline Library interview, December 16, 1998.

Joe Danoff, Cline Library interview, January 27, 2000.

Gloria Emerson, interview with the author, February 13, 2000.

Ed Foutz, Cline Library interview, March 9, 1998.

Ed Foutz, interview with the author, September 28, 1998.

Jay Foutz, Cline Library interview, August 12, 1998.

Loyd Foutz, Cline Library interview, August 12, 1998.

Russell Foutz, Cline Library interview, April 3, 1998.

Michael Gross, interview with the author, October 29, 1999.

Mildred Heflin, Cline Library interview, July 15, 1999.

Bruce Herr, interview with the author, October 31, 1998.

Grace Herring, Cline Library interview, February 11, 1998.

Robert Hilgendorf, interview with the author,
    October 25 and November 8, 1999.

Evelyn Jensen, Cline Library interview, February 10, 1998.

Edith Kennedy, Cline Library interview, March 12, 1998.

John W. Kennedy, John D. Kennedy, Cline Library interview, December 16, 1998.

Jack, Evelyn (Sammie), and Snick Lee, Cline Library interview, August 18, 1998.

Marie Lee, Cline Library interview, July 14, 1999.

Bill Malone, Cline Library interview, August 14, 1998.

Jack Manning, Cline Library interview, March 12, 1998.

Jewel McGee, Cline Library interview, February 11, 1998.

Jewel, Leona, and Lavoy McGee, Cline Library interview, February 11, 1998.

Ruth McGee, Cline Library interview, February 11, 1998.

Paul D. Merrill, Cline Library interview, January 26, 2000.

Richard Mike, interview with the author, January 31, 2000.

Betty Rodgers, Cline Library interview, July 14, 1999.

Walter and Alice Scribner, interview with the author,
    November 17, 1979, and October 19, 1998.

Jay Springer, Cline Library interview, December 1998.

J. B. Tanner, Cline Library interview, August 12, 1998.

Joseph Elwood [Joe] Tanner Sr., Cline Library interview, March 30, 1999.

Stella Tanner, Cline Library interview, July 16, 1998.

Charles Tansey, Cline Library interview, March 10, 1998.

Eric Treisman, interview with the author, November 8, 1999.
Tobe Turpen, Cline Library interview, March 1999.
Sallie Wagner, Cline Library interview, December 15, 1998.
Clarence Wheeler, Cline Library interview, March 10, 1998.
Les Wilson, Cline Library interview, March 31, 1999.
Tom Woodard, interview with the author, December 9, 1998.
Tom Woodard, Cline Library interview, December 14, 1999.
Cecilia Yazzie, interview with her daughter, Arlene Tracy,
    June 3, 1999. Translated from the Navajo by Arlene Tracy.
Colina and Raymond C. Yazzie, Cline Library Interviews, January 26, 2000.
Peterson Zah, Cline Library and author interview, March 16, 1999.

J·L

BIBLIOGRAPHY

Aberle, David F. 1991. *The Peyote Religion Among the Navaho*. Norman: University of Oklahoma Press.

Adair, John. 1994. *The Navajo and Pueblo Silversmiths*. Norman: University of Oklahoma Press.

Adair, John, Kurt W. Deuschle, and Clifford R. Barnett. 1988. *The People's Health: Medicine and Anthropology in a Navajo Community*. Rev. ed. Albuquerque: University of New Mexico Press.

Adams, William Y. 1971. "Navajo Ecology and Economy."

———. 1963. *Shonto: A Study of the Role of the Trader in a Modern Navaho Community*. Washington, D.C.: Smithsonian Institution, Bulletin 188.

Amsden, Charles A. 1934. *Navaho Weaving: Its Technic and History*. Glorieta, N.Mex.: The Rio Grande Press, Inc. Reprint from The Fine Arts Press, Santa Ana, Calif. in cooperation with the Southwest Museum.

August, Jack. 1994. "The Navajo and the Great Society: The Strange Case of Ted Mitchell and DNA." *Cañon: The Journal of the Rocky Mountains American Studies Association* 1(2):8–28.

Baca, Lawrence R. 1988. "The Legal Status of American Indians." 230–37 in *Handbook of North American Indians*, vol. 4, William Sturtevant, ed. Washington, D.C.: Smithsonian Institution.

Bailey, Garrick, and Roberta G. Bailey. 1986. *A History of the Navajos: The Reservation Years*. Santa Fe, N.Mex.: School of American Research Press.

Batkin, Jonathan. 1999. "Tourism Is Overrated: Pueblo Pottery and the Early Curio Trade, 1880–1910." 282–370 in *Unpacking Culture: Art and Commodity in Colonial and Postcolonial Worlds*, Eds. Ruth B. Phillips and Christopher B. Steiner. Berkeley: University of California Press.

Bedinger, Margery. 1973. *Indian Silver: Navajo and Pueblo Jewelers*. Albuquerque: University of New Mexico Press.

Begay, Myrtle. 1977. "Myrtle Begay." 56–72 in *Stories of Traditional Navajo Life and Culture by Twenty-Two Navajo Men and Women*, Ed. Broderick H. Johnson. Tsaile, Navajo Nation, Arizona: Navajo Community College Press.

Biderman, Paul. 1973. "Consumer Class Actions Under the New Mexico Unfair Practices Act." *New Mexico Law Review* 4:49–63.

———. 1979. "The Impact of the Revised New Mexico Class Action Rules Upon Consumers." *New Mexico Law Review* 9:263–85.

Blue, Martha. 1988. *The Witch Purge of 1878: Oral and Documentary History in the Early Navajo Reservation Years*. Tsaile, Ariz.: Navajo Community College Press.

Boyce, George A. 1974. *When Navajos Had Too Many Sheep: The 1940s*. San Francisco: Indian Historian Press.

Brugge, David M. 1980. *A History of the Chaco Navajos*. Albuquerque: National Park Service, U.S. Department of the Interior.

Caskey, John P. 1994. *Fringe Banking: Check-Cashing Outlets, Pawnshops, and the Poor*. New York: Russell Sage Foundation.

Coffey, Walter C. 1918. *Productive Sheep Husbandry*. Philadelphia: Lippincott.

Drefkoff, Max M. *An Industrial Program for the Navajo Indian Reservation: a Report to the Commissioner of Indian Affairs*. Washington, D.C.: Government Printing Office.

Eddington, Patrick, and Susan Makov. 1995. *Trading Post Guidebook: Where to Find the Trading Posts, Galleries, Auctions, Artists, and Museums of the Four Corners Region*. Flagstaff, Ariz.: Northland Publishing.

Francisconi, Michael J. 1998. *Kinship, Capitalism, Change: The Informal Economy of the Navajo, 1868–1995*. New York: Garland Publishing, Inc.

Gilbreath, Kent. 1973. *Red Capitalism: An Analysis of the Navajo Economy*. Norman: University of Oklahoma Press.

Gillmor, Frances, and Louisa Wade Wetherill. 1952. *Traders to the Navajos: The Wetherills of Kayenta*. Albuquerque: University of New Mexico Press.

Graves, Laura. 1998. *Thomas Varker Keam, Indian Trader*. Norman: University of Oklahoma Press.

Gross, Michael P. 1973. "Reckoning for Legal Services." *Notre Dame Lawyer* 49:78–104.

Harris, Neil. 1978. "Museums, Merchandising, and Popular Taste: The Struggle for Influence." 140–74 in *Material Culture and the Study of American Life*, ed. Ian M. G. Quimby. New York: W. W. Norton & Company Inc.

Harvey, Byron I. 1996. "The Fred Harvey Company Collects Indian Art: Selected Remarks." 69–86 in *The Great Southwest of the Fred Harvey Company and the Santa Fe Railway*, eds. Marta Weigle and Barbara A. Babcock. Phoenix: The Heard Museum.

Hegemann, Elizabeth C. 1963. *Navaho Trading Days*. Albuquerque: University of New Mexico Press.

Hill, W. W. 1948. "Navajo Trading and Trading Ritual: A Study of Cultural Dynamics." *Southwestern Journal of Anthropology* vol. 4:371–96.

Iverson, Peter. 1981. *The Navajo Nation*. Albuquerque: University of New Mexico Press.

James, George W. 1974. *Indian Blankets and Their Makers*. New York: Dover Publications Inc.

Johnson, Broderick H., ed. 1977. *Stories of Traditional Navajo Life and Culture*. Tsaile, Ariz.: Navajo Community College Press.

Johnson, Earl Jr. 1974. *Justice and Reform: The Formative Years of the OEO Legal Services Program*. New York: Russell Sage.

Johnson, Troy R. 1996. *The Occupation of Alcatraz Island: Indian Self-Determination and the Rise of Indian Activism*. Urbana: University of Illinois Press.

Kelley, Klara B. 1983. "Ethnoarchaeology of Navajo Trading Posts." Paper given at the Annual Meeting of the American Society for Ethnohistory (Albuquerque, N.Mex., Nov. 1983).

Kelley, Klara B., and Peter M. Whiteley. 1989. *Navajoland: Family Settlement and Land Use*. Tsaile, Ariz.: Navajo Community College Press.

Kirk, Tom. 1979. "The Kirk Clan, Traders with the Navaho." 147–58 in *Brand Book No. 6, Corral of the Westerners*, San Diego, Calif.

Kluckhohn, Clyde, and Dorothea Leighton. 1974. *The Navaho*. Garden City, N.J.: Anchor Books, Doubleday.

Lamphere, Louise. 1977. *To Run After Them: Cultural and Social Bases of Cooperation in a Navajo Community*. Tucson: University of Arizona Press.

Left Handed. 1995. *Son of Old Man Hat*. Recorded by Walter Dyk. Lincoln: University of Nebraska Press.

Leupp, Francis E. 1910. *The Indian and His Problem*. New York: Scribner's Sons.

McNitt, Frank. 1962. *The Indian Traders*. Norman: University of Oklahoma Press.

———. 1972. *Navajo Wars: Military Campaigns, Slave Raids, and Reprisals*. Albuquerque: University of New Mexico Press.

Nash, Philleo. 1988. "Twentieth Century United States Government Agencies." 264–75 in *Handbook of North American Indians: History of Indian-White Relations*, vol. 4, Wilcomb E. Washburn, ed. Washington, D.C.: Smithsonian Institution.

Newcomb, Franc J. 1966. *Navaho Neighbors*. Norman: University of Oklahoma Press.

Parman, Donald. 1976. *The Navajos and the New Deal*. New Haven, Conn.: Yale University Press.

Rapoport, Robert N. 1954. "Changing Navaho Religious Values: A Study of Christian Missions to the Rimrock Navahos." Reports of the Rimrock Project Values Series. Papers of the Peabody Museum of American Archaeology and Ethnology, Harvard University, vol. 41 no. 2. Cambridge, Mass.: Peabody Museum.

Reichard, Gladys A. 1997 (1934). *Spider Woman: A Story of Navajo Weavers and Changers*. Albuquerque: University of New Mexico Press.

Reno, Philip. 1981. *Navajo Resources and Economic Development*. Albuquerque: University of New Mexico Press.

Roberts, Willow. 1987. *Stokes Carson: Twentieth Century Trading on the Navajo Reservation*. Albuquerque: University of New Mexico Press.

Rushing, W. J. 1992. "Marketing the Affinity of the Primitive and the Modern: Rene d'Harnoncourt and "Indian Art of the United States." 191–236 in *The Early Years of Native American Art History: The Politics of Scholarship and Collecting*, ed. Janet C. Berlo. Seattle: University of Washington Press.

———. 1995. *Native American Art and the New York Avant-Garde*. Austin: University of Texas Press.

Schmeckebier, Laurence F. 1927. *The Office of Indian Affairs: Its History, Activities, and Organization*. Baltimore, Md.: The Johns Hopkins Press.

Schmedding, Joseph. 1951. *Cowboy and Indian Trader*. Caldwell, Idaho: The Caxton Printers.

Schrader, R. F. 1983. *The Indian Arts & Crafts Board: An Aspect of New Deal Indian Policy*. Albuquerque: University of New Mexico Press.

Shepardson, Mary. 1971. "Navajo Factionalism and the Outside World." 83–89 in *Apachean Culture History and Ethnology*, eds. Tucson, Ariz.: University of Arizona Press.

Southwest Indian Development Inc. [1969]. *Traders on the Navajo Reservation: a Report on the Bondage of the Navajo People*. Window Rock, Ariz.: Southwestern Indian Development Inc.

Underhill, Ruth. 1956. *The Navajos*. Norman: University of Oklahoma Press.

U.S. Bureau of Indian Affairs. 1949. *Report to the Commissioner of Indian Affairs on Navajo Trading*, prepared by Moris S. Burge. Washington, D.C.: Government Printing Office.

U.S. Bureau of Indian Affairs, Navajo Area Office. 1976. *Navajo Area Progress Report 1975*. Window Rock, Ariz.: Bureau of Indian Affairs, Navajo Area Office.

U.S. Congress, Joint Economic Committee, Subcommittee on Economy in Government. 1969. *Toward Economic Development for Native American Communities: a Compendium of Papers Submitted to the Subcommittee on Economy in Government of the Joint Economic Committee, Congress of the United States*. Washington, D.C.: Government Printing Office.

U.S. Department of Agriculture. 1935. *Navajo Trading: A Report*. Prepared by Bonney Youngblood. Washington, D.C.: Government Printing Office.

U.S. Department of the Interior. 1948. *Report of the Navajo—A Long-Range Program of Navajo Rehabilitation*. Report of Secretary of the Interior, J. A. Krug. Washington, D.C.: Government Printing Office.

U.S. Federal Trade Commission. 1973. *The Trading Post System on the Navajo Reservation*. Staff Report to the Federal Trade Commission. Washington, D.C.: Government Printing Office.

U.S. Senate. 1937. *Survey of Conditions of the Indians in the United States*. Washington, D.C.: Government documents.

Vogt, Evon Z. 1951. "Navaho Veterans: A Study of Changing Values." Reports of the Rimrock Project Values Series. Papers of the Peabody Museum of American Archaeology and Ethnology, Harvard University, vol. 41 no. 1. Cambridge, Mass.: Peabody Museum.

Weigle, Marta, and Barbara A. Babcock. 1996. *The Great Southwest of the Fred Harvey Company and the Santa Fe Railway*. Phoenix: The Heard Museum.

Wolf, Eric R. 1982. *Europe and the People without History*. Berkeley: University of California Press.

Young, Robert W. 1961. *The Navajo Yearbook 1951–1961, A Decade of Progress*. Report No. 8. Window Rock, Ariz.: Navajo Agency.

———. 1968. *The Role of the Navajo in the Southwestern Drama*.

———. 1978. *A Political History of the Navajo Tribe*. Tsaile, Ariz.: Navajo Community College Press.

Young, Robert W., and William Morgan. 1980. *The Navajo Language: A Grammar and Colloquial Dictionary*. Albuquerque: University of New Mexico Press.

Archival Sources

Federal Trade Commission Archives, made available by the Archivist, U.S. Federal Trade Commission, Washington, D.C.

Records of the United Indian Trader Association (UITA) MS 299 at the Cline Library, Special Collections, Northern Arizona University.

Sam Day Papers, the Cline Library, Special Collections, Northern Arizona University.

The Trader Project, Chaco Center Archives, Zimmerman Library, University of New Mexico, Albuquerque, New Mexico.

Newspapers

Albuquerque Journal, Albuquerque, New Mexico.
Farmington Times Hustler, Farmington, New Mexico.
Gallup Independent, Gallup, New Mexico.
Los Angeles Times, Los Angeles, California.
Wall Street Journal, New York, New York.

INDEX